T0158562

HOW TO BE
AN AUTHOR

Join the community:
facebook.com/groups/howtobeanauthorinaustralia

HOW TO BE AN AUTHOR

THE BUSINESS OF BEING A WRITER IN AUSTRALIA

GEORGIA RICHTER & DEBORAH HUNN

 FREMANTLE PRESS

Contents

List of acronyms

ABDA	Australian Book Designers Association
ABN	Australian Business Number
ALAA	Australian Literary Agents' Association
ASA	Australian Society of Authors
CALD	culturally and linguistically diverse
CBCA	Children's Book Council of Australia
FAQ	frequently asked questions
IPEd	Institute of Professional Editors
ISBN	International Standard Book Number
ISSN	International Standard Serial Number
LGBTQIA	lesbian, gay, bisexual, transgender, queer (or questioning), intersex, asexual
MC	master of ceremonies
MEAA	Media, Entertainment & Arts Alliance
NED	National edeposit
NLA	National Library of Australia
ONIX	ONline Information eXchange
PR	public relations
Q&As	questions and answers
RRP	recommended retail price
SCBWI	Society of Children's Book Writers and Illustrators
SPN	The Small Press Network
YA	young adult

About this book

A writer who dreams of being published understands that there is more to being an author than getting words down on the page. A writer is a creator but, if they also wish to be published, at least some of the time they may also need to be their own office manager, marketing and public relations person, and perhaps even distributor and bookseller.

In this book, we are going to assume that you are one of the writers who actually writes, rather than someone who only thinks or talks about writing. We are also going to assume that you would like to be published and are keen to to receive some industry insights on all the ins and outs of the business of being a writer.

Every writer has their own personality and method, and every writer exists somewhere on the spectrum of introvert to extrovert, orderly to shambolic. Whichever kind of writer you are, we know that across time and with practice, you will come to understand all the wonderful, messy and chaotic aspects of your own creative process. You will participate in the steady accrual of hours at the desk – amassing words, creating poems, stories, novels, non-fiction. And you will understand how writing time can be painful and exhilarating, pointless and purposeful.

How does a writer become a published author? First, maybe, they dare to think of themselves as *a writer*. Amidst discarded drafts and changes of direction, and with a growing understanding of voice and which ideas are big enough to sustain a poem, a story, a novel, every writer begins somewhere. Many writers remember the first thrill of recognition upon sharing their work – of active encouragement, of reading to an audience, of winning a competition, of being published online or in a journal. Many writers begin by writing alone, but along the way find a trusted mentor or a community of writers around them.

We can't help you turn up at the desk to write, but we *can* help you with all the other business of being a writer who is aiming for publication, and we can certainly give you our most useful tips and assist with some perennial pickles.

The questions we answer in this book are ones we have heard in classrooms, on panels and in writing workshops. They are the questions emailed to us or posed while waiting in the queue at the ice-cream van at writers festivals. They are questions about inspiration and choosing a genre, about research and writer's block, about building an author brand and how to know when a manuscript is ready for submission, about how to create and maintain a social media profile and find the right publisher.

In this book, we answer these questions from a teacher's perspective and from a publisher's perspective. Creative writing lecturer Deborah Hunn concentrates on the business of being a writer prepublication, while publisher Georgia Richter looks at the things you need to know after a manuscript has been submitted and accepted for publication.

This book includes tips from Fremantle Press marketing and communications manager Claire Miller, whose role it is to coach authors on how best to present themselves effectively to media and to their audience. It also contains advice from booksellers and self-published authors and other industry specialists.

And you will hear from writers themselves. The eighteen authors who responded to our questions in the 'Ask an author' sections have one, two or many published books to their name. Each started out as someone who wanted to write, and each works hard at being an author. Each has a sense of their own brand, and regularly interacts with their audience. These writers represent many genres – from children's picture books, junior fiction and young adult fiction, to literary and commercial fiction, narrative non-fiction, biography and poetry. However, the questions we put to them were intentionally not genre specific but aimed at drawing out their personal experiences about writing process and practice, and inviting them, as published authors, to share with new writers what they have learned along the way.

This book looks at the business of being a writer from the very beginning – all the things you might want or need to know, for instance, about the business associated with writing a manuscript, approaching publishers, the editing process, and promoting your work. This book is also designed to be dipped into and consulted as you move into different phases of your own writing practice. If you are contemplating self-publication, we look at this subject specifically in Chapter 5. Primarily though, while much of this book will be useful to writers who would like to self-publish, *How to be an Author* is aimed at those interested in finding a traditional publisher for their work. For further reading, in Chapter 11 you will find a list of the organisations and resources mentioned throughout the book (and a few more besides), along with the top three resources recommended by each contributing author.

Every writer understands the deep, expanding pleasure of laying down words, the drive to inhabit internal worlds and to create characters, and that almost mystical feeling of participating in a process that can feel close to immortality. And many writers feel the need not only to create, but to share their writing with readers.

If you are one of these writers, then this book is for you.

1. In the beginning

- Writers are readers
- Inspiration and ideas
- Some triggers for creativity
- How to know when there is enough material to begin
- Dedication to the craft of writing
- Establishing a routine
- Choosing a genre
- Finding a voice

A creative writing teacher has frequent encounters with students new to the writing practice. Students often know they want to write, but going about it can seem a daunting task. The role of the creative writing teacher, and the role of this book, is to help you navigate some of the terrain the new writer invariably encounters. In the first four chapters we will address some of the questions commonly asked by new writers as they begin to think about their practice as something to get serious about. A life of writing can be glorious and exasperating, rewarding and confronting. But before we dive in, please remember that your health and wellbeing should always be a top priority. While the business of being a writer can be challenging, none of it should be soul-destroying. At different times in your life, it may be enough just to write and not to publish, or to not write at all: remember that you always have a choice in what you do.

Writers are readers

If writers are the ones who write, they must also be the ones who read. No musician ever composed in a vacuum; no artist ever painted without reference to the art that came before and that is being made around them. If we are lucky, books and stories are some of the earliest artforms we are exposed to. We listen to books and fall in love with stories long before we begin to dream that we can be storytellers ourselves. For people who are attuned to words and drawn to write, there comes a time when we begin to read consciously, and as if we are apprentices. We begin to ask why masterful prose is so masterful, and why less successful executions of language do not work.

Through reading, we never stop learning about the art of being a skilled wordsmith. Throughout this book, you will hear from writers how important voracious, thoughtful, constant reading is to the writer's craft. So: reading is crucial. As for writing – where does one begin?

Inspiration and ideas

Some individuals appear to hop into writing with ease, knocking out a novel in no time. Is it really that easy? Some of them might be bluffing. Others may just be freakishly fortunate. For the rest of us, writing requires hard work. If you are new to establishing your writing practice, turning up at the desk is one thing, but wondering how and what to put down on the page can be quite another.

Just write is sound advice, and some of the lucky ones do. You may often feel time-poor and the pressure of other aspects of your life calling. If you want to write, you must set these aside, for the time being, and begin.

So, let's start at the very beginning of any writing project – with ideas and inspiration. If you attend writers festivals or listen to author interviews, you will often hear two questions posed by those interested in the writing process. One of these, which we will return to later in this chapter, is about the author's methods or routines. The other question will take the form of something like:

- Where do you get the ideas for stories from?
- What inspired you to write about …?
- What was the inspiration for that moment in your book where …?

The answers to such questions are varied – ideas can indeed come from anywhere. While some of what you come across may seem a little daunting (you're unlikely to be sitting atop Mount Everest or chatting over dinner with a Nobel Prize winner anytime soon), a lot of it is comfortingly relatable, and will possibly already be part of your everyday life. This may be so even if you don't yet recognise precisely what shines out or how you can use it. It is that capacity to identify the kernel of an idea that matters, as much as the idea itself.

Jane Austen, drawing on her own inspiration for novel-writing, famously provided the following advice to a would-be writer about seeking ideas for stories: 'Three or four families in a country village is the very thing to work on.' Austen's near contemporary William Wordsworth was inspired by his sensory encounters with the natural environment during long walks in the countryside. Another writer of the same era, Mary Shelley, is sometimes thought to have found the genesis of her novel *Frankenstein* in the tragic death of her own infant child and her longing to bring her back to life. Of course, the factors that go into building sustainable ideas are not often singular – Austen too found inspiration in nature and place, Wordsworth built on personal suffering and *Frankenstein* famously draws on the myth of Prometheus, while all three authors were, in differing ways, highly conscious of the philosophical, aesthetic and political debates of their times. Whatever the impetus, each writer was able to catch the potential of imaginative sparks that were present in their own lives and creatively transform them into works that, some two hundred years later, maintain an enduring hold on readers.

Children's author Deb Fitzpatrick notes encouragingly that 'ideas can come from anywhere', but she adds a crucial proviso – 'if we are open to them.' It is essential to be an active and curious observer, alive to significant details and open to the potential for stories that surrounds you.

It is equally important to develop a system for recording your ideas. Because, while that flash of inspiration – the one that comes suddenly as you wait for a train or watch two shoppers fight over the last roll of toilet paper – may seem so extraordinarily unique that you will never forget it, the specifics of such eureka moments can fade easily. In the same way, the potential usefulness of some observations – a line of conversation overheard in a pet shop, the sight of a fire engine on your street when there's no fire – may only provide a springboard when you think about them sometime later. So, arm yourself – whether with a small notebook and pen, a digital memo on your mobile, or a journal to jot your ideas and observations in each evening – and make sure you keep a fresh record.

Some triggers for creativity

Historical fiction writer Natasha Lester says, 'I've learned that inspiration can come from anywhere; it's a matter of being tuned into the possibility and exposing yourself to other media that might spark ideas.' Poet Caitlin Maling recommends a life of literary crime: 'I'm a magpie: I collect and steal things to feather my nest. Or maybe a butcherbird, because what I like to steal is song – I am always listening to the peculiarities and particularities of speech wherever I am. Weird things bring me joy, like the Australianism of shortening words. I try to lean into the parts of language that, for whatever reason, cause pleasure.'

Below is a list of suggestions to trigger creativity:

- Family lore and history.
- News stories.
- Observation of daily life in busy places that are rich in variety of people and activities – shopping centres, public transport, beaches, sporting events, markets and fairs.
- Places and activities – walking, cycling and running can provide a powerful impetus for freeing the imagination into loose associative play. Inevitably we do these things in particular places – whether it's a park, a beach or just around the block – and this can produce heightened observations or a strong instinctive sense of atmosphere that can prove creatively generative.
- Dreams, desires and fantasies.
- What-ifs – projecting alternative versions or outcomes of events that have actually happened, whether in your own life or those of others. This is particularly useful as an imaginative trigger if you are seeking to add difference and depth when transforming autobiographical material into fiction.
- Ask the question, 'How would an outsider see it?' Try to observe the world around you from the perspective of an outsider who knows nothing of places, customs or people that you take for granted. Write some diary entries from that perspective. Don't worry at this stage about self-censoring: these triggers are just for you.
- Freewriting – an exercise for writers seeking to generate a flow of ideas. The aim of freewriting is to write quickly, without censorship or judgement, as spontaneously and loosely as possible, without concern

for logic but being open to dreamlike wordplay and association. It works best if you set a relatively short time limit; a prompt can also be helpful (such as the first object you see; a word or sentence chosen randomly from a book). Freewriting can break through the constraints of judgement or self-criticism that can stifle imaginative play essential to the early generative process.

Don't be hard on yourself if you are seeking story material but feeling low on inspiration and unable to produce impressive work like glossy rabbits from a hat. Sometimes a pause occurs because your mind is still working something out and, providing it's not a precursor to procrastination, if you leave the page you're sweating over and instead spend an afternoon gardening, taking the dog for a walk or playing computer games, you may well find an idea asserting itself when you least expect it. The creative mind is extraordinary in this way.

You will also find that the sources for your ideas and inspiration will change over time, reflecting different phases in your own writing and life, and also changes in subject matter and genre. Caitlin Maling, for instance, recalls:

> When I started out, I wrote pretty consistently about myself, often about things or experiences I was having trouble processing. I used to feel that poetry came from a deep well of language and emotion, but as I kept writing, I (thankfully) stopped having enough trauma to fill my writing and I had to find other ways to write. It was interesting for me to learn that my writing impulse was actually separate from this font of emotion. I still use writing as a way to filter and understand my experiences, but I've come to believe that good poems are always doing more than this, particularly in the relationship they form with language. I altered the questions I was asking in my poems: instead of them being questions about myself, I tried to write from asking questions about the world. I write a lot about places and the extra-human world.

Remember that there is no one-size-fits-all template: you need to find what works for you.

Ask an author: Where do you find inspiration or ideas?

Brigid Lowry says:

They say that everyone who has survived childhood already has enough material to last a lifetime. One's own life and experience provide an abundance of good raw material. I have found this to be true for writing memoir fiction, essays and poetry. It no doubt applies to writing plays and film scripts, too, although I have never written either of these.

Other people's lives are also rich material. It pays to be interested, and ask people things. How did you feel about leaving home? Who do you like most, your mother or your father? What is your biggest regret? Have you ever made cheese?

Travelling is a good way to produce ideas. Living a full life and having interesting adventures has many benefits, including providing seed material.

Ideas are not hard to find, actually. They can be found on the street, in the park, at bus stops, in cafés, at railway stations. Further sources include but are not limited to the following: overheard conversations, strange things children say or ask, newspapers and magazines, and dreams.

Sometimes God or the universe magically channel material into my brain. Ideas arrive, inexplicably, often at the oddest times, which is why a writer should always carry a pen and a notebook. (Margaret Atwood advised carrying two pencils in case one breaks or you can't get to a pencil sharpener.) Who knows where these lucky ideas come from, or why they arrive just at that particular moment. Creativity and imagination are mysterious.

Deb Fitzpatrick says:

Inspiration and ideas for my novels come from a variety of places. Sitting at a café people-watching is a great place to start. Sometimes, the experience of watching a film or reading a book can make me feel incredibly creative and motivated to write; other times, simply walking through streets lined with homes, wondering what might be happening beyond those front doors is enough. I also do a lot of walking in bushland and along the coast, and find this very creatively 'opening'. I love weaving these landscapes into my writing.

I've had some of my clearest ideas, though, from real-life events I've heard about on the news. I'm a news addict and will watch or listen to several (choice) news services every day if possible. The tragic death of an experienced glider pilot in the Stirling Range National Park in 2011 was one such story; I simply couldn't get it out of my head and it formed the basis of my novel *The Amazing Spencer Gray*. Western Australia's deadliest natural disaster, the 1996 Gracetown cliff collapse, was something I wanted to explore creatively in my adult novel, *The Break*. And a story I heard on the news while driving my car, about a young child left on a Sydney family's doorstep, is at the heart of *At My Door*.

Of course, like many writers, I blend my fiction with a good dose of the personal – camouflaged where necessary! If I write anything that has happened in my own home with our kids, I always make sure they read it and have the opportunity to ask for changes.

Natasha Lester says:

These days, I usually find my inspiration in the research I'm doing for another book. I'll find a fact or an event that will seize my imagination, but it won't fit in the book I'm currently writing. For example, when I was researching *The Paris Seamstress*, I came across the story of *Vogue* model turned war photojournalist Lee Miller. Her life fascinated me, so she became the inspiration for the main character in *The French Photographer*, my next book. I also find my ideas in newspaper articles, podcasts, movies, television programs, books, art galleries; lots of other places.

The idea for one of my earliest novels, *If I Should Lose You*, came from a newspaper article I read about donor coordinators: nurses who have the incredibly difficult job of caring for a patient on life support while at the same time discussing the possibility of organ donation with the patient's family.

The idea for *The Paris Seamstress* came partly from the movie *Dior and I*. When I was watching the movie, I suddenly had a very vivid picture form in my mind of a mother and daughter working together in a Parisian atelier. The other part of the idea for that book came from a podcast about the growth of the ready-to-wear fashion industry in Manhattan during the 1940s after France was occupied by the Germans and Parisian fashion was no longer accessible to the world.

And Brendan Ritchie says:

I generally avoid actively searching for inspiration or sitting down to think of ideas for writing. Instead, I just try to stay open and receptive to what is happening in the world around me and to recognise when something starts to tug at my subconscious. I had a long list of what I thought were very workable ideas for a debut novel, all extracted from regular sources such as newspapers, memories and anecdotes, but stumbled on the idea that eventually sparked my novel while watching a band play at a music festival. A more recent idea came thanks to a Qantas commercial on television, another while thinking of the route I would travel to arrive at a town in the South West. Each of these experiences reminded me that the relationship between a writer and their body of work is often mysterious and fluid.

Writers regularly talk about how their mind is subconsciously working on creative problems while they're away from their work. A complicated narrative issue can seem impossible to solve while sitting at the computer, but somehow the answer manifests while walking the dog or preparing dinner. Perhaps there is something to be taken from this in relation to ideas and inspiration. Many writers are inquisitive by nature, so giving free rein to this trait and living a life away from the desk seems like a viable way to encounter the kernels from which a novel may be born.

How to know when there is enough material to begin

The short answer to this is: you will not know until you try. And, as we said in the introduction to his book, we assume that writers are the ones who have a drive to write and will turn up at the desk no matter what. This doesn't mean that turning up is always easy. Procrastination can be self-doubt in sheep's clothing. So can the sense that one does not yet have enough material to begin. But ultimately, the only way to know whether you do or don't have enough material is to start writing.

The fascination with ideas and inspiration is understandable given that without these all-important seeds, a story cannot begin to grow and thrive on the page. Remember, though, the seeds themselves are not the full-grown tree or even the sapling; once you have an idea, you still have plenty of work to do.

Fiction, poetry and life writer, Brigid Lowry observes:

> I find that I can trust life to provide ideas. Getting them is not the problem. Remembering them and turning them into something worthwhile is another matter. One can help ideas germinate by minimising distraction and by showing up at the desk every day.

Nonetheless, at some stage, you may be required to assess the worth of material collected and what is required of you to move into the process of writing. In the following chapter, we will look in more detail at the nuts and bolts of research and planning, but for now let us consider how a writer can ascertain whether the material they have collected is worth investing precious time in.

As a journalist, Anne-Louise Willoughby was trained in assessing the weight and merit of her material. It is a practice she has carried into her own writing:

> I think I am always unconsciously switched onto high alert for a story. Inspiration comes in the moment that I engage with an interesting person – something resonates and begs to be explored. But what can be just as challenging as trying to find an idea is actually being able to determine if the idea has legs. Can it carry the weight expected of an extended work, as opposed to an article?
>
> I have always travelled and I am naturally inquisitive. I was introduced to the subject of one of my projects, a cowboy then in his eighties, by friends in the country near San Antonio, Texas. I knew that he was a legend in the region, but also reticent. His unassuming nature and charismatic smile immediately told me that a story was quietly sitting inside him, waiting to be told. Getting closer to discovering if the idea is worth pursuing is all in how you talk to people you want to get to know. Don't scare them off by getting excited and making big statements about the book you're going to write. Building trust is paramount. To start with, it might be slow going, and you might just find it was not a great idea after all! But don't give up straightaway; listen to your instinct. If the hairs on the back of your neck won't lie down when you think about your idea, you can be pretty sure there is something to tackle.

Dedication to the craft of writing

At some point, the writer must roll up their sleeves and commit. Author and illustrator Ambelin Kwaymullina says:

> Ideas are easy: they are everywhere. Many, many people have good ideas for books. Far fewer ever actually write one. One of the important aspects of being a professional writer is understanding that inspiration is usually the smallest and easiest part of the writing – that it's not about the pursuit of some amazing idea, but about the work required to take an idea and shape it into a book. Inspiration is art but writing an actual book requires dedication to craft. I suggest to aspiring writers that they spend less time focusing on ideas and start considering how to turn ideas into story; when they are reading books they love, start paying attention to all the tools the author uses to shape their ideas and convey them to the reader.

What Kwaymullina refers to as dedication to craft involves both familiarising yourself with a range of writing techniques that will prove essential in your writer's toolbox, and judging which techniques will prove most useful for your particular purposes. When you are setting out on a new work, you could find yourself asking some of the following questions:

- Do I use first-person point of view, third-person limited or omniscient, or multiple points of view?
- How will I handle narrative time? Is my work to be linear or circular in structure? Will I incorporate flashbacks?
- What genre will best convey my themes and plot?
- Should my research be channelled into fiction or non-fiction?
- Do I incorporate research into my manuscript as direct quotations or will I paraphrase, fragment or absorb the material in some other way?
- How do I translate my ideas into compelling characters? Discussions of characterisation have long emphasised the importance of exploring what drives your characters – their aims, desires, fears, beliefs etc. – and the tensions that underpin and complicate these. Emphasis too is given to the following components of characterisation:

- » appearance (showing what a character looks like)
- » thought (showing what a character is thinking – in fiction not all characters' thoughts will be explored, so consider who to prioritise)
- » dialogue (how characters speak aloud and to each other)
- » action (the way a character acts: what they choose to do, whether consciously or unconsciously, in particular in testing situations).
- How long do I envisage the work to be? How many chapters and/or sections? Do I need to mock up a plan so I can visualise what goes where? Or will I just see where it goes?
- Do the poems I have been writing have something in common and therefore belong in a collection? What gaps do I see if I bring them together?

As you build material, you may start sharpening your technical skills through writing exercises and through successive drafts. There are many how-to books and websites on methods of honing your skills – some of our contributors' favourites are listed at the end of this book.

Writing occurs by trial and error. It can be a series of false starts and abandoned enterprises. Some hours, and some days, will definitely be worse than others. Your progress may stutter or leap.

Sometimes thinking about what you are doing is important, but most times, turning up at the page is the only way to work it out.

One of the most useful mindstates might be: progress is not linear and you are not what you write. Just because what you are doing doesn't seem to be working, it doesn't follow that you are worthless as a human being *or* as a writer. You are finding your way towards a thing, and the only way to get there is through. Every writer must have a process, and that process is rarely easy.

Dedication to craft means discipline and persistence, and can be most productively achieved by establishing a routine that ensures you write regularly and maintain focus.

Establishing a routine

Once you have an idea you wish to pursue and a determination to bring it to fruition, it may help to envisage a routine – one that will assist you to structure the task ahead and facilitate the methods of your creative process. Of course, it could be that you already have these in place, and are conscious of how and why they work for you. If not, it is certainly worth reflecting on what works best for you and then laying down a plan for a regular and productive process.

To do this, here are some of the questions you could ask:

- Should I set aside certain times each day to write?
- Should I create a schedule blocking in writing time, research time and downtime?
- What practical arrangements will I need to make to ensure I have the time to write without distraction?
- Is it better for me to go work in the library or a café rather than face the distractions and responsibilities of home?
- Can I break my project down into a list of tasks I can tick off as I go?
- Am I a morning person or a night owl? Should I work on writing fresh draft material in the mornings, and use the afternoons for review? Or should I write at night and ease into the day with research or rereading?
- Do I need to mark off certain days or times for research only?
- Should I turn off my phone or my alerts and notifications while writing?
- Am I going to write my first draft by hand and move to the screen later?
- What access to technology do I require (printers and other hardware) and how can I get it?
- How will I redraft and edit? By printing off a hard copy and marking up changes, or working directly on the screen?
- What method will I use for saving and dating copies of my files as my work progresses?
- How often will I back up my work?

Remember, just because something feels difficult, this doesn't mean it's the wrong approach. Advances are often made when things are uncomfortable. It may take time and experience to understand whether creativity pains are an inevitable part of your process or something that is unnecessarily restricting you. Your method may seem anarchic, messy and slow, but that might just be part of your creative process. Identifying your own method and routine may only occur with practice, and in the next chapter we will dive further into the interesting subjects of plotting, planning and getting stuck. Knowing the answers to the 'big' questions of what kind of a writer you are can assist you in your day-to-day writing practice, even if the answers themselves change over time.

It can definitely help to consciously create the space and time in your life in which to make writing fit, and it can signal to others around you that the business of being a writer is systematic, disciplined and task oriented – just like many other jobs.

No two writers' methods or routines will be alike. But it can help to be a magpie about this part of the practice too. Insight into the habits of others might inspire you to make a change or try something else if you feel stuck.

Ask an author: What writing routine do you use and has it changed over time?

Natasha Lester says:

I wrote my first three books in two-hour blocks of time while my babies were having their day sleeps. I hated it at the time, but now I'm so grateful for that experience. It taught me not to wait for inspiration, that inspiration can often come at other times of the day when you're not at your desk. That the work of writing is not in getting inspiration, but in sitting down at the desk and being disciplined enough to actually write sentences and paragraphs and chapters. It taught me not to waste time because I didn't have any time to waste.

Those learnings have stood me in good stead. My children are now all at school, but I've been able to maintain the discipline of those early years. I'm not easily distracted and I use my time wisely. I write in half-hour blocks with about a ten-minute break in between each block – sitting for long periods is very bad for your back, so it's a great idea to get up and move around regularly. Also, if I know I'm just sitting down for half an hour, I'll be as productive in that half hour as I would be if I sat at the computer in an unfocused way for two hours.

I use school terms to break up my writing year. I write a draft of a book during the school term and then have two weeks away from it over school holidays to get some distance and perspective. Once school goes back, I sit down at the desk and redraft. I usually submit my sixth draft to my publisher. The first draft takes up about 20% of my writing time; 80% is in rewriting.

And Brigid Lowry says:

I began writing professionally when my son was seven, so I wrote while he was at school, and aimed for five hundred good words a day. If I had time, in the evening I might edit or write a bit more. Nowadays, my routine is more organic. I aim to write for an hour a day, and enjoy it. If the work takes hold, I write for longer. Sometimes I write in the morning after I have finished my morning routine of meditation, yoga, breakfast, email and general mucking about. Then, after groceries, walking, errands and lunch, I may find I am drawn back to writing in the afternoon, but not often. More usually, if I get a second wind, it will be at night. I have learned over many years of listening to other more famous persons at writers festivals, and by reading books about writers and their methods, that whatever works for you is the correct routine. I know writers who work on two books at a time, and writers who write like stink for days then party for weeks. I know of saintly writers who get up at 5 am and write before their kids wake up. I know people who begin at 9 am, write until lunchtime, then eat a sandwich and diligently write some more.

Enjoy the flow of your own way of doing things. Be flexible, because life is a long game and circumstances will change. The only absolute thing is that if you want to be a writer, you must sit down and write.

Choosing a genre

Finding a voice and selecting a genre are two aspects of being a writer that are intertwined – but let's take a moment to look at them separately.

If you are serious about being a writer then you will likely be thinking about what type of book/poem/story/collection you are seeking to create. Or perhaps you have written something and are not sure what it is. If you went looking for your hypothetically completed work in a bookstore, by what genre would it be classified? Crime or true crime? Horror, romance or science fiction? Literary fiction? Young adult? Fantasy? A hybrid of some of these?

Why choose a genre at all? Some writers have a very definite sense of the genre they want to work in and are well versed in its conventions because it is what they read and love. For this reason, Alan Carter feels that he has no choice about choosing to write crime:

If I'm not in control of that, I'm not in control of anything, I suppose. I'm an avid crime fiction reader. In my other life as a TV documentary maker, I was also interested in stories to do with law and order, and crime. It's a popular genre across many platforms: books, podcasts, TV, movies. The stakes are always high, there is conflict and excitement, often a puzzle to solve, and they are peopled by great characters often flawed and usually driven. Crime fiction (and true crime) tends to be about some very Old Testament universals in life: greed, lust, envy, ambition, revenge and betrayal. They are both plot- and character-driven tales with compelling forward motion and the kind of resolution between the forces of good and evil that is often missing from real life. What's not to like?

Should you actively choose your genre? If you are open to writing in any genre, then you can be targetted what you choose. Crime sells better than poetry but each form has its own freedoms and limitations. Women's historical fiction performs strongly but may not leave you the space to explore your love of the absurd. Genre choosing is like matchmaking: Are you in it for a bit of fun, or something more serious? To what extent are you and a genre really compatible? Can a particular genre assist your long-term goals as a writer or is it a frivolous diversion? Actually: are frivolous diversions what you want to write? Are you writing the kind of book you want to read? Is there a certain kind of audience you would like to attract for your work, or are you happy to take all comers?

It may be a matter of thinking about what you are predisposed towards. You have a set of experiences and areas of expertise that are unique to you. You know that your mind works in a particular way. You may have studied certain subjects and been engaged by certain things. You don't need to limit yourself in how you deploy your knowledge and your particular – even peculiar – curiousity about the world. Margaret Atwood is widely known as a poet and writer of literary fiction, but she has written in the genres of historical fiction, science fiction, dystopian fiction and realist fiction. Liz Byrski has published popular fiction, narrative non-fiction, reportage and memoir over a long and varied career. Tim Winton crafted numerous award-winning works of adult literary fiction while offering up the adventures of Lockie Leonard to kids.

As an early-stage writer, try not to allow anxieties about genre overwhelm you, as this is an aspect of your writing that will remain potentially variable throughout your career. Nevertheless, be aware that genre *does* matter to readers, and finding the right genre can facilitate your capacity to tell the story in the way that best suits your aims, subject matter and abilities. Some questions that may help you answer this are:

- What do you enjoy reading and why?
- What genres do the authors you most admire work in?
- What sort of genre best suits the idea you are seeking to develop?
- Are there conventions of genre already inherent in your work?

Remain an active and curious reader, and don't be afraid to be flexible with genre. Sometimes, if you are stuck, it may be worth switching genres: for instance, if you're writing true crime, you might find you work more fluidly with the material if you write it as a crime novel; you may be stuck in a young adult story when really your content is better suited to a younger demographic. Trying to use your trip to Mongolia as a basis for a novel and making no progress? Maybe what you really need to write is a narrative non-fiction travel memoir. Try changing direction for a bit and see what you feel works best; perhaps show the different approaches to a trusted reader.

And of course, if you do find yourself changing direction entirely, mid-career or via simultaneous publications – say gardening author and writer of erotica – you can always choose a pseudonym, to ensure your brands don't clash. (We will look more at author brands in Chapter 3.)

Below are some questions new writers ask in relation to genre. These are not exhaustive – you should look to a writing book for those. But they are frequently asked questions that relate to submission and publication.

What is the difference between fiction and non-fiction?

Fiction refers to writing that, even where it may use 'real life' as a starting point, stems from the writer's imagination. Fiction uses setting, dialogue, plot and characters, and accommodates a wide range of styles. Fiction's forms include novels, short stories, novellas and scripts. Fundamentally, the reader understands that the content is not 'true' and a fiction work will be marketed in this way.

Non-fiction, on the other hand, is based on true events, often has an air of objectivity and is often supported by research and references. Forms include history, biography, autobiography, popular science, sport, gardening, as well as books featuring photography and fine art.

What is narrative non-fiction?

Like non-fiction, narrative non-fiction tells *true* stories but moves away from the objective tone, unembellished style and factual emphasis of non-fiction. This genre is typically subjective, told from first-person point of view, and its writers draw on devices commonly associated with fiction to tell their story. These can include:

- Figurative language.
- Recreated dialogue.
- Non-linear, juxtaposed and fragmented structure.
- Plotting.
- Imaginative speculation.
- Composite characters.
- Incorporation of writing fragments in other genres and styles.

The narrative non-fiction writer is often upfront about their personal focus and any significant imaginative deviations they may be making away from non-fiction (i.e. the truth). The reader engages with the work understanding the story is essentially 'true' (in the manner of non-fiction) or, where it deviates from pure facts, is still relaying an emotional truth.

In this genre, the *meaning* of the story should be bigger than the story itself, so that a more universal point is also made. A surf travel memoir, for instance, may be a vivid account of the surfer's travails and ecstasies, but may also be an exploration of the way humans can find themselves helpless in the ocean's thrall while feeling simultaneously drawn to be its vigilant custodians.

Sub-genres include memoir, personal essay, true crime and travel writing. Narrative non-fiction approaches can also be found in biography, food writing, cultural commentary, nature writing, blogs and sports writing.

What categories of children's fiction are there?

Children's fiction is generally divided by age group but may be categorised slightly differently by different publishers and booksellers. Broad categories include board books (newborn to age 3), picture books (3–8), first chapter books or junior fiction (6–9), middle-grade books or middle readers (8–12), and young adult (YA) novels (12 and up, or 14 and up).

Should I write my book with a secondary destination in mind, like film or television?

It can be tempting to pen a work that you believe down the track will make a great screenplay or a perfect television series. Our advice, though, is *don't*. A book that is reaching to be something other than itself, or is focused too much on visuals, is only going to feel uncommitted or shaky; it may pay insufficient attention to dialogue, character or plot. With entertainment streaming companies like Stan, Netflix and Foxtel Now competing for market share, a great deal of new content is required, and such businesses are coming to publishers for well-developed stories set in well-conceived worlds with strong characters and compelling plots. In this context, the role of the book remains simply to be the best it can be on its own terms rather than straining to inhabit another form simultaneously.

Should I write my book according to what's trending?

Vampires come in, and vampires go out; Nordic sweaters are all the rage and then characters can't shuck them off fast enough. Unless you are able to predict a trend several years in advance, then the ship full of vampires in Nordic sweaters will have sailed by the time you are ready to submit your manuscript. So our broad advice is: don't bother to write about what is fashionable now just for its own sake. On the other hand, if you see a gap in the market and you are excited by the possibility of filling it, this could be a reason to choose some particular subject matter over another. When it comes time to submitting your work to a publisher, your accompanying material can certainly state that you believe yours is a work that will provide readers with something they can't get anywhere else.

Ask an author: Do you choose your genre or does your genre choose you?

Rachel Robertson says:

My genre – creative non-fiction – definitely chose me. I write personal or literary essays, lyric essays and memoir. Actually, when I was younger, I always dreamed of being a novelist or poet. I wrote and published some poetry and short fiction but I really found my form when I started work on my book *Reaching One Thousand*, which is a collection of autobiographical essays ordered by theme. The desire to use my own experience and research as the basis for my work helped me find the genre that suited me best. Interestingly, it was at that point that I realised I had spent the past seven or eight years reading memoir and creative non-fiction, rather than the literary fiction I had previously always enjoyed best. It was as if my unconscious had been preparing me to write non-fiction before I knew that's what I wanted to do.

What I love about creative non-fiction is the way it is grounded in history or current affairs, or an individual or family life, but is written using imagination and literary and creative flair. In writing memoir and autobiography, I believe in honouring Philippe Lejeune's notion of the 'autobiographical pact': I want to tell a truth of some sort and will not deliberately falsify events (though memory and interpretation are never reliable). I am now writing pieces that I would describe as lyric essays; these works are more allusive and less tethered to my own life or particular events. They leave more for the reader to do.

Nandi Chinna says:

In some ways I think your genre chooses you. When I was young and still in high school, I thought I wanted to be a novelist. I read a couple of seminal books such as John Steinbeck's *The Grapes of Wrath*, which had such a profound impact upon me and the way I thought about social justice, that I really thought I wanted to write fiction. But later when I started trying to write something for myself, it was poetry that seemed to come out of the pen via the unconscious. For me, poetry is essential: it holds the story and the metaphor in such a compressed and powerful way, and can brilliantly speak straight to the heart of things. I think poetry chose me. Poetry was there to help me navigate the bewildering landscapes of my own self, as well as the absolutely incomprehensible inequities and tragedies of living in the world. We return to poetry in our most joyful moments and in our most horrendous, inexplicable pain. I feel like I'm still learning what poetry is, still trying to learn how to make the best of it.

Anne-Louise Willoughby says:

The genre of biography quietly sidled up to me. Most journalists probably like to think they have a book in them and I thought mine would be a novel. But when it came down to it, the first book I felt compelled to write was the story of Nora Heysen, a woman who had been underrated for her career as an artist. Writing a life was a logical progression for me because journalism is life writing in snapshots: the how, what, where, why and when of a life event. Biography is the extended version: the movie as opposed to a scene. My career training over many years involved research and stringent fact-checking, and it provides a solid platform for the rigours of biography. I'm naturally inclined to want to talk to people, and that same curiosity propels the drive required to write a life. A certain patience is necessary, too, when the research leads to an unexpected path. You must follow up the unexpected and my experience as a reporter and journalist prepared me for that. That all said, while the genre of biography suits me, it doesn't mean I won't write fiction. So much of life forms the basis of a cracking tale.

Daniel de Lorne says:

The genre you choose to write in is likely to come out of your own reading preferences. Perhaps you're attracted to its conventions or the possibilities for creating something new or better. Whatever the reason, there's something that draws you to it in the first place. Whether it ends up being the genre you publish in isn't always guaranteed.

You may find that publishers (if you're going down the traditional route) or readers aren't there for your twist on a longstanding genre, or that the market may be so flooded with sparkling vampires it's hard to cut through. This may be an opportunity for you to stretch yourself as a reader and as a writer, finding a new-to-you niche or one that you've previously shunned. Explore. Discover.

Using myself as an example, I started out in paranormal and horror and thought I would only ever write in those genres (perhaps with a side of fantasy thrown in). I then realised that most of my ideas had a romantic element to them that could be expanded upon, and as such could position my writing within the romance genre. From there I've written in paranormal, horror, romantic suspense, rural and contemporary. If I had been so against stepping outside my comfort zone, my opportunities for publication would have been limited.

Meg McKinlay says:

I think the genre/s in which we write are a function of many things, among them our own particular interests as individuals and as readers. We may not consciously choose aspects of our writing – genre, audience, form – but they're still an outcome of choices we make or have made in the past.

As someone who has written across a broad range – speculative fiction, contemporary realism, historical, crime – genre is often the last key element upon which I settle. In general, I start with one small seed of inspiration – an image, a character quirk, a line of dialogue that won't let me go – and play creatively until it accretes enough material to acquire a kind of momentum. I've described myself in the past as an 'accidental' writer of both speculative fiction and crime fiction, because the genres of the novels in question emerged organically as I followed, respectively, a character trait and a setting. Neither of those are genres I would have consciously set out to write, for a range of reasons, but not least because I am not an avid reader of either.

Some might interpret that process as a case of genre choosing them, or at the very least choosing a particular project, but I'm sceptical of that way of framing things. I suspect it's most accurate to say that genre emerges from the pre-work I do, from that initial period of creative play. I may not be conscious of the process, but in the end I'm the one putting those building blocks in place.

Something I would stress is that however you come to a particular genre, you should treat it with respect. If you write in a field, you must read in it, familiarising yourself with its traditions and tropes. Subscribing to the notion of a genre having chosen you should never be a justification for a lack of thoughtfulness in its execution.

And Sasha Wasley says:

My genre very much chooses me, but I have had to wrangle my writing so I have more control. If my writing heart had its way, my books would be a melting pot of mystery, romance, literary and psychological thriller genres. In fact, my early books were just that: if I had a new idea, no matter whether it was urban fantasy or whodunnit, I would merrily shoehorn it onto whatever novel I was working on at the time. It took me a long time to learn that some ideas should be noted down and left to ferment for another novel.

I've now learned that, if I'm writing a series or contracted for a multi-book deal, I must respect my readership and be cognisant of my brand. In a series, I must stay true to the genre or I will lose my readers. If I'm writing the third book in a trilogy, I can't segue from young adult paranormal romance to crime fiction. In those situations, I have to choose my genre and resist its efforts to choose me.

While writing a three-book rural romance series several years ago, I got distracted by a psychological thriller idea. Luckily, I had the discipline to write the third novel in my rural romance series before diving into the new idea. I'm really happy with the psychological thriller but it doesn't suit my brand or my progression as a commercial fiction author, so it will probably be shelved for a couple of years. It would be too jarring a shift for my readers. The next book for me will be a commercial women's fiction based largely in a small country town – which is a more natural shift from rural romance for my readers.

Finding a voice

As an emerging writer, you may be struggling to develop your voice – that intangible yet palpable melding of style, spirit and focus that is unique and distinctive, identifiable by others as running through the writer's body of work, yet capable of growth and variation over time.

Finding a voice can be fundamental to facilitating the writer's control of their process and, as the authors' responses below suggest, finding one's voice assists in establishing confidence and enabling progression. A writer's voice marks their particular appeal to their readers – familiar but never formulaic, individual and engaging. If considered in the context of the business of being a writer, your voice will be a crucial and identifiable component of your brand. That said, finding a voice will take time, so don't panic if it does not emerge overnight. Some observations about voice:

- Finding a voice involves trial and error, patience and practice.
- It is not something you are simply born with – beware the myth of natural-born genius and remember even the inherently gifted need to nurture their talents.
- Don't worry if you feel your writing is initially too close to the voices of writers you admire; the influence of exemplars is a very useful part of

the development process. Many writers, including those whose views appear below, acknowledge the formative significance of influences, and of reading widely, to the evolution of their own voices.

- Think about the writers you admire. What is it that is distinctive about their work that appeals to you and distinguishes it from the work of others? Read some reviews. What qualities do critics and reviewers draw attention to?

- Don't become overly self-conscious about voice as you write. This can be very inhibiting. A burst of freewriting could be a circuit-breaker if you find you are falling into this trap.

Ask an author: How do you find your voice?

Brigid Lowry says:
Finding your writing voice is a question that can't really be answered rationally. It is possibly more a case of letting your voice find you. It seems to me that everything that you are and all that you believe in will contribute to the writer you become. Are you deeply intellectual, or maybe quiet and odd? Where were you born? Who are your ancestors? What genres do you read? What are you interested in? You are a product of your time, your place, your society, and possibly your star sign and Enneagram as well, and your writing voice will reflect this.

The more fully you own your originality, the more the world can shine through you. Being who you are and claiming your voice can feel like an unwanted gift at times. Perhaps you long to be Haruki Murakami but find that you are actually Banana Yoshimoto. Your job is to claim your Banana fully. Ben Elton writes like Ben Elton, Tim Winton writes like Tim Winton, Jeanette Winterson writes like Jeanette Winterson. Be in favour of originality. Say what you want to say. You are you, and will write as you once you stop trying to be anyone else. This is the miracle.

Liz Byrski says:
A good way to begin finding your voice is to write a short opinion piece or column. The art of the columnist is to find a voice that people want to read on a regular basis. It is the reliability and credibility of

the voice that brings them back, even if the opinions expressed are not always the same as their own. Readers learn to trust a voice and to rely on it.

In non-fiction, your own voice – honest, confident, well informed and consistent – is always best. It's important to remember that voice is different from style. Voice is about you as a writer; it is how people recognise you – a combination of vocabulary, syntax, tone and the way you structure and organise your work. It is also about your point of view, what you believe in and what you choose to write about in both fiction and non-fiction.

You may find it useful to try reading aloud what you have written, recording it and playing it back. Remember, you are listening for style and content, and whether you have conveyed a message. When you have captured your own voice, you will have established a platform for your writing in whatever genre you prefer. This is just as true for fiction as non-fiction. Know your own voice, and then you will be able to create other voices to help you tell your story.

Holden Sheppard says:

Agents and publishers will often say what they are looking for is a fresh, new voice: someone who tells a story in a new and refreshing way. Finding your voice as a writer is important to make your writing appealing to readers and publishers. Here are a few tips on finding your voice as an author:

- Read books and authors similar to how you think you'd like to sound and learn what works for you and what doesn't.
- Write a regular blog – this enables you to practise writing often but without the pressure of completing a whole novel, and along the way you'll organically discover what you sound like on the page.
- Write like there are no sacred cows – that is, forget what your spouse or family or friends or boss or your god or whoever would think about what you're writing, and just write how you feel. Not only is this liberating in a personal sense, but it often unlocks an authentic voice, because you're not trying to make your manuscript 'good', you're just trying to write honestly.

For me, these three steps all helped me discover my own authentic voice – something that was missing from my earlier manuscripts when I was more focused on writing something that would 'work' for the market. To reference a quote attributed to American jazz musician Miles Davis, 'Man, sometimes it takes you a long time to sound like yourself.'

David Whish-Wilson says:

Paradoxically, perhaps, I think the best way to find your own voice as an emerging writer is to begin by inhabiting deeply the voices of writers you admire. This of course requires finding those writers who you think are exemplars of the kind of writing you want to undertake, reading as much as possible of their work and thinking about the craft behind the way they construct their stories, but also, more importantly, allowing their voice to sink deeply into your own. Initially at least, this might make your early attempts at writing feel inauthentic and borrowed, except that it won't be over the longer term, because your own voice will emerge naturally and inevitably the more you write, and the more you commit to your writing. Writing is a reader's craft, after all, and it's an intuitive process as much as it's a conscious process. Learning to read critically is important, but so is allowing a writer's voice to subconsciously guide you in the process as you make your first steps as a writer. An established writer friend of mine still begins every morning's writing by reading a couple of paragraphs of Virginia Woolf. My friend's voice is very much her own, but that habit of opening herself up to another voice that she admires, to loosen up the mind, as it were, is still an important part of her routine.

And Caitlin Maling says:

It's a cliché, but reading other people's work is the most important part of developing your own. I recommend reading as broadly as possible, with three particular streams: things you love (can be anything), things considered great (what's canonical – think about why), and things that are getting big press now (why is something hitting the Zeitgeist). I often think poetry is just reassembling the same ingredients as every other poet in a new way – for you to be able to do this you have to do as much prep as possible. When I first got into poetry, I bought several huge anthologies (think *The Norton Anthology of Modern and Contemporary Poetry*) and I would flip through them, pausing where a poem or poet really struck me; this helped me get across what had come before me and refine my taste.

Lean into the things you know better than anyone else. Are there weird realms of words and knowledge you have access to? If so, use them. I do believe the best poems come from knowledge or questions that have been personally processed by the poet. Often when I watch sport or dance, I think about the idea of physical intelligence and how it's a type of flow state similar to what I enter when my poetry is working well. But having that intuition is also about having practised your arse off, so write as often and as weirdly as possible. Take a notebook with you everywhere, start poems on trains and planes, notice where you do your best work and repeat it. In first drafts, and when you are starting as a writer, is the time to let it all hang out. Editing is where you take your bundle of weird words and fashion something from it.

So, now you have a voice, a genre and a project – or at least are working towards some of these things. You may also have the beginnings of a method and routine, or perhaps you are working them out as you go.

In the next chapter, we will look at some of the things to think about beyond the process of creation: those facets of the business of being a writer that you might encounter when you are away from the page.

2. The process of creating a manuscript

- Research
- Plotting and planning
- Getting stuck
- Building a community and finding peers
- Mentors
- Feedback and workshopping
- Opportunities for gaining experience

Not everything covered in the first chapter will necessarily happen at the beginning of your writing process. Certain aspects, like routine, voice or genre, may be arrived at osmotically or gradually. In this chapter, we will look at what to do once you have found a subject you wish to pursue, and how you might build a network of support around you while you do.

Research

Not every new work requires research to be undertaken, but quite a lot does. The research that writers do as they embark upon a new piece of writing generally involves library and internet research, but, dependent on genre and aims, can also include:

- Observational research – attentively deploying the senses and gathering material by immersion in a place, activity, event or experience.
- Talking to interview subjects and experts related to the subject matter of your work, through structured interviews or informal conversations.

Observational research skills are fundamental to travel writing, and anyone working in that genre should not leave home without them. Some forms of observational research (for instance, visiting the local beach or night market) can be easily undertaken, though nothing will be achieved without close attention to significant details using all the senses, plus a good note-taking process.

More complex experiential scenarios in which you might also participate in an activity (such as spending time with the night shift in an emergency department or being present at a rally) as well as almost all interview research, can require formal consent from your subject (see p. 107) and may have attendant moral, ethical or legal considerations (see Chapter 4). This type of research can be time-consuming to organise and undertake, so forward planning is essential.

The most common mode of research for writers, however, is through exploring written, aural, visual and audio-visual resources, predominantly through libraries and the internet.

Using the internet for research

Search engines like Google provide gateways to a plethora of information, some of which could be very useful indeed, but all of which should be approached with critical scrutiny and attention to accuracy and provenance. Ask yourself:

- Who wrote this?
- What are their qualifications and experience to be offering this opinion?
- Who runs/owns/endorses this website and what might they stand to gain from disseminating this information?
- Should I cross-reference by seeking out a couple of different resources to see if they are consistent?
- Is the information logically presented and supported by sources?
- To what purpose am I putting the information I'm seeking?

Whether you are writing a historical novel that explores the disappearance of Harold Holt in 1967 or a biography of the late Amy Winehouse, you should be aware that you will need more than a Wikipedia article, a blog dedicated to conspiracy theories or a fan site on Tumblr to inform your knowledge of the subject or to persuade readers that you, or perhaps your characters, know what you/they are talking about. Of course, these resources can have their uses: Wikipedia can be a good starting point for basic information or a gateway to further resources; maybe you are debunking conspiracy theories, or maybe you are building some characters who believe them; and fans can be the guardians of obscure facts about their idols or provide intriguing insights. Google Maps and Google Earth can be perfect tools for confirming distances between places or checking, for instance, whether the butcher's shop window is visible from the front doorstep of the police station in a certain town.

However, if you are drilling down deep into a subject, then take full advantage of the rich array of high-quality resources that the internet has to offer, from free or partially accessible quality newspapers and journals, to open-access out-of-copyright books, to the websites of medical and scientific research organisations, rich with links and resources, to the blogs of lauded writers and to TED Talks by innumerable specialist speakers across a diverse range of professions.

Using libraries for research

The interconnectivity between library and internet research is invaluable for the contemporary writer. Internet searches will direct you to information about books and other resources that you will be able to seek out through a library, whether local, state or university. Libraries are increasingly blending shelf-based and digital resources, and their catalogues can be searched offsite, allowing you to save time by knowing which library you need to go to, whether the item is available, whether your local library can recall it or order it in for you, and if one library has a greater range of resources in your area of interest than others.

The National Library of Australia (NLA) provides an extraordinary online resource in the form of Trove, which is an ever-growing repository with digitised access to cultural texts including books, newspapers, journals, theses, data sets, physical objects, images, music, videos, interviews and maps from libraries, museums, archives and research organisations around Australia.

Many libraries offer links and guidance on how to find web resources. They also offer computer terminals to search from, power points for your laptop, free wi-fi, desk space, heat in winter and air-conditioning in summer. But don't forget that actually browsing the books on the library shelves can lead you to serendipitous discoveries that may even reset the entire direction of your writing. Following the research trail laid down in the works you are reading is also invaluable. Ask yourself: What books and articles have they referred to? Do they look useful? Where can I find them?

It may be that your research points you towards such primary resources as unpublished diaries and letters, government documents, photograph albums, oral histories, court transcripts, military records, explorers' maps, home movies or old documentaries. Primary resource research will usually require forward planning and can be quite time-consuming. Some primary materials may have been digitised and made available online for easier access, but in many cases you will only be able to find them in archival collections or special collections, often housed in state or university libraries. You will need to notify designated library staff or archivists managing the collections to book a time in which you can access the documents, usually in a closed-off reading area. Be mindful that you won't be permitted to photocopy fragile documents, though you might be able to take digital photos, and you might be restricted to a pencil and notebook for note-taking. For speed of access and to assist the library professionals, make sure you research and record as much as you can of the identifying details of what you are looking for in advance, using the library catalogue or internet resources for background.

Some genres, such as biography or historical fiction, will be inherently grounded in deep and lengthy study, but, as the writers whose opinions appear below make clear, all writing requires some kind of research. Curiosity fuels creativity. Realising imaginative worlds requires attention to small details, and credibility is integral to the authenticity of a piece. It is worth keeping in mind that research isn't linear: dead-ends, U-turns, and false starts are all part of the game. As with so many other things to do with writing, adaptability, resilience, lateral thinking, perseverance, dedication and doggedness can be qualities just as important as research skills themselves.

Ask an author: What types of research do you do and how do you go about it?

Liz Byrski says:
In writing fiction, the research always begins for me with working out who the characters are, what sort of backgrounds they come from, and what has influenced who they've become. As most of my characters are over fifty and often much older, I have pretty good

personal knowledge of key national and international events that would have affected the characters, and also of the way the world has changed over their lifetimes because I am at the higher end of that age group, but I still have to do research.

For example, at the moment I am writing about a character who had polio as a child, and now, in her seventies, suffers from post-polio syndrome. I began by talking to a friend who had polio as a child and now has post-polio syndrome and had written his PhD on it. Then I searched online to find several other personal stories, and more general information. But reading is only part of the research; the most valuable information comes from interviews. I have searched for and found several other people who told me their stories of polio in the past and its impact on their lives in their sixties and seventies.

For previous novels and non-fiction books, I've interviewed a wide range of people, including police officers, a lawyer, ex-servicemen, members of parliament, a nun and a former nun, a chef, belly dancers, the owner of a lavender farm, a high court judge, a couple of miners, a welder and many more. I always do some background reading in advance so that I can ask informed questions. This makes it easier and more effective for both the interviewee and for me.

I also do a lot of research online to clarify any historical events or periods. It is also valuable for landscape and the atmosphere of places. By looking at coloured photographs or short documentaries, I can get a good sense of place. I also use locations I know well or have visited. Images, short films or travel documentaries also help me refresh my memories. My most recent book was set in the Blue Mountains and I found all my information on the internet because I have never been there, but many readers have assumed that I know the area well. Don't overlook the facilities of your local library. Most librarians enjoy helping people find what they need and suggesting other possibilities.

Nandi Chinna says:

Research occurs every day in varied and unexpected ways. Research can be listening to the radio, going for a walk, reading a book, dreams, chance encounters, overheard conversations and stories that other people tell you. My biggest research tool is probably my senses. When I go out walking, or indeed at any time I'm awake, I'm listening closely to sounds, using my olfactory receptors, noticing activity at all levels – tracks on the ground, what's above in the sky or trees, not just what is in front of me. I'm always touching textures, tasting leaves, examining shapes and forms. Research is really having a healthy curiosity about being in the world.

More formal research sources I use include archives, libraries, the internet, resource books and histories, journals and bird and plant reference books.

Apart from stumbling upon random stories that interest me, my research usually begins with an idea. I usually have ideas about writing projects while I'm out walking. I find the practice of walking is very stimulating to the unconscious and it's when ideas surface and pop out into my conscious thinking process. A few lines of poetry may arise; a memory or an idea that I want to pursue. I usually do start with journal writing and then I might do some research to follow up on some of the known knowledge about particular subjects. Although I'm beginning to realise how Eurocentric my research is and I'm trying to expand the cultural parameters of my research as well as move to a more raw and pure associative kind of writing.

Amanda Curtin says:

The *immersive research stage* is about the accumulation of knowledge – the big, essential things and the little details. Immersion in your subject/place/time/issue gives you the material from which to write something authentic and credible, something readers will trust.

At first, the research seems unstructured. You have some idea in mind – for example, a place or an issue – and beyond the desire to understand everything about it, you might not know what it is you're looking for. Begin with the obvious, and then move beyond that. Look for context. Look for connections that align facts and details with the senses and emotions. Follow tangents – they are often where the magic lies. Be alert for anything that makes your heart race – these *aha* moments are signals, messages, signs that say 'dig here!'

Common sources for immersive research include libraries, archives, photographic collections, newspapers, museums, films and documentaries, interviews, maps. Site research – travelling to places, walking, taking photographs, making observations, listening, feeling – is invaluable if you're able to do it. If you're not, use whatever technology is available (e.g. webcams, Google Maps) and seek out the impressions of others (e.g. through memoirs, artworks).

In the *reactive research stage*, you *do* know what you're looking for. You want answers to specific questions: How much did an orange cost in Lerwick in 1906? Did convicts wear underwear? How many women artists exhibited in the 1911 Salon d'Automne? Common sources for reactive research include internet searches, consultation with individuals and organisations identified during immersive research, and libraries and archives.

James Foley says:

I do a few types of research, including *subject matter research*. If I'm working on a book with a specific topic (e.g. Vikings, robots, dung beetles, space travel), then I'll do a lot of research before I start writing. Sometimes a lovely nugget of knowledge turns up that can be turned into a plot point. I take lots of notes in my sketchbook; I save folders full of web links and playlists of YouTube videos. Often I have to go back to the research during the writing or illustrating phase when I realise I need to check facts or get more information.

That brings me to another type of research – *image reference*. When I'm illustrating, I need to know how to draw things I've never bothered to learn how to draw before – that could be a rabbit, or a hotel lobby, or a 1955 Chevrolet Apache. Google image search is an illustrator's best friend.

Illustration involves a bit more research too, if you could call it that – or maybe it's better classified as *experimentation and preparation*. When planning a new book, I need to spend some time testing out the illustration style – perhaps I need to practise using a new medium, or find new ways to use tools I'm familiar with. Then I need to figure out what my characters will look like. I always draw some character turnaround sheets, i.e. a template for each character, drawn from a few different angles. This also lets me set their costume and colour scheme. I also prepare a cast sheet: this is like a police line-up with all the characters standing in a line, showing their relative heights. This also lets me double-check that each character is unique; each character in a story has to be instantly recognisable and can't be confused for anyone else in the cast.

Rachel Robertson says:

I do plenty of research because I almost always write non-fiction. I find myself undertaking three types of research. First, there is subject-based research. For example, I was recently writing about a porcelain jug I inherited, and for that I did research on porcelain, types of clay, the history of the particular company that made the piece, the history of when such jugs were used and so on. Secondly, I do personal, familial or archival research. So, in this example, I tried to find out when my family bought or received the jug, and when it was used. Memory work, looking at photographs and letters, and talking to others is part of this type of research. Then, thirdly, I will usually do some more theoretical or literary research. For me, this is more about linking a personal or historical story with a larger idea or theme. It is often a more haphazard and opportunistic type of research, involving going down lots of rabbit holes. For example, for the porcelain jug essay, I read Edmund de Waal's *The White Road* (Vintage, 2016), looked at lots of still-life paintings of pots, read some works about colour glazes and so on. Often, I read a particular theorist – in this case, I read bits of philosophy, because various thinkers have written about jugs and vases. (This turned out to be a red herring in the end, but I had to read it to find that out.) In this way, I do a lot of research, but may end up using only a couple of facts or a quote or two in my final work. I don't ever feel it is wasted, though; the research and thinking are all part of the process and I believe they help me towards a deeper engagement with my theme and story, and ultimately a more powerful work.

Anne-Louise Willoughby says:

As a biographer, detailed, forensic research is the main component of my work. I start by creating a linear timeline of events and notable moments, and a visual map of phases in my subject's life. Ending up looking like a Venn diagram, this document holds the names of people who I've identified to be either close or peripheral to my subject. As the map expands, it functions as a quick character referral tool and as a check on gossip versus fact. If a particular anecdote, rumour or suggestion recurs in diagram intersections, I know I am in solid territory and need to investigate further.

I search public institutions (and, of course, Google) for archived materials relating to my subject's personal and professional lives, as well as those of people they were close to. Letters proved to be invaluable in writing *Nora Heysen: A Portrait*; the National Library of Australia holds an extensive archive.

After determining who of the key people are still living, I approach them for interviews. I research the lives of deceased figures in social, political and historical contexts, and how my subject interacted with them.

Thinking laterally and having persistence are critical. Reading widely is essential. Cast the net wider than you'd think and you'll have better chances of discovering unexpected information and narrative links, as well as finding credible sources to verify details. Trove, the NLA's online database, allows researchers direct access to newspapers, journals, books, maps, personal papers and born-digital content.

And David Whish-Wilson says:

One thing I learned early was that both fiction and non-fiction projects require an equal amount of research to do them justice. Sometimes the research is crucial to capture the finer details of a project and at other times it's more about becoming immersed in a world with its own distinct voices and senses of place. My favourite kind of research, where possible, is to speak to people directly – to listen to their stories. This can help to flesh out a story, but can also lead to surprising new directions that mightn't have been obvious to begin with. Beyond that, I employ the standard research methods of trawling the net and local and university libraries for texts (books, articles, films, documentaries) about my developing idea, learning as much as I can. The trick is knowing when to leave the immersion in the world of research and start writing. Sometimes, too much research can be paralysing. For this reason, once I'm confident in the broader research, I begin writing as soon as possible, researching alongside the writing, opening myself up to the possibility that I might stray away from the fixed details of the research and allowing myself to do that – it can always be returned to later.

Plotting and planning

So, now your research is somewhat underway, or maybe it's positively humming along. Sooner or later, the time must come to write. Writers preparing to make this leap are sometimes described as either *planners* or *plungers* in their approach to the writing process. The terms *plotters* and *pantsers* are used too, but the basic meanings are the same: writers who meticulously map out the specifics of the work (such as structure, plot and themes) and who must have their strategy in place before they start to write; or those impulsive souls who grab the flash of an idea and jump right in, finding direction as they go. In truth, the set division between the two approaches is not fixed: some writers incorporate a bit of both as they ease into their task, or find that certain genres or topics lend themselves more to one or the other. Crime writer Alan Carter notes that he does 'permutations of both, to a greater or lesser degree', while Brendan Ritchie, the author of two YA dystopian novels, reveals that he has tried both methods and 'found that plunging brings a momentum and energy to my writing that I haven't yet experienced when planning'. However, after the rush, 'backtracking and redrafting' is required – a move back to planning and coherence.

Are genre and reader expectations a factor that you need to consider when determining your approach? Rural romance author Sasha Wasley has particular advice when approaching a series:

> The only time I think you really need to have some sort of road map or plot framework down on paper before you start writing is when you are writing a book series with a single overarching plot. I have been caught out a couple of times when I didn't do this and it made writing the final (or even the middle) books very difficult. There were things I wished I had or had not written in earlier books that would have made the series much stronger. If you want to write a series, I recommend spending the time doing plot work in advance.

Brendan Ritchie suggests that dystopian fiction may be better suited to a plunging approach, as this synthesises the characters' chaotic and uncertain existence for the author. Of course, as Ritchie notes, the plotting side of the equation will become a factor as the revision process develops.

The choice of planning or plunging, or the combination of both, seems to be a matter of individual preference among writers, a question of experimenting to see what works for you, rather than a purely genre- or reader-driven imperative.

Ask an author: Is plotting and planning your manuscript a good idea, or is it better to plunge straight in?

Alan Carter says:

Yes. That really is the answer to both questions and there will be authors who swear by one or the other. Thriller writer Lee Child, for instance, claims that he never plans ahead; he'll just sit down and write and write until he's finished. He also claims to never need to 'backfill' – that is, to go back and fill in some holes or plot points, or logic issues that become apparent after early readings. That's, well, phenomenal. Other authors will pre-plot down to the very last detail and know way ahead every single twist and turn. I find it useful to have at least a big picture in my head, for example, with my first novel *Prime Cut*, it was a cold-case murder combined with a contemporary crime that drew attention to the dark side of the mining boom. Or with *Marlborough Man*, it was a former undercover UK cop in hiding with his family in remote New Zealand being hunted by the gangsters he tried to take down while himself trying to solve some child abductions in the area. In both cases I had the framework in my mind but didn't know until well into the story whodunnit, why and how. There's something to be said for sitting down for a day's writing and allowing yourself to be led somewhere unexpected.

Brendan Ritchie says:

This is a personal creative decision that need not determine the quality of a finished manuscript. There are plenty of successful writers who swear by the security and diligence of the planning approach, just as there are others who can feel hemmed in by knowing too much before the writing begins. The terms architect and gardener are sometimes used in place of planner and plunger. I like gardener as a substitute for plunger as it suggests some purpose in how a writer chooses to begin, or what they choose to plant and where. From that point the writer nurtures their seedlings and watches to see how each will grow and interact with the others. Which plant will fight and struggle for a footing? Which will spread wildly and engulf the others? Will flowers bloom and seeds be thrown out to propagate new growth? They're not perfect metaphors, but perhaps the patience required by both architects and gardeners is similar to that of the writer.

And Sasha Wasley says:

Being a plotter or a pantser is such a personal choice and I'm a strong believer in maintaining the magic of writing – which means you should follow your heart and love what you write. If you try to be something you're not, you might kill the magic. Some people create extremely detailed plots before they start writing; others just plunge in. Plotting and pantsing are completely equal in my view. There's one exception which I'll cover in a moment.

I am 75% a pantser. I start with a premise, concept or character and begin writing, and watch the story unfold as I write. Often, much of my plotting happens in my head while I write the first couple of chapters. I become a daydreamer while I am writing a novel and spend much of my time thinking about my characters and what they will do next.

The other 25% of me is a plotter. Whenever I find myself in a plot tangle or if I get a bit of writer's block, it's time to sit down and do some behind-the-scenes work. I will develop character files with their motivations and arcs, write a timeline and story structure, and write some possible outcomes for whatever problem I have come up against. This process usually gets me through any big plotting problems.

Getting stuck

Even the most assured and prolific writers admit to experiencing what is sometimes known as writer's block: a creative paralysis during which their ideas dry up or their capacity to creatively transform ideas into writing flounders in a sea of self-doubt and inaction. It could be less ominous perhaps, given the negative associations that the term 'writer's block' has accumulated, to think of such periods in the writer's journey as simply getting stuck.

What is the difference between getting stuck and procrastination?

Simple procrastination is something you can overcome when you commit to the writing; indeed, you may well recognise this even as, and precisely because you are, procrastinating. You might play computer games for an hour, or find yet another reason to hit the shops, precisely because this lets ideas to percolate in the back of your mind. You're not writing, but you are also not *not* writing.

A number of things can get you going again. The penny drops and you find the way forward. Or a deadline bites, or you get fed up with your own inaction and sit down and start writing. You might just need a few jump-start strategies to get you going: a burst of freewriting for ten minutes, or building up momentum by re-reading and making minor edits in the last few pages you wrote before blasting off on fresh material.

In effect, such procrastination may well be part of your writing process, and you will perhaps come to recognise it as such. Getting stuck is something rather different, because the usual routines to overcome procrastination don't break through.

What is the difference between getting stuck and burning out, and can one be a symptom of the other?

Blockages do not only manifest themselves in procrastination. You could find yourself glued to your laptop or bent over a notebook for what seems like an eternity, trying heroically to get the words you need out, to no avail. But how do you know if you're actually creatively drained because you're burnt out? The simple answer is to take a break and see what happens. Turn your writing meter off, do something you enjoy, get some rest, de-stress your brain. Writers need to practise self-care in mind and body, just as athletes do. You might find you come back to the desk refreshed, and resume your writing smoothly, or else perhaps you'll spot that problem – in plot, character, structure or research – that is also a part of what's been hampering you.

'Stepping away', as Alan Carter calls it, and knowing when you need to do so, is but one of a number of options to bear in mind when you get stuck.

Ask an author: What do you do when you hit a snag during the writing process?

Alan Carter says:

Have a cuppa, surf the net, mow the lawn, go for a swim. Write a different book or story. The essence is that stepping away for however long it takes is usually worth the while. If it's writer's block then, as Louise Doughty advises in her excellent book *A Novel in a Year* (Simon & Schuster, 2007), try writing about the time you, for example, broke your thumb, or fell off a ladder, or got lost or got stood up. They are exercises that can unblock the creativity drains (so to speak) and may even be scenes that survive into your finished novel. Also don't be afraid to write out of sequence. If a current scene is troubling you, jump forward to a later one and write that instead. In *Getting Warmer*, I was determined to have a key scene involving an ambush set-up at a place called Capo D'Orlando Drive by the harbour in Fremantle. As my ever-astute editor pointed out, it was the least logical place geographically to have such a scene, but I was determined nevertheless because it just seemed such a cool place. So I walked around there, jogged around there, thought and thought about how to make the illogical into the logical. So, step away for a while, pretend to do something else, then when the problem thinks it's got you beaten, you come at it from a different angle and put it in a headlock.

Nandi Chinna says:

I always find that doing something physical helps to untangle snags in writing. Generally I go for a walk, a gym session, a bike ride or a swim, or I clean the house. Another helpful thing is doing some research by consulting books or websites to increase your knowledge about a subject and trying to find different ways into the piece you're writing. Look at different perspectives and voices. You can try to approach the piece in different ways, for example first-, second- or third-person voice. Think about the tone of the piece: are you leaping straight in? I find this is usually the best way to start something. Are you giving too much information or not enough? Do you hold a lot of implied knowledge that your readers will not have? Do you need to give them more information? Are your metaphors too obscure or too obvious? There are many questions like these you can ask yourself about a piece if it is not working.

You can ask trusted friends or colleagues to have a look and see what they think. They might ask you, 'What are you really trying to say here? Are you really communicating your intention? Are your characters and dialogue believable?'

Most commonly, I leave the piece of writing for a week or two. Start working on something else for a while and leave the tangle, and come back to it later with a refreshed mind.

Brigid Lowry says:

The healing benefits of a cup of tea and a sit in the sun can be profound. A long walk can really help. Solutions to technical problems can arrive by themselves if given some fresh air.

Sometimes research helps. Reading what other writers have to say can be useful. Sometimes I ask some questions of the text. What seems to be the actual problem? What am I really trying to say? Am I writing clichés? Are my characters working? Would some dialogue help? Would this work better in first person? Is the tense working? Am I over- or under-writing? Is this a novel or merely a good idea that isn't sustainable in a long form? I try to come up with questions from the sensible, grown-up part of my brain, and find answers in the same location.

It could be time to seek professional advice, because if it is a technical problem, someone else can often see what is needed. If you have an editor, now is the time to use them. Otherwise, find a few trusted friends you can call upon to read your work and offer intelligent suggestions.

If none of this works, put the writing away for a while. Clarity may emerge, given some time and distance. Occasionally, like all writers, I have had to admit that something just isn't going to work. Boohoo, but never mind. Start again, take up floristry, or begin drinking too much. The choice is yours.

And Brendan Ritchie says:

Returning to the overarching motivations of the characters can provide a lot of guidance and affirmation during difficult writing junctures. Any writing theorist, from Aristotle to Stephen King, will suggest that characters, like people, have things in life that they want: escape, acceptance, survival, fame, financial security – the list goes on. Their journey to obtain these things often gives shape to a narrative and propels the writing forward.

Problems within the writing process can sometimes surface when a character's actions don't align with their broader motivations. Or perhaps their motivations have shifted, yet their behaviour hasn't adjusted accordingly. Or their motivations are vague or underdeveloped, leaving them feeling arbitrary and directionless. Characters aren't robots. They will, and should, be full of nuance, complexity and contradiction, but they still need to be headed towards something larger for a narrative to maintain its trajectory. With this in mind, consolidating a character's motivation can assist a writer to locate problems in a manuscript or see a way forward when things feel difficult. Some questions to ponder in these situations may be: What does my character want in life? Has this altered from the start of the narrative? What is my character doing to progress towards this goal? What obstacles are they facing (needless to say, obstacles are crucial)? What could they feasibly try next? Considering the answers to these questions can often help to solve broader issues relating to plot, setting, dialogue and many other things.

Many of these tips are getting, as you can see, into the nuts and bolts of writing itself. While it is not the aim of this book to be a writing manual per se, there are certainly places that you can go to resolve those issues that relate to the writer's craft.

Building a community and finding peers

Writing is often (though not always) a solo activity. Many writers go it alone, preferring to keep family for nurture and encouragement and no-one or just a few close writing friends for creative sustenance. Others thrive by finding what YA author Holden Sheppard terms their 'tribe' and immersing themselves gregariously in a writerly community.

Whatever your preference, you will find that even self-confessed loners agree that building connections with fellow writers and engaging with writing networks provides a vital pool of information, resources, opportunities, encouragement and shared experience. And sometimes finding even just one ideal person to comment on your work can make all the difference, whether you are stuck or writing well. This role may be filled by another writer who 'gets' you and your work. Sometimes these relationships are reciprocal and you find that you are learning together; sometimes your levels of writing experience can be quite different – and we will look at what it means to have a mentor in a moment.

As you begin to write, you may already be forging a supportive group of writing peers and engaging with writers' networks through university studies or TAFE, or through like-minded friends and family members, or through attending a writers group or workshops at community writers centres. Online engagement, in particular through social media, is also a good method of community-building. If you feel at a loss about where to start – whether offline or online – then you could begin by contacting your local writers centre, local or state library, or the peak writing body in your state.

Mentors

A mentor is akin to a 'life coach' for writing. Their role is quite different to an editor or manuscript assessor (see p. 110). The mentor helps a new writer to develop their potential and can offer experience, insight and assistance in and around the writing process. The mentor–mentee partnership may be organised by a writing organisation or writers group or through an educational institution; a more experienced writer may informally assist an emerging writer for the pure satisfaction of sharing what they have gained and learned along the way. The mentor may be paid for their services, or they may not. They can be involved with their mentee for a short duration or over years. The mentor is often involved with the writer long before a contract for publication and perhaps even before a manuscript comes into being. They can be particularly valuable for people who have a story to tell but are entirely new to the writing process.

Mentors assist with the development of a work in general terms, answering questions, perhaps about research, or how to approach subject matter and genre choice. They may have advice on where and how to seek funding, or offer simple encouragement when a writer feels stuck or discouraged – in short, they provide their experience in order to ease the writing process for a new writer. Where the relationship works well, mentors can continue to operate as a cheerleader and supporter to

2 THE PROCESS OF CREATING A MANUSCRIPT

individuals over a long period of time. They can derive great satisfaction from the success of the writers they have helped, and mentees can similarly find themselves wanting to 'give back' in the same way. We will look again at mentorship programs in Chapter 4 but for now, if you are a brand-new writer starting out with no community around you, and think that you would benefit from the support of a mentor, then approaching your local writers centre is a good place to start.

Ask an author: What are your tips for building a supportive writing community – offline and online?

Alan Carter says:

Online, obviously, you need to connect with and follow all the various writing groups relevant to what you do, along with publishers, agents, fellow scribes, bloggers, reviewers and such. For instance, I am linked with crime and general writing groups in Western Australia, New Zealand and Tasmania. Encourage, applaud and share the initiatives and successes of those you are linked with and hopefully they will do the same in return. But it's not only about marketing and profile building – you can get tips about opportunities and resources out there, plus you can share your own similar tips. Offline can be even better! Hopefully you'll get to meet some of these people at festivals or industry gatherings; hell, you might even like each other and become actual real friends. Then you might be able to offer mutual support in the form of early manuscript readings, shout-outs at book release time, or including each other in your annual top ten reading recommendations. The possibilities are endless. Or, like me, you might just sometimes catch up with them for a beer and a yarn about how things are going.

Meg McKinlay says:

First, ask yourself what form that support would ideally take for you, and what the relationship would be between it and your creative work. I'm an introvert and a loner by temperament, and well-meaning advice I received early on – that I absolutely *must* join a writing group of some kind, that finding 'critique partners' was essential – was anathema to me. The relationships that now support me in my creative practice also sustain me as a person and have grown slowly over time, in the way of any friendship.

The best advice I can give is rather trite: be yourself, in all things. Attend events that genuinely appeal to you, engage in conversations – both online and off – on topics and with people that have specifically piqued your interest. Seek genuine connections rather than number-gathering/following/retweeting/signal-boosting for the sake of it. Even if you're seeking support in the form of tangible outcomes such as follow-backs, reviews, retweets or book sales, I believe those things flow from meaningful exchange, from being yourself, or at least some version of it. We certainly don't need to give our whole self away on social media, or indeed in real life, but if you engage in ways that are natural to you, and do so in your own voice, a meaningful community will form around you.

A note of caution, too, particularly for those starting out: remember that while engaging with the writing community – getting out to launches and festivals and bantering back and forth on Twitter – can be fun and motivating and professionally useful in all sorts of ways, in the end it isn't writing. With social media at our fingertips, it can be easy to fall into the trap of being part of the writing community while neglecting the creative work at its heart.

Holden Sheppard says:

I'm a big advocate for writers finding their tribe, both for personal wellbeing – feeling understood by fellow authors – and professional development – that is, having ongoing discussions about writing craft as well as the business side.

These days, social media is often at the core of building such a community. I have found Twitter the best platform for meeting fellow writers, especially as a newbie author. Before I had anything published, I had no book to tweet about, so I would tweet about the daily grind of the writing process, using hashtags like #AmWriting or #WritersLife, and this is how I found other writers at similar stages of their careers.

Initially, though, I would just tweet and wonder why nobody was liking anything I put out there. Eventually I realised that Twitter is just a giant playground: if you're going to make friends with new people, you need to actually interact with them, too. It sounds a bit naive, but it can be helpful to think less cynically about 'building an audience/

community' and more about finding friends and supporters. The best way to find a friend is to be a friend. So, most of my social media time is actually not spent on uploading my own posts, but on chatting to other people, sharing their successes, commiserating their low ebbs, laughing at funny memes and communicating via GIFs. The best way to find supporters is to be a supporter to others. Friendly writers will gladly reciprocate the support you give them.

Most of the same principles apply offline. Be yourself when you go to events. Spend time chatting to new people. Support others in their good times and the bad. By being a part of their support network, they become a part of yours. Writers are excellent at lifting each other up.

Rachel Robertson says:

Developing and maintaining close writing friendships is important. Like many writers, I am a bit of a loner, but I do have a small group of friends who are writers or artists. I know quite a few painters and printmakers, and I find it nourishing to talk to them about the creative process. I have also been fortunate to have several writing mentors. As I get older, I aim to pass on some of what I have learned from them to other, newer writers. But I suppose what is most valuable for me is just to know people who I can talk to about my work, and sometimes share draft work with, in order to keep the creative space alive. Many of my writer friends and colleagues are active online and I really admire that. I think it is a great way to make good contacts with other writers, with publishing outlets and with readers. Ultimately, though, writing is a solitary activity. As Helen Garner said in her keynote address at NonfictioNow: 'Loneliness is the natural companion of the writer' (RMIT, 2012). I agree; I'm often lonely and I often struggle with writing. At such times, it is good to remember that I have the contents of my bookshelves to inspire and comfort me, as well as my real-life friends.

And Caitlin Maling says:

It's okay not to have a writing community. Nearly every writer I know is lonely in some way. I'm not going to romanticise it like some writers do and say loneliness is essential to poetry, but more that writing is solitary work. So, for me, it is less about a supportive writing community and more about making sure you have a supportive community in general. My husband and family understand the work I do, and provide me with nourishment and support in order to undertake it.

That being said, it is useful to know other writers, so you don't feel completely isolated and because it makes your work better. The connections I have made have been through institutions. Studying creative writing is not for everyone and does have its definite downsides – for example, it can promote a certain homogeneity in work: there can come to be a similarity of output between writers who study together and, in addition, a similarity of output between writers who have studied creative writing at a tertiary level across programs, as most tertiary study is quite similarly organised. Even so, completing my Master of Fine Arts in poetry was the first time I felt truly surrounded by people interested in pursuing a creative life. In addition to having studied and taught creative writing at a tertiary level, I participate in a lot of artist residencies nationally and internationally. I find the hothouse atmosphere they provide, in terms of being surrounded exclusively by other creative practitioners and doing nothing but creative work, can sustain me for the extended periods of time I'm back in the 'real world'.

One thing I would heavily advocate is to be as generous and kind as possible to your peers. There can be a tendency to feel stress and a sense of competition regarding the paucity of opportunities (and the perennial squeeze on these opportunities) for writers in Australia. This lack is not the fault of the writers, but more a fault of trying to fit a writing life into a capitalist, rationalist, cost-benefit system. Try to be happy whenever someone you know receives an award, grant or residency.

Feedback and workshopping

One of the benefits of building a writing community is that it gives you opportunities to revise your drafts and to obtain feedback from your peers through a process called workshopping, where fellow writers read your work and hopefully provide constructive insights.

Workshopping can also allow you to read the work of other writers, breaking a sense of isolation in your endeavours and allowing you to develop your skills as an attentive reader, commentator and editor. By doing this, you will find much to enhance your understanding of your own writing process.

So, what are some of the elements of constructive workshopping?

Set up clear protocols

Ask: how will this workshop work? That's up to you and your group, but some kind of structure and a mutually understood set of protocols helps to ensure you know what you need to do and when to do it. There are many options:

- You could exchange drafts, read and comment during the workshop. This can be effective for short pieces of work, when the group is small, participants are pressed for time and you can set aside several hours to meet in a quiet space. (A crowded café is not the best environment. Your local library may be prepared to offer you a room on a regular basis – it's worth asking! You may also choose to meet online if that is more convenient.)
- You could set a deadline to distribute drafts to each other via email, allowing sufficient time for the group to read each other's work and make notes prior to the workshop, whether that be face to face or online. This allows for more considered reading and feedback, in particular for longer pieces. You can cut straight to the chase in discussion. To make this work, all those involved need to stick to the deadline.
- You could set up a rotational arrangement whereby two or three writers nominate to provide drafts each session and the group focuses only on those spotlighted writers and their drafts. This breaks up the pressure to produce work each session and allows for a very closely focused preparation by the selected writers and the readers.
- Decide whether it would be useful for the group to have a facilitator.
- While it is ultimately a matter of personal preference and a matter of group consensus, if you are working in a face-to-face group you will likely find working with hard copies the most productive and group-friendly method. It is far easier for a group to discuss, share and add to the feedback collaboratively and swiftly when hard copies can be passed back and forth. Marked-up material can also be returned to the writer after the discussion.
- If you are using hard copies, make sure you provide your group or workshopping partner with a legible copy of your draft. Picking up a

few typos is part of the feedback process, but no-one appreciates having to decipher a scrawl. Trying to figure out whether a page is missing is also a waste of time.

- Members of your group may wish to practise marking up work using Track Changes in Microsoft Word or on Google Docs. This kind of editorial interaction may be good practice for working with an editor in a publishing house. Your local writers centre, society of editors or TAFE for short courses may be able to assist with upskilling.

Whatever your group chooses, it needs to work for everyone, and everyone should try to adhere to the same process. If not, dysfunction and resentment can set in. For instance, you can't just expect to receive feedback without reciprocating in kind. The same is true in reverse. Good communication about the workshop process, as much as about the content, is key.

Giving feedback

Giving and receiving feedback are two sides of the same coin. When you are giving feedback, remember to deliver it in the same spirit and with the same level of consideration that you would like to receive it.

The best way to be a good reader is to understand and respect that the work you are reading is that of another writer: it is not yours. You may, for instance, love sci-fi and loathe romance, but that does not mean someone else should transform their writing in accordance with your genre preferences. A good reader reads and comments on the work in terms of what it is, rather than what they want it to be. A good reader is also attentive to the aims and concerns of its writer. If you do not feel yourself to be the right reader for a particular work, then perhaps you are better not to offer feedback at all.

A reader is at their most useful on their first encounter with a work. At this stage, as a reader, it is invaluable to take note of your initial reactions to the work throughout the reading experience. These might be positive reactions, like:

- Being able to see the characters when you hear them speaking.
- Eagerly anticipating what happens next.
- Being impressed by a fresh image.
- Laughing aloud.
- Being moved or surprised by the ending.

If your reading is slowed by aspects that are working less well, take note of these things too. Your responses to a work while reading may include:

- Wondering who is talking.
- Finding the pace slow.
- Finding a line, verse or piece of work to be oblique and elusive.
- Having to read a sentence three times.
- Feeling unsure you understand what the writer is trying to do.

When thinking about your responses at a certain point in the text, it is constructive to then ask *why* you have reacted in a particular way. Ask what makes the pace slow. What would make the work pacier? What is it that stops you from understanding a sentence? Your answers will provide the basis of feedback. Give feedback that blends parts of the first, positive list above with parts of the second. Offer praise on what is working, then constructive comment, then more praise.

When determining what feedback to give, you may have more overarching questions about the piece – and some of these may require input from the writer. These questions could include:

- What stage is this writing at – raw and early or advanced and refined?
- What is the genre and who do you think the intended readership is?
- Is the world-building persuasive?
- Is there consistency in time, place and genre?
- Has research been sufficiently absorbed into the work?
- Are there anachronisms in terms of content, detail or dialogue?
- Is the lexicon (set of words chosen) appropriate for this piece?
- Does the dialogue work?
- Does the pace work?
- Does the plot hold up?
- What is the point of view in this piece and is it consistently maintained?
- Does the point of view serve the themes and plot effectively?
- Does it feel as if anything is missing from this piece of writing?
- Has the author asked you to concentrate on any specific areas?

A reader's perspective or insight can locate something in the work that may not have occurred to the writer. But it is always up to the writer, not the reader, to make a change if they feel it is warranted. In order to be a good reader, remember the following:

- It's your role to pose questions not to provide solutions.
- Be positive and constructive in both your written and verbal feedback.
- Pose potentially thorny feedback as questions rather than flat assertions.
- Use 'I' statements where possible (I feel …, I wonder …).
- Sometimes the most valuable thing you can do is to ask questions.
- General, broadbrush feedback can be useful.
- Explicit feedback can give the writer areas to focus on, though line-level responses may be better delivered in writing than verbally.
- Written responses can lead to misinterpretation of tone and intent. If you are working online, re-read your responses before sending.
- Don't be so anxious about upsetting a writer that your feedback becomes bland and ineffective.
- Avoid workshops that collapse into mutual admiration societies, which will leave participants unsatisfied, disengaged or complacent.

When giving feedback, give some thought to how you feel about *receiving* feedback. If you are someone who is unfazed by sharp remarks or blunt criticism, it's worth remembering that not everyone is the same. Inevitably, groups are made up of a diverse range of individuals with different temperaments, ages, cultural backgrounds and experiences. You're a writer after all, so remember to bring your observational skills and imaginative empathy with you to the workshop table.

Receiving feedback

Feedback gives a writer insight into how readers receive and perceive their work. If one person feels that way, it is possible other readers will too. Having a reader look at your work can enable you to see it with fresh eyes. It is not uncommon to feel relieved by suddenly being 'allowed' to delete a passage or character or scene because someone else tells you what you already secretly suspected. This aspect of self-editing is sometimes referred to as 'killing your darlings'.

In advance of workshopping, think about what you want from the feedback and convey this to your readers in advance, whether these are macro or micro issues. These could include plot progression or glitches, dialogue authenticity, handling of flashbacks, anachronisms, unnecessary tense shifts, the strength of the ending, distracting content, mixed metaphors, clichés and appropriateness for the intended audience.

Here are some other things to consider when seeking feedback:

- Only provide work once you feel it is ready to be seen.
- Be open to insights about aspects of the draft that you have not high-lighted for consideration.
- Ask for clarification if you don't understand the feedback.
- Remain aware that not all feedback is right for you. After the session, think through the feedback you've been given and consider whether it is in tune with your aims.
- Enjoy the positive feedback.
- Try to think of 'criticism' as opportunities to improve your work.
- Understand that differing opinions in a group may not be resolvable.
- Provide your peers with the next draft for feedback on your changes.

Whether giving or receiving feedback, remember that workshopping, like writing itself, is part of a process, not an instant solution.

Ask an author: What are your tips for constructive workshopping?

Brigid Lowry says:
The publisher Ray Coffey once shared with me something really useful about being edited and receiving feedback. He said that there are two sorts of people who are hard to work with. The first are those who won't take any advice on board. Everything they have written is already perfect. The other sort of difficult writer is the one who totally accepts everything you suggest, without thinking it through, and just lies down like a wet daffodil, agreeing to all your feedback. Working with an editor, or getting feedback in a workshop, is supposed to be an intelligent dialogue between the parties involved. Sometimes the wisdom and insight offered is invaluable. Sometimes you need to think about it for a bit. Sometimes it just doesn't sit right and it never will. Ultimately the work belongs to you and you don't have to change anything you don't want to; however, if ten people tell you you're drunk, sit down.

Being workshopped can be painful. Writers are fragile creatures. We put our lives, words, heart, blood, sweat and tears on the page. We are very needy, and we want you to love us very deeply and furthermore love every word we write. It is good to remember that it is not personal. People love you, but you probably need to face it: your poem is too mysterious.

Rachel Robertson says:

When I have a full draft of an essay that I've taken as far as I think I can on my own, but which I don't feel confident is finished or ready for publication, then I find it helpful to share it with one or more other writers who can give me feedback: what is working, what is not working, what is missing and what is confusing or obscure. At this stage, a small group of committed and respectful writers who can constructively comment on each other's work can be really helpful.

If I am facilitating a writing group (for example when teaching), I will work with participants to set some clear boundaries and ways of working at the start. I like to have these noted quite formally, so that everyone understands the purpose and parameters of the group, how it will work and the logistics of it. I often provide a series of prompts to encourage those giving feedback to do so in a helpful way. Or I might provide a handout: a useful one, for example, is 'Twenty Ways to Talk about Creative Nonfiction' by Perl and Schwartz in their book *Writing True: The Art and Craft of Creative Nonfiction.*

The biggest problems I've seen arise in writing groups result from: participants having different ideas about the purpose of the group; a focus on copyediting or sentence/word-level editing (which I don't think can be done usefully in a group); misunderstandings about different genres (e.g. when someone told a non-fiction writer that she should change the personality of one of her 'characters' because she 'wasn't very nice'); and, of course, personality clashes (which is why having a facilitator can be a good idea).

David Whish-Wilson says:

As a writer, you'll need to develop a thick skin and a degree of trust in both your own opinions as to the value of your work, and the opinions of those whose job it is to guide you towards getting your manuscript to a publishable stage. Some people are lucky enough to have friends or family in the broader industry and others need to go out and find those people. Either way, it's a truism that the more you work on a piece of writing, the more its subtle faults and opportunities for improvement become invisible. It's also a truism that as an emerging writer, the chances of getting a manuscript 'right' without having gone through a process of drafting and redrafting is very slim. Time away from a story can bring freshness and clarity, but just as important is having people whose opinions you value cast their eyes over your work, with a mind to offering constructive criticism. Workshops can fill this function, as can small writing groups where writers share their work with one another. It's a brave thing to offer up your writing to scrutiny, and criticism always stings, but there's no way around this part of the process. By the time you get around to submitting your work for publication or to a competition, you need your manuscript to be as good as it can possibly be, and that invariably means drafting and redrafting your work based on constructive feedback from forthright and qualified people.

And Caitlin Maling says:

When you send something out for feedback, you need to be ready to hear feedback. This involves being aware that what is being critiqued is the writing, not you as a person. If you cannot take feedback as separate from you as a person, you need to rethink putting that piece up for criticism, and if you can't take it at all, then perhaps a writing life is not for you.

That being said, one key thing about developing your voice is owning your intention with your work and being able to articulate it. This will allow you to filter feedback, to see whether it's useful to you in terms of refining your work so it can be the best version of what you want it to be. Often you can identify whether or not someone is a good reader for your work. When you find someone who is, try to set up a regular exchange with them, but be understanding if they say no – writers, especially writers who also work teaching creative writing, can often be overwhelmed by the sheer amount of work they are needing to read and respond to. If someone says they don't have time to read your work, it's not a reflection on you or your work – they are probably just busy. Whenever anyone does take the time to offer you feedback, unless you are paying them, this is an act of generosity and should be treated as such.

Opportunities for gaining experience

Long before you have a book contract, there are many opportunities available to get your work out to readers – most 'new' authors or manuscript award winners will have a solid body of shorter works and accomplishments behind them.

Submitting your work to journals as well as writing competitions can be a good place to start. Even if you don't win a prize or have a piece accepted for publication, these things provide deadlines around which to organise your writing, forcing you to actually finish a draft, polish and proof it. Remember to read both the advice for contributors and the actual creative content of any journal to which you submit. Try to read the stories and manuscripts that do win once they are published to see what may have given them the edge.

There are a number of forums available in capital cities and some larger (and even smaller) country towns for reading your work in public, in particular if you write poetry. Try your state's peak writing organisation, library or local writers centre for information about poetry groups that meet regularly for readings. These may be at a writers centre or in a pub or café. The format usually combines featured guest spots for established and emerging poets, with open mic sessions where unscheduled readers, including new poets, can step up and share their work. This provides an opportunity to make yourself known to your tribe, to hear experienced poets reading their work and to read your own work to that audience.

In the last decade, poetry slams have become popular events, and a nationwide poetry slam competition now sees heats run in every state in capital cities, with some opportunities in larger regional centres. State winners compete at a national final held in Sydney, with the Australian winner competing internationally. The combination of paid travel, prize money, publicity and online promotion of the winning poets performing their work presents a marvellous opportunity for experience and building a profile. If slams, performance poetry and other spoken word events are proving crucial pathways to success for some poets – for example, British writer and recording artist Kate Tempest – then social media too has figured as an equally crucial launch pad. This is evidenced in the case of Canadian poet Rupi Kaur, whose work in Instapoetry (short poems designed to fit in an Instagram post) and consequent accumulation of millions of admiring followers led to the publication of a poetry collection that spent more than a year on the *New York Times* bestseller list.

Emerging writers can be understandably nervous about reading to an audience, but it is something you will need to do in your later career when promoting your work. Try practising reading by finding a friendly listener or a group that you feel comfortable with. Remember to project your voice if you are without a microphone, to find opportunities to practise with a mic before you use one, and to seek advice from those who have. If you are not a natural performer and, in particular, if you are shy, then do take comfort in the knowledge that others similarly placed have found that, eventually, things do become easier.

Ask an author: What practical steps can new writers take to build a profile and gain experience as they start out on the road to publication?

Nandi Chinna says:

The path to publication is very different now than when I first began publishing my work in the 1990s. I followed a fairly traditional path to publication, starting off in journals, newspapers and anthologies until I finally got my first small collection published by Five Islands Press. Today, there are many other options such as online journals, your own webpage or blog, Instagram. My best advice to writers starting out on their publishing journey is:

- Find a mentor who you trust and whose work resonates with you. Having a good mentor can save you years of learning the hard way through getting your work rejected time and time again. A mentor can help you to identify what you are really trying to achieve, and help you to develop the tools you need to achieve your writing goals.
- Try to get published in reputable journals such as *Westerly, Meanjin, Cordite Poetry Review, Island, Australian Book Review* and *Plumwood Mountain*. There are a lot of smaller zines and journals out there that will publish you, but I feel it's better to be published in journals in which your poetry is peer-reviewed, and which will only accept a high standard of work. The goal of publishing is that you are entering a milieu of other writers and readers. When you have read other writers' work, and you've

worked hard on your own writing, then you can send it out into the world to do its job, to find its audience, connect with readers, and join the community of writers who offer their services to the world.

- Set yourself some realistic goals and look for opportunities such as mentorships, residencies, new publishing programs and scholarships. If you have a goal to work towards, such as a publishing opportunity, it helps to set yourself deadlines and make sure you are staying on track with your writing projects.

David Whish-Wilson says:

If you're a writer determined to focus upon short-form writing, then clearly it's in your best interests to know what other people are writing, but also what the benchmarks are for the different outlets available to you locally, nationally and internationally. Every journal, zine, mag or literary competition can have its own texture and flavour, and finding the one you aspire to publish in or enter a piece of work into is a great start. If it's a local journal, magazine or competition, this is even better, in the sense that it also opens you up to a real rather than just virtual community of writers and readers. Things such as reading nights, spoken word or poetry slam events are important for the same reason, hopefully allowing you to find your fellow writers, your people, but also the editors and publishers from the same local outlets. It's also sound advice, of course, having established the flavour, form and style of your favoured journal or literary competition, to make sure that you pay strict attention to their style guide and entry guidelines. Editors and judges are generally overworked and underpaid, and the difference between the story that gets selected and the one that doesn't can often be very subtle – sometimes even coming down to a matter of formatting. More broadly, even if your long-term ambition is to write long-form prose texts, having a CV that contains a few publications is an invaluable thing as you go out into the world to secure an agent or a publisher, and might make the difference between your submitted work 'catching the eye' or not.

Daniel de Lorne says:

Before you consider sending anything out for publication, know your craft and know your genre. This also includes knowing what your readers want.

Accept that editing and revisions are part of the process and cannot be ignored. This is not just about spelling and grammar but about structure as well.

Get an outside opinion before you seek publication. Find a critiquing partner or group, or go for a paid manuscript assessment.

Learn how to pitch and how to write query letters and synopses. These skills will stand you in good stead with publishers and agents. Look for pitching opportunities and practise your pitching skills. Twitter pitches are a thing, so keep an eye out for them via publishers or agents.

Contests can lead to publication. While it's great to win money, at the early stage of your career, the best contests are those that provide industry exposure and/or feedback. If the judge (hopefully an editor or agent) likes your work, it may result in a request for more. Feedback from contest judges is worth its weight in gold, as it helps you find out what the judges (and publishers) are looking for, as well as how to improve your work.

Attend writing conferences and festivals. They may have opportunities to pitch to agents or publishers. Network with other writers and those in the industry. You never know who you might talk to and what can come of it.

And Caitlin Maling says:

Read, read, read, read. Submit, submit, submit, submit. Be okay with rejections. It's a hell of a lot of admin to be consistent about submissions, but maintaining a spreadsheet of submission windows and doing regular updates will save you a lot of missed opportunities. I personally believe in only submitting to publication and competition opportunities in which you get paid – writing is work and should be treated as such.

There is no shame in submitting to anything, nor in being rejected. There is no sudden point at which you become a 'real writer'. Aim for things you think you definitely can't get; it's so subjective that all you have to do is hit the right reader on the right day. I think most of my success is simply down to always having my hat in the ring.

Open mic events are great for poets (although they can be terrible to sit through). I always like to use these to read work that I'm unsure of; it gives me the greatest sense of how an audience might respond to it. Attending readings also gives you an insight into what is currently

> being written and how people are receiving it. If you find yourself reacting strongly against something being read, stop and think about why.

Workshopping and performing your work can be first steps in testing and refining it in front of other readers. At what stage should you focus on who you are writing for? We will dive into the distinction between readers and audience in the next chapter.

3. Readers and audience

- When to think about your readers
- The relationship between genre and reader expectations
- The difference between readers and audience
- How to identify and connect with your potential audience
- Tips for finding an audience
- The relationship between audience and author brand
- Tips for establishing an author brand
- How and why to pitch
- Tips for preparing pitches
- Pitching practice

Sooner or later, if you want to be a writer whose work is read by others, it makes sense to think about your *readers*. As you begin to refine your manuscript, you will also need to start thinking about your *audience*, which can be rather a different thing. Who is your audience? And what is your author brand? The answers to these questions are not confined to any single book you write. Before we look at author brand, let's first explore the distinction between readers and audience, and the kinds of steps you can take to reach them.

When to think about your readers

Imagine someone who gets your work, totally loves it and tells you that it fulfils all their reading expectations. This is your 'ideal reader'. Thinking about them can help you interrogate your own work as you revise it. Focusing on your ideal reader's expectations prompts you to ask whether you have delivered the content clearly for them in terms of genre delivery, language choice, pace, character and plot.

When you ask yourself such questions, you are being not so much a writer as an editor. When you have answered as many as you can, you may turn to actual readers to help advance the current draft. Such readers can include beta readers – unpaid people (often friends) who read your work to give you feedback about what is working and what needs revision. (Be sure to be gracious and grateful to these generous individuals!) They can include the workshopping peers we discussed in Chapter 2, who review your work in a structured, reciprocal feedback situation. It may include sensitivity readers you have chosen because they are qualified to consider and advise on cultural or gendered representations, misrepresentations, bias, racism or stereotypes. (More on this in Chapter 4.)

When should you start to think about these readers – ideal or real? If you care too much too early about what your theoretical reader thinks, the result can be paralysing. It's often a good idea to write your draft first – to just get it down and say what you want to say without giving two hoots about grammar, plot, character, tense or point of view. Use the first draft to write for yourself, and the second (or later) to write for your readers.

The writers we asked suggest that thinking about readers shouldn't come too early in the equation, and shouldn't usurp the author's creative momentum or their sense of voice: these writers clearly distinguish between the drafting stage and the editing stage.

Ask an author: When is it time to think about your readers?

Amanda Curtin says:

I don't think about readers at all while I'm writing. I write what I feel compelled to write, exploring what intrigues or confounds or deeply unsettles me, and I try to keep the faith that what's important to me might be important to readers like me.

I'm not even sure that readers know what they want until they read it, although I concede there are exceptions: series fiction, for example, and genres where there are specific generic conventions and expectations. But for the most part, I think we underestimate readers if we imagine they simply want more of the same; we have the best possible chance of writing something they will engage with if we concentrate on character and story and the raddling question of what it is to be human, rather than on trying to anticipate what the market might want.

It's in the editing stage that I do consider readers. By then, of course, I'm not considering *what* but *how*. I look at my manuscript analytically, thinking about how I've put everything together. Are readers likely to understand what I'm trying to achieve – meaning and nuance, plot and subtext, layers of character and story? Are there better ways of structuring my work to engage readers? Are there potentially distracting elements? What about language, tone, voice, point of view? Is there enough rhythm and pace to keep readers reading? Have I said too much or not enough? By paying attention to these matters you give readers the respect they deserve.

Meg McKinlay says:

Thinking about readers is not a conscious process for me, at least in the early stages of drafting. Because of the way I write, the question of what I 'want to say' is something that develops during, and as a function of, the drafting process itself. I never set out with an agenda, something in particular I want to get across. In the beginning, I'm just playing with something – perhaps an image or a line of dialogue – that won't let me go. Theme and audience develop alongside each other as part of that process and I redraft with those factors in the front of my mind. It's really only at that stage that I take a step back and think more objectively about the reader – about their age and language level, about what sorts of things are likely to make them laugh or cry or wonder, about whether I've been too vague or too expository or longwinded or self-indulgent at various points. I find it very easy to be ruthless about my work at this stage, and I think this is because I am so entirely voice- and character-driven early on; this means that whatever I do later – however I cut and shape – the bedrock of the work feels authentic to me, alive in a way that is deeply personal.

Liz Byrski says:

I think this is where voice is particularly important, and of course there are some differences between writing fiction and non-fiction here.

It is unrealistic to think that in non-fiction you can always say what readers want to hear without damaging your credibility. Inevitably you will have to say things that some readers will not want to hear, but if you have established a credible and honest voice, your readers will accept that. Saying what people want to hear, even if it is not what you believe, will not help your writing and will eventually lead to your losing readers. I am constantly thinking about the readers and their expectations and trying to hold their attention, but not necessarily their agreement or approval. I don't compromise in order to please, but I do try to explain why I hold a particular view, and to acknowledge that others hold valid opinions different from mine.

In fiction, I am always writing for a readership of which I might otherwise be a part, and this makes it a lot easier than writing for a new and different audience. I try to create credible, contemporary characters with distinctive voices, realistic lives and opinions. My fiction is a form of social realism. Through the characters, I explore social and personal issues, and the positive and negative aspects of ageing in contemporary society. Any areas of restraint are around my personal sensitivities. I have never tried to hold back to appease readers, but I do try to be aware of others' sensitivities and treat them with respect. I would never change what I believe or want to say to accommodate my readers.

And David Whish-Wilson says:

When it comes time for you to write your own work, you certainly don't want to be thinking too much about, or second-guessing the desires of, an invisible readership, when you should be focusing solely upon your work at hand. One way around this is to find your own 'ideal' reader. It might be a writer friend, or an editor, or a teacher, who knows your work and the genre that you're working in, and whose opinions you value. Asking yourself, 'What would so-and-so think of this passage of writing?' or, even better, actually showing your writing to this person when it's ready, is both a practical strategy and a release from the worry about how your work might be received by an illusory (at this stage of the process) 'reading public', when your work might be months or years away from being fully realised.

The relationship between genre and reader expectations

In Chapter 1 we looked at how, when and why writers choose a particular genre. This time we are considering the question of genre through the framework of how, and by whom, your work will be received.

What are a reader's expectations within a particular genre? How will you accommodate them in your own writing? If you *don't* think about reader expectations at all, is it possible to find yourself stranded with a peculiar hybrid work that has no logical destination?

If you are choosing to write within a well-established genre, it makes sense to be informed about its conventions. The aficionados of any genre (crime, sci-fi, romance etc.) who will form a core group of the actual readers of your work (and often its best word-of-mouth endorsers) will be more than competent at the rules of the game. So, as they weigh up where you, an unknown, fit within a field populated by their favourites, they will be scanning for genre competence and how your work lives up to and surpasses their expectations. David Whish-Wilson observes:

> Aside from its obvious pleasures, reading the work of writers you admire is a constant reminder of the bar that has been previously set. The writer you admire might be highly commercially successful or quite the opposite – someone writing distinctive, niche material that nevertheless appeals to you. Either way, the fact that you admire this person's writing means that others likely do as well. There is a balance to be found between being aware of reader expectations within a genre while striving to produce work that says something interesting and original.

As you consider why and how to situate your writing within a genre, and if you are thinking of how to make your work stand out in a crowded field, you will need to know the rules of the game so you can decide whether to break or keep them.

When you are ready to think about readers, look closely at the books in your proposed genre that have been successful in appealing to readers. Ask:

- What are their characteristics of voice, style, tone and themes?
- What has worked for these writers and why?

- To what extent do you want to absorb these considerations into your own work?
- How much are you prepared to strike out on your own and bend, blend or break the rules of a genre?

If you know you are writing for readers of a specific demographic, then it is crucial to identify the voice, language, tone and themes appropriate to them. This need not, however, be stifling or prescriptive, as Meg McKinlay notes on the subject of writing for children:

> When writing for children, the best way I can describe it is that I have some version of my own child self in mind. Or perhaps, more accurately, that I drop into the mind of that imagined child, and write out of that. I find this relatively natural and tend to trust my instincts, having faith that the feelings and concerns and idiosyncratic voice of that persona will connect authentically with readers. Not with *all* readers, of course, and I think it's important to bear that in mind. There is, of course, no single idealised child reader.

Holden Sheppard adds:

> Before you begin, you at least need to have a general sense of what genre you're writing and whether it's pitched at adults, young adults, middle-grade readers or young children. As a teenager, I wrote stories pitched at a young adult audience, and this is where I landed as a writer. Even as an adult, I remained interested in YA. This is now mostly what I write, and my books will tend to be realist contemporary fiction with a raw, gritty edge.
>
> That said, at first draft stage, you don't need to go too deep into locking in this audience or categorisation. Use these rough guidelines, but allow your first draft to be an exploration. Write freely. The writing itself will help you work out what this story is, more so than agonising over your outline or plan. Once you get to a second draft, that's the time when you need to get a firm handle on where this book would fit on a bookshelf. Is this book actually young adult or middle grade? Is it leaning more towards sci-fi or dystopian fiction? Are you a romance author, or a contemporary fiction author whose books just have a romantic element to them? What do *you* want to write? Who would read it?

Regarding YA fiction specifically, there are often questions around what content is appropriate for teenage readers. I personally don't censor or sanitise my writing because I remember what it was like to be a teenager, and I know young people can handle more than some conservative adult guardians might believe. If anything needs to be brought into line for the market, that's where my publisher would step in to tell me what will and will not fly when it comes to bookshops, libraries and schools wanting to buy the book. For my novel *Invisible Boys*, I suspected my publisher might tone down the sexual content, but thankfully they didn't. The only thing I had to edit out was loads of C-bombs until I had only two left, for impact.

No harm can come from feeling free enough to write whatever you choose without thinking about readers at all. Don't become so preoccupied by reader considerations that you stifle your writing before you've built momentum. If you are confident in your voice and your subject matter, then the question of reader can wait. As long as you are excited and energised by your work, then it is likely that others will be too. It may be that, rather like the productive dynamic between plotting and planning described in Chapter 2, you will start to find a sense of who you are writing for through the process of writing itself. And then, at some stage, *really* thinking about who you are writing for is one of the things that differentiates the serious emerging writer from the rest.

The difference between readers and audience

As a published writer, your *audience* will consist of those people who will or might buy your book, along with those who may promote your book in some way. This audience is not necessarily the readers your book is targeted at. Think about picture books. Would it be better to market a picture book to babies and children aged zero to five, or instead market it to the parents, teachers and grandparents most likely to get the book into the hands of the infant reader for you? The people who *buy* your book are not necessarily the people who will *read* your book. They include a more diverse range of people, like the gift buyers (such as the accountant buying a DIY carpentry book for her mother at Christmas time), the compulsive bedside stack topplers drawn to your book because it is pretty, and the receptionist charged with choosing coffee table books for the waiting room.

This is perhaps a kind of creatively freeing proposition: when you are at your desk, you need only think of your ideal reader and yourself, rather than your audience. It is when you are away from your desk and thinking about the other business of being a writer that you can focus on audience and ways of connecting with them.

The other freeing proposition is that, when all is said and done, a book can't actually define its audience, but an audience *may* define what they think the book is and where it fits in the marketplace or genre. Audience appeal can be diverse and unpredictable. Regardless of what target or theoretical audience a book enters the marketplace with, some books do cross over, appealing across age groups and/or usual genre preferences to reach those for whom they may not have been primarily intended. Cases in point include Mark Twain's *Adventures of Huckleberry Finn*, Tolkien's *The Hobbit* and J.K. Rowling's Harry Potter series. This is why some books, when reprinted, are redesigned and remarketed to better fit the audience they have found.

Nonetheless, let us proceed with looking at the kinds of things you as a writer can be proactive about in identifying and then connecting with an audience.

How to identify and connect with your potential audience

When your book is published by a publishing house, the promotions team helps find the book's audience by pitching it to sales reps (the people or companies who sell to bookshops on behalf of publishers), booksellers, festival programmers and reviewers. The publisher has a wealth of experience in the matter of finding audiences for books, and they will package your work (including cover design, price point and the book's physical dimensions) accordingly. The promotions team will market it so that it reaches the people most likely to buy it. This audience could be wider than the one you envisaged, for example, an education market for your poetry book, or a literary fiction market for your speculative fiction or crime novel.

But even right now, as the author of a future publication, you can support your future publisher by reaching out to your audience in that realm where humans connect and talk about books. The business of audience building never ceases. *Any* person you meet or interact with offline or online is a potential member of your audience. Someone who has never heard of you may meet you at the launch of someone else's book, then later buy your book and become an avid fan. A school may book you to run a workshop and down the track order your book for the school library. Some future child brings it home, a parent reads it – another member joins your audience. Every positive connection and interaction is a possible future sale. And when your actual book is in someone else's hands, or someone else's house, that buyer and your book are both potential ambassadors, possible future salespeople for an ever-broadening audience.

Thinking of the audience as the kind of group that might be added to, however and whenever possible, should be reason enough for you to engage with warmth and enthusiasm with strangers in any situation where you have cause to talk about your work, and it is wise as a writer when away from your desk (where you may only be thinking about your ideal reader) to give some thought to these things. At the beginning, or across time, you may even actively shape your writing practice or genre choice around endeavouring to reach a certain group of people, whether that is your identified readership or a broader audience.

Ask an author: When you began as a writer, did you identify a particular audience you wanted to write for?

Liz Byrski says:
Yes, I did. I was working as a journalist at the time, so I was aware of the importance of targeting an audience. I had written a number of successful newspaper and magazine features, so I chose a topic on which I had done a lot of research: the impact of alcoholism on families. In writing my features, I had not been able to find a simple, non-academic book suitable for family members and others whose lives were affected by one person's drinking. I decided that this was my audience. I did more research – especially interviews with partners, parents, children, other relatives and colleagues. It proved very successful.

Years later, when I started to try my hand at fiction, I spent a lot of time wondering where to begin, what sort of fiction I wanted to write. At the time, I was searching for contemporary Australian novels about the lives of women over fifty, but all I could find were books about younger characters. As a freelance feature writer, I had learned the value of identifying a gap in the market and then writing to fill it. I decided to try to write the sort of novel I wanted to read. So, I was an example of the readership I wanted to write for. It worked. My first novel was a great success and readers wanted more. Now, fifteen years and ten novels later, I am still writing for this readership, although I also have many younger readers, even some teenagers.

Alan Carter says:

I knew I wanted to write for an adult fiction audience, and that I would be writing in the crime fiction genre. I have been an avid reader of crime fiction for a long time, and if I were to aspire to anything, it would be that. In particular, I tend, as a reader, to favour contemporary-set police procedural series and themes addressing gritty social issues. I was never going to try my luck at deep science forensic crime fiction – I was terrible at science at school and I'd just never be able to pull it off. One of my first resource books was *Forensics for Dummies* – that's the level I operate at. But give me a handful of interesting characters, a great setting and something to get on my soapbox about, then watch me go.

Ambelin Kwaymullina says:

My first book was a picture book, so I had an obvious audience in mind. More broadly, however, I think audience is important. This is especially the case for anyone who wants to write for children and young adults. A failure to properly consider audience is a mistake I often see being made by aspiring YA writers. Simply having a teenage protagonist does not mean a book is a work of YA. It must be written in an age-appropriate voice (both in terms of the character's voice and of a voice that will speak to the audience). In this regard, small things can make a big difference. To give a simple example, I've often seen aspiring authors write a character who describes people in their late twenties as 'young'. No teenager thinks someone of that age is young; that is very much the voice of the author speaking.

It is also extremely important to consider audience when dealing with difficult and sensitive material. It is a hallmark of good writing for teenagers and children that sensitive material is only ever dealt with in a way that is age appropriate.

Natasha Lester says:

This might sound naive – and it probably was! – but I gave no thought to audience at all when I began writing my first book, *What Is Left Over, After*. Figuring out how to actually write a book was the most important and difficult thing for me back then, without the added pressure of considering audience.

I wrote because I loved writing, and I wrote a story that I loved. I wrote a book I wanted to read rather than a book for any specific group. It was the same when I switched to historical fiction and began writing my first novel in that genre, *A Kiss from Mr Fitzgerald*. I wrote a story that was begging for me to write it; I didn't ever sit down and consider who the audience for the book might be. In fact, I had a major panic midway through the writing when I realised the entire story was set in America, which perhaps wouldn't appeal to Australian readers, and also when I understood that the book was so different to what I'd written before that I'd need to look for a new agent and a new publisher. Luckily it all worked out, so I would say: if you write what you love, the audience will feel your enthusiasm and then they will love it too.

And Sasha Wasley says:

Understanding my audience has been a learning curve. When I started out as a writer, I had the innocent pleasure of writing for myself. I was my own target reader!

Later, I came to recognise that I wanted to become a professional writer, so I started to think more about my audience. I wanted to write for readers of innovative, intellectual literature; however, when I look back, I realise I was not writing literary fiction. This probably explains why none of those novels ever got published.

My first published work was a young adult novel intended for the commercial fiction market. Perhaps the reason this book got published was because, for the first time, I wrote for my audience. I thought about the things that would interest and engage teenage readers, how teens speak and the distinctive self-consciousness of those years. I kept my sentences succinct and accessible, built plenty of humour into it and ensured there was the right amount of romantic angst I loved so much in my adolescence.

When I started writing commercial romance, I didn't know much about my readership. Readers of rural romance in Australia are most often women aged thirty-five to seventy-five – and there's a quiet group of male readers in there, too. Now that I understand more about my readership, I find myself being considerate of them. I think about individual readers I have met, feedback they've given me, and the bits of my books they like. I want to please them, whether that's by moderating the swearing or including rich, multifaceted characters of all ages.

Actively connecting with your audience is more important than it used to be. Once, an author was a distant thing: the subject of a book review or arts column, up on stage at a festival, someone to be reached via fan mail. There was formality and structure to the reader–writer relationship. Today, social media has made this relationship much more informal. The lack of structure requires more work from the author in relationship-building and connection, because expectations make it so. Publicist Claire Miller has some tips on how, even early on, writers can identify and connect with their audience.

Tips for finding an audience

As a writer, you will be adept at listening, and will have some solid research skills at your disposal. You can be interacting with and building an audience while you're still writing, and this may even help you find a publisher. Consider setting aside one or two hours a week for this process:

- *Identify like titles.* Go to a bookshop and find look-alike titles. What recent releases are similar to yours? Make a list of those books and be sure to include at least one bestseller, at least one local title (from your state or nearest city) and a title that is lesser known and has flown under the radar.
- *Identify the publisher.* Who publishes those books? Which publishing houses and which publishers from within that house? Be aware that some publishing companies have multiple imprints – different trade names under which they publish works to distinguish between different consumer demographics.
- *Follow the publisher.* Follow relevant publishers or imprints on social

media and keep notes on the kinds of ways they are marketing your comparison titles.

- *Set up Google Alerts.* Watch which media outlets are covering like titles. Look at the outlet's audience by visiting the advertising section on their website. Though it contains information aimed at prospective advertisers, it nonetheless can provide you with an overview of that outlet's demographic. If you're writing non-fiction on a particular topic, set up a Google Alert on this topic and find out which journalists are writing about it. Follow them on Twitter. Keep notes of ongoing stories that are relevant.

- *Follow like authors.* Find authors of books similar to yours on social media, follow them and watch how they interact with their audience. Which social media channels are the most popular? What are people saying and what are they engaging with the most? Who are those people, demographically speaking? What have they made public about themselves?

- *Follow local authors.* Once you have a list of local authors, start going to some of their events so you can meet their audience directly and interact with them.

- *Become a member of at least one online book club.* Follow your look-alike books online. Which groups are reading them on Goodreads, Better Reading or Amazon Books? Read the comments and reviews – what key words and phrases are readers using? Start keeping a record of the way your potential audience members use language and what words they use.

- *Enlist local experts.* Befriend a number of booksellers and librarians. Tell them you're writing a book, and ask them about how your look-alike books are going. What kinds of people are buying or borrowing them and how popular are they? (We will revisit the matter of relationships with booksellers in more depth in Chapter 4.)

- *Be broadminded about audience.* If you're a children's author, make sure you consider both the child readers *and* the gatekeepers as your audience – the parents, grandparents, teachers and librarians who will be buying your books on behalf of children. Follow mummy bloggers and sign up to education newsletters.

- *Listen to feedback.* If the people you're connecting with aren't connecting with your book or manuscript, are they your audience members?

The relationship between audience and author brand

The reason you need to think about audience early is that your audience will always be bigger than any single book you will write. In buying your book, people will also be connecting with your author brand.

Once your work has begun to shape up and you feel ready to talk about it to others, you can also start thinking about how to present yourself and your work to prospective readers, as well as to others who may be interested in your work (journalists, booksellers, book reviewers, podcasters and bloggers).

The first thing to keep in mind is this: your author brand will be bigger than the book you are writing. Marketing and communications professionals work every day on understanding and articulating author brands and helping authors to define and refine their own brand. As with identifying an audience, your publisher may see ways of promoting your brand that have not occurred to you. The more you understand about yourself – the self that relates at least to the work you are writing – the more opportunities you will have to promote your work and yourself as a package, and the more potential a publisher will see in you and your work.

Let's look at what an author brand *isn't*. It's not an evil phrase. It's not a logo. It's not you pretending to be something you're not. It's not you trying to look like a corporation or an influencer or a product. Children's author James Foley says, 'Whether you try to have an author brand or not, you are going to have one anyway, so you have to control it.' In choosing how you are going to depict yourself, it makes sense to be authentic. Remember you are a storyteller. Your author brand is the story of who you are. It has a narrative and it has a voice. Each story you share about yourself has a why, what, where, when, who and how.

An author brand can be visual. If you're going to have multiple online platforms, what consistent visual elements can you have? This doesn't mean you need glamour shots. What kinds of images represent you? Is there a particular type of content that you are attracted to for curated materials? Some authors go as far as picking an iconic article of clothing or style for their appearances before live audiences and on social media – think China Miéville's shaved head, piercing and tatts, Dan Brown's turtleneck and tweed jacket, and Dale Spender's entirely purple wardrobe.

You are not static. Your opinions, vulnerabilities and strengths change over time, and so should your author brand. A strong brand is a flexible one. And if you write within multiple genres under different pseudonyms you may have multiple brands.

How much of yourself you choose to reveal, and in what way you reveal it, is something you can think about and plan. For instance, which parts of yourself are going to engage the community that may become your audience? Which parts will attract support from the industry and other writers? Which will make you attractive to those who award grants and residencies?

Tips for establishing an author brand

Thinking about your author brand and refining and defining it (while recognising that it is a dynamic thing) will begin to shape how you interact with others as an author. Here are some suggestions from Claire Miller for when you are starting out:

- *Know yourself!* The better you know yourself and your relationship to your work, the better you will be at establishing a consistent author brand. Anything you choose to reveal about yourself should be honest, real and represent your values.
- *Write down notes about your vision and your values.* What do you stand for? Think about this in relation to the topic of your book as well as in relation to the book industry. Craft stories about your vision and values and start sharing them in person and on social media. Telling people what you stand for should be a regular part of nurturing your author brand.
- *Take people along for the journey.* Lisa Shearon – digital marketer, journalist, copywriter, blogger and social media mentor – recommends sharing what it is like to be an aspiring author, and says that it is okay to occasionally show a little bit of vulnerability, particularly when used with humour. You don't have to be the all-conquering hero all the time (unless that's who you really are). You don't have to be upbeat all the time. Showing a range of emotions creates empathy and a sense of common feeling.
- *Don't be afraid to make mistakes.* Be ready to embarrass yourself some of the time. Don't let fear stop you from trying to connect.
- *Make a list of the people who help you along the way.* Share with others how they helped. You are not an immaculate conception. An authentic

thank you to acknowledge assistance from community members connects you to more communities. Asking people for assistance in a courteous way can also create connections.

- *Know your audience.* Who are they? What do you like about them? What do you find hard to take? What is it about you that they are likely to relate to, and what won't they relate to? Think about how to connect with them and how to challenge them.

Ask an author: When you were starting out, how did you establish your brand as a writer?

Alan Carter says:

Winning a Ned Kelly Award with the first book helps! I think what seems to have worked for me is tying my fiction writing partly to my other career as a documentary filmmaker, and highlighting the social conscience aspect of both. But both also demand an ability to entertain as well as inform, so I look to create authentic and engaging characters, realistic and occasionally funny dialogue and situations, and evoking a strong sense of place. What draws me again and again to the series I like to follow is place as much as character and plot. I'm happy to revisit Rebus's Edinburgh, Robicheaux's Louisiana and Faraday's Portsmouth over and over. With my Cato Kwong series, locals and outsiders can claim Fremantle and other Western Australian locations for themselves, so the characters and the setting are an integral element of the brand.

Daniel de Lorne says:

My brand is still evolving as the number of books published goes up. When I first started, I thought I would write only on the darker side of things, even in romance. However, as opportunities have come up and my willingness to try new things has grown, I have expanded what I promise to my readers.

In establishing a brand I considered what I liked to write and how it could be classified. I looked at what were the common elements in what I was writing that I could turn into a brand. I'll admit that it now needs some updating as time has gone on, but in general I write emotional stories with complex characters in the gay romance genre.

I then use images, text and content that support that brand – 'gay romance with emotional stories and complex characters' – across my website, social media, newsletter etc. For example on social media I might share photos of dark, brooding (and often well-muscled) men, or write a blog post about the Top 10 Broodiest Vampires. And in my newsletter I'm unlikely to talk about my favourite recipes, but will focus on the latest dark fantasy series I'm reading. Book covers also form part of that brand and speak strongly to the genre they're in.

And Sasha Wasley says:

Starting out, I didn't have a clear brand as an author. This was largely because I didn't know how important it was, but also because I prefer to write in a variety of genres. I wasn't even very strategic about choosing my author name. I simply went with my initials (S.D. Wasley) at first because I saw my publisher had another Sasha on their author list and didn't want people to get confused. It turned out to be a poor choice because when I signed with Penguin, they wanted me to use my full first name ('it looks prettier on the cover').

This meant I suddenly had two author identities. At first, I thought that could work because I could be S.D. Wasley for my YA and paranormal work and Sasha Wasley for my contemporary women's fiction. But as time goes on, I sometimes wish I had chosen another name altogether for my romantic and women's fiction. Some readers are happy to cross genres; others are adamant that they 'hate' romance or paranormal.

I still want to write across various genres, but I have had to settle on a solid and distinctive brand, name and voice for myself. I present myself as Sasha Wasley on social media and occasionally refer to my works published under the S.D. Wasley pen-name. Having two separate social profiles would diffuse my following. Going forward, my hankering to write mystery and psychological novels must sit on the backburner while I establish my brand in the commercial (women's) fiction market. I will need to decide what to do about my pen-name if and when I start publishing in those other genres.

In Chapter 8 we will return to the matter of refining your brand once you are a published author.

How and why to pitch

Being able to talk about your work is just as important as establishing your brand. Even while you are still writing your manuscript, you can start to hone your pitching skills in moments when you come across someone who may help your career. This will be good practice for later.

Some pitching skills are actually the same skills required of a writer when gathering material for their work. Writers need to be alert, attentive, good readers of people, good listeners, able to shape a story and able to change the content to accommodate every particular audience. So practising pitching can even strengthen your writing, even when you are not at the desk.

According to Claire Miller, a lot of what we call 'pitching' is just being able to tell a good story to the right person at the right time. You want it to become something natural – something that no longer feels like a pitch but is incorporated into how you talk about yourself and your work. Good pitches, like good stories, have a beginning, a middle and an end. Good pitches are targeted and streamlined, without waffle. There is no 'one pitch fits all' – you need to be able to tailor your story for a variety of different people.

Good pitches create a genuine sense of connection and become a conversation between two people. Sometimes it's better to spend your time getting to know the person you're pitching to rather than going straight in with a hard sell. Take the trouble to read the mood of the person you're pitching to – if they are not receptive to hearing a pitch but you pitch anyway, you're harming rather than aiding your cause. But if, in the course of listening and conversing, you discover that your story aligns with what the person is saying about themselves – that's the time to go for it.

Tips for preparing pitches

- *Prepare interview questions.* One of the most powerful things you can do is to put yourself into the shoes of the person you are pitching to. If you were them, what would you want to know about you and your book? Prepare a set of questions as if you were a publisher, agent, bookseller, event programmer, other author, book buyer, your publicist or a journalist. What are the top three to five things they could ask you?
- *Practise interview answers.* Switch it around and think about how you could answer those questions. Think about each answer being a mini

story – a couple of lines with a beginning, a middle and an end. Be as open and as honest as you can, and use anecdotes and examples to help you tell the story. Develop different answers and stories for each of the people mentioned above. Then think about what you may need to know before jumping in with a pitch. If you meet a publisher you've never heard of, how will you determine if they are the right publisher to pitch to? What will you ask them?

- *Attend pitch sessions.* Local writers centres and festivals sometimes have pitch sessions where authors can pitch to publishers – go along, watch the pitches and evaluate them. Use this to learn how to refine your own pitch.
- *Network.* Each time you go out to a networking event, introduce yourself to three people, ask them about what they do or what they read and get their business cards. Remember who they are so you can reconnect with them later.
- *Engage.* Remember that every single person you come across is a potential reader or book buyer. Do not underestimate or dismiss someone just because you think they might not be in your core audience. If you decide they are of no use to you, then each interaction is an opportunity lost.

Below are some questions for honing your material for pitching situations. You may like to practise responding to these questions with a friend who likes asking them, or as an exercise in your writers group. This exercise will alert you to areas you might not wish to respond to, and work out stategies to avoid them, or help you practise answering them in a way you are comfortable with.

Pitching practice

By way of preparation, practise answering the following questions yourself, either in writing, or out loud. Next, find a friend who can act as a journalist interviewing an author for the first time. If possible, reverse your roles as well, so that you learn to understand what makes an answer interesting and what loses a listener's attention. When interviewing, see if you can home in on the points or angles that you think may interest people in particular and direct your questions accordingly. Help them tease out story angles. Make brief notes as you go.

Use the questions below, and ask additional or alternative questions so your interviewee can clarify key points and try to be as expansive as possible.

- What is your book about?
- Where is it set?
- Why did you write it?
- Why did you think it was important to tell this particular story?
- What makes it unique or timely?
- What kinds of stories have been in the news that relate to your work – what are possible hooks?
- When writing it, did you have a particular kind of reader in mind – who were you writing for?
- What do you want people to know about this work?
- What are some ways the content relates to your life – what are its possible angles?
- Why were you the best person to tell this story?
- Which books inspired you during the writing of this book?
- Where were you born and where did you grow up?
- Where did you go to school?
- When did you decide to become a writer, and why?
- Who helped you become the writer you are today?
- How did your own background inform the writing of this book?
- What is a typical day for you?
- What advice would you give to other new writers?
- Is there anything else you'd like to add?

In this chapter, we've looked at when thinking about readers should become an element of your writing process. We have also considered the importance of consciously connecting with that more disparate group, your potential audience, as well as how to begin thinking about your author brand.

In the following chapter, we will look at some of the other matters you may need to tend to in the intervals when you are not writing, as you move closer to preparing to submit your work for publication.

4. Approaching submission

- Bookshops for beginners
- What booksellers do
- Tips for building relationships with booksellers
- Grants, residencies, awards and mentorships
- Tips for applications
- Copyright and moral rights
- Moral and ethical obligations
- Own voice considerations
- Obtaining a subject's consent
- Self-care
- Defamation
- Seeking a manuscript assessment before submission
- How to know when a manuscript is ready to submit

Once your work is rolling along (or even just chugging or sputtering), there are other aspects of writing that you can attend to in your creative downtime, including relationship building with booksellers and applying for funds to support your work. And some of the moral and ethical aspects of your writing practice that we discuss in this chapter go to the heart of your responsibilities as a writer.

Bookshops for beginners

We began Chapter 1 with the observation that serious writers need to be serious readers. Serious writers also need to be serious about supporting the industry that sustains them. This includes becoming a meaningful member of the community that exists around the hub of their local bricks-and-mortar bookshop. Bookstores, particularly independent ones, are much more than just a retail outlet: they are a place for like-minded people – readers and writers – to gather. Booksellers are curators and reviewers of books, and creators of events that are centred around books. They are professional salespeople in *your* line of business. A single bookshop can have a powerful effect on your sales.

Thinking, acting and buying local is in part a philosophical position, and some writers will be just as happy to buy heavily discounted books online, while some print-on-demand and self-published books may actually only be available online. Nonetheless, many traditionally published and self-published writers derive huge satisfaction from walking into a bookshop and seeing their book on the shelf. Now is a good time, as your work develops and advances, to connect with the people who work in the places where you may like to see your own book sold.

What booksellers do

A great deal goes on in a bookshop that the customer does not see. To the casual observer, a bookshop is an oasis of comforting orderliness through which the public drifts and browses and chats with the bookseller and fellow book lovers about recommendations and favourite reads. But behind the scenes, *a lot* is going on. A bookseller is always working to meet the demands of regular and casual customers to ensure repeat custom. Another ongoing and important function is seeing and speaking to publishers and sales reps. Other activities of booksellers include:

- Reviewing and ordering the books that will be published in three months time (or longer, for lead titles).
- Replenishing backlist orders (topping up the stock of books that are not new releases but which continue to sell).
- Stocking shelves, stickering books and creating displays.
- Pulling from shelves titles that have not sold and preparing them for return to distributors (sale-or-return is a method of holding stock in bookshops).
- Organising and setting up events.
- Maintaining their website and customer database
- Creating and publishing a newsletter in print and/or online.
- Providing customers with information and taking individual orders.
- Hand-selling favourite titles to walk-in customers.

If you are a regular customer who interacts with bookshop staff, your support will be noted and appreciated. If you come in to talk about books, buy them, and recommend the store to other readers, then you are gaining future credits as an author who can one day be supported in return. This is not a cynical exercise: the bookshop is a delicate ecosystem that requires preserving for the survival of readers, writers and booksellers alike.

When choosing which bookshop to start your relationship-building with, it makes sense to select one that sells the kinds of books you are writing and hope to publish. The content and emphasis of every bookshop is different, and is partly driven by the subjective curatorial approach of its manager and staff. Each bookshop bases its stock on what the readers in their area want to read, or on a specialty area (such as foreign languages, erotica, graphic novels, or children's books and games) to which readers will travel in order to buy or browse.

Tips for building relationships with booksellers

At this point of your writing career, *ask not what the bookseller can do for you, but what you can do for your bookseller*. Get serious about your reading, get in touch with your local bookstore, buy books from them, talk to them, go to bookstore signings and events, be a familiar face – this is something to do before, during and after you've been sent a contract for a manuscript. Do it when your manuscript is just a distant gleam in your eye; do it now! But keep in mind that booksellers are busy people. When it relates to matters not linked directly to being a customer and champion of the bookshop, choose the timing of your approach with care. Some other practical actions suggested by Claire Miller include:

- *Become a part of the bookshop's community.* Go to launches and events to meet other writers. Talk to the people behind the counter and the author who has just been published. Scope out what bookshops do for other authors. Choose the events for authors with books most like yours and use the opportunity to learn from them. Go to events that interest you (such as books in bars, YA book clubs, poetry readings, library talks) to meet readers and other writers.
- *Reflect on your interactions.* Treat your bookshop outings as social occasions and as research opportunities. After events, ask yourself: What are the elements of a successful book launch? How did a particular

author connect with their audience, and with the bookstore host? What worked, and what needed refining?

- *If you are based in a regional or remote area, develop online relationships with booksellers.* Make contact with their customer service people, buy their books, thank them when they do things well, ask for book recommendations. (Don't be overzealous – one short email every few months will do.)
- *Engage with bookshops on social media.* Join competitions, comment on the posts you like, tag them when reviewing books you purchased from their bookstore, join in on Love Your Bookshop Day or Australia Reads or any other online promotion that happens annually. Show booksellers you are a valuable audience member before you become someone who wants your book in their store.

Grants, residencies, awards and mentorships

Two universal afflictions for writers are the absence of time to write and the money to do it with. Until we live in a society where artists are appropriately remunerated, these conditions will go with the territory. There is, however, a number of philanthropic organisations and state and federal government programs to help ease the financial and time deficits of writers. There are many different kinds of support available. Each can represent a meaningful component of a writer's income or method of practice in a given year. So, let's take a look at what these are and how to access them.

An *award* can be bestowed on a writer based on the quality of their entry or through merit for a work or career achievement. Awards can be given for published or unpublished work, and there are some lucrative manuscript prizes in Australia for new and established writers. They can come in the form of honorary peer recognition, a publishing contract or a cash prize. Some are aimed at young writers, or at different genres like romance or speculative fiction, or different forms like novels or novellas or essays. After your work has been published, your publisher may enter your book into awards, or alert you as to what awards are available in case you should choose to enter.

A *grant* is often specifically project-focused. It can give writers the time and capacity to travel or provide some other writing-related cost in order to research, begin writing, or consolidate a work that is already underway.

A *residency* provides writers with a place to write and can be offered by a philanthropic organisation, teaching institution, or writing or community centre. Some residencies include the provision of travel expenses, food and lodging; others just a room in which to write. Residencies can come with no strings attached, or with reciprocal obligations, including that the writer conduct workshops or interact with the attached community in some way.

Mentorships from an experienced practitioner are another form of professional development offered to writers to advance their project, and may be part of a residency arrangement, or otherwise something you apply for as part of a project grant. Some organisations like the Australian Society of Authors (ASA) or Varuna, The National Writers' House have formal mentorship programs or offer mentoring sessions. Access to these may vary depending on how advanced your manuscript is. Tertiary courses can be another portal of access to the kinds of people who may be able to operate in a mentoring role, and creative writing postgraduate thesis supervisors can also offer some of this kind of support.

Some grants and residencies require the submission of project proposals, budgets, itineraries, sample materials or letters of support. Many also require acquittals, where you report on how your time or money was spent, as well as what outcomes you achieved. Not all residencies are funded – some have small stipends, but all can give you space and time to write and to advance your career.

Where can I find these opportunities?

It is a good idea to start with your own context and locale – for instance, your own writers centre – and then broaden out from there. Schools and tertiary institutions and arts centres or even your local council sometimes offer writing residencies. It's worth investigating and asking around. Next, start googling (and see Chapter 11). Listed below are just some places to begin your search, which will give you a sense of the possibilities on offer:

- Your state peak writing body will often collate lists of available opportunities for writers.
- Asialink enables cultural exchanges throughout Asia, with residencies for two to three months.
- The Australia Council website has information about residencies and programs on offer, including the Keesing Studio in Paris and the

B.R. Whiting Studio in Rome. The Australia Council also offers an array of career development grants, fellowships and grants for residencies and mentorships, and is very open to self-devised or self-managed residencies based on a proposal of your own choosing.

- The ASA has a Writers Benevolent Fund for authors in financial need.
- The Copyright Agency commits 1.5% (about two million dollars) of its annual revenue to funding grants and fellowships for mid-career or established authors.
- The National Library of Australia offers Creative Arts Fellowships for research work within the library's collection.
- Res Artis is an aggregation site that lists 400 residencies for the arts, including literature, in over eighty-five different countries.
- Varuna, The National Writers' House offer a wide variety of residency programs and professional development opportunities, including a First Nations Fellowship residency.
- If you are a First Nations or CALD (culturally and linguistically diverse) author, you will find special publication and mentorship opportunities with arange of journals including *Overland*, *Peril*, *The Lifted Brow*, *Mascara Literary Review*, *Westerly*, *Kill Your Darlings* and *Australian Book Review*, along with Sweatshop in Western Sydney.

How do I prepare a successful application?

A great deal of preparation goes into the most successful applications. The secret is to find a compelling project that is uniquely yours. The application should be delivered in the same way you would deliver a tender to build a new bridge: here's what you are offering, these are the project's parameters, and this is why you are the best person for the job.

An application is not the same as a pitch. Assessing panellists don't want to hear about the hook of your book ('a stunning saga that will chill and thrill!'). They want to hear about the nuts and bolts of your project and what you require to make it happen. When applying for a residency, the more concrete information you can supply the better: where you are going and for how long, how you will get there, and how the destination or request fits with your project. The time spent putting together a proposal can be fruitful whether or not you are successful. It can clarify what your particular project is about, and why you are prepared to devote months or years to it.

Tips for applications

When considering applying for a grant, residency or mentor program, it is good to first gain some clarity about what it is you require. Ask yourself what you *need* at this stage of your work, what it is you would *like to do*, and what is *feasible to achieve* in the time you are asking for. Once you feel you understand the parameters of your project, ask whether you need

- A project grant to get you started.
- A mentor to help you through this stage.
- A supported residency or a solo residency.
- A time and a place to write.
- A destination to do your research.
- Time to do your research.
- Money to buy you time.

In selecting what you are applying for, be strategic, informed and authentic. And, critically, get as much advice as you can from relevant project officers by phone, email, or a meeting online or in person.

What does an assessing panel look for in an application?

Assessment panels are generally made up of experienced peers, with a regular turnover of assessors. For most projects, panellists will be looking not at who you are, but at the merit of the project itself. This is good news for new writers!

Funding bodies are looking for projects that are plausible, interesting and convincing, and compatible with what is being asked for. People assessing grants are often writers themselves who understand what a writing project looks like and feels like. They want substance, not a sales pitch. They are looking for a submission that conveys:

- Your passion.
- Your awareness of where the work sits in terms of its genre.
- That you can identify how your work is doing something different and why it is worthwhile for you to pursue.
- That your work fits in with the goals of their organisation.
- That your work is worthwhile for the organisation to invest in.

What are the benefits of receiving grants, awards or residencies?

When a writer applies for a grant or residency, it is generally with the belief that the main benefit will be to achieve time and money to write. However, other benefits often last well beyond the time of the project itself. They can include:

- An affirmation of your hard work to date.
- The realisation that you are not alone because you find yourself in a community of other writers.
- Giving you a break from trying to write and survive.
- An addition to your résumé.
- Networking: making links and connections with peers or mentors.

Copyright and moral rights

As a writer, it is good for you to have an understanding of the rights you hold over your own work, the legislation that protects authors and their work, and what steps to take if you are including the work of other creators – such as writers, songwriters, photographers, artists and illustrators – in your own. In essence, any written material that you produce is automatically copyrighted upon its creation and for seventy years after your death. After seventy years, copyright lapses and your work enters the public domain, available to be used without permission. Copyright similarly protects the work of other creatives where you might be wanting to include extracts from another author in your own work.

Note that the information below and elsewhere in this chapter is not intended as legal advice. The Australian Copyright Council is a non-profit advocate for Australian creators. Their website has lots of information about copyright and moral rights. Another good resource for questions about copyright and other legal matters is the website of the Arts Law Centre of Australia, a not-for-profit organisation that provides free or low-cost advice to Australian artists and arts organisations. (For details and links to fact sheets, see Chapter 11.)

What is copyright and how is it created?

Copyright law in Australia is set out in the *Copyright Act 1968*, and has been amended a number of times since. Protecting a creator's rights in their original work gives people incentives to create new material for the benefit of others, and to retain control over the use of the content they create.

Copyright protection occurs automatically upon the creation of a work – the instant a poem is penned or a song written down. Copyright protection is free and there is no system of registration in Australia. No creator is too young to hold copyright in their work.

A creator's copyright is a valuable asset. The copyright holder has the exclusive right in their own work to reproduce it, make it public for the first time or communicate it to the public via social media, email, pamphlet etc., as well as the right to perform their work in public or create an adaptation of it.

Copyright can be sold or licensed to others, so that party can use the copyright material and benefit from its use, as in the case of a contract for publication.

How long does copyright last?

The answer to this question is that it depends on when the material was created, whether it has been published before, and whether the identity of the author is known or not known:

- Until 1 January 2005, copyright in Australia in a work lasted for the life of its author, plus fifty years (the year ending on 31 December of the fiftieth year).
- In 2005, under the Free Trade Agreement with the United States, the term of copyright was extended to last for the life of the author plus seventy years.
- The seventy-year timeframe can vary where the duration is marked not from the death of the author but from the first year of a work's publication.
- Changes made to the *Copyright Amendment (Disability Access and Other Measures) Act 2017* stipulate some variations in how the timeframe applies in relation to material never before published and only made public after an author's death and before 1 January 2019.
- Copyright in some material held in libraries may also be under certain restrictions. (Copyright aside, libraries may restrict certain uses of public domain materials for other reasons, such as in cases where there are donor restrictions, Aboriginal and Torres Strait Islander cultural requirements, or the material itself is physically fragile.)

Do I need permission to quote the work of others in my own work?

In simple terms, the answer to this question is yes: when an author wants to quote or reference material that is still in copyright, they must obtain legal agreement from the work's publisher or its copyright holder (such as the author themselves, or their estate) in the form of permission or a licence. The agreement can include a fee for usage as well as limitations of usage based around territories or print runs.

There are a number of instances where you do *not* need to seek permission to reproduce somebody else's work or part thereof. This may be because copyright has expired, or because an exception or statutory licence applies, say for educational or government use. The Australian Copyright Council sets out what constitutes 'fair dealing' in Australia, which applies when quoting from a work for the purposes of comment, review, criticism, parody, satire, research, study or reporting. (Note that under United States copyright law, 'fair use' applies as a defence to a claim of copyright infringement, but is not an applicable defence in Australia.) If your usage falls outside these purposes, then infringement of copyright can be said to occur where a 'substantial part' of a work is used in a way exclusively reserved to the copyright owner. A 'substantial part' is not defined by the number of words used but rather by whether it is an important, essential or distinctive part of a work. Even if the extract you want to use is only five words long, the publisher or copyright holder may deem that extract to be significant in its own terms. And the only way you can discover what constitutes 'substantial' is by applying to the copyright holder for permission to reproduce their work.

Quoting from others, or reproducing their images in your work is a less pressing concern *before* you make public or publish your own work. Down the track, your editor can advise you what material you will need to seek permission for. Formally seeking permissions is a task that can be left until after contracting when you have all the relevant publication details (see p. 169). But it can save you a lot of time later to compile as you go a comprehensive list of primary source material used and referred to in your work.

Note: there is no copyright in a title – you are free to quote the titles of books and songs and poems. That is good if you have a character who wants to read a book or sing a song. But quoting lyrics from songs can be expensive. Your character may prefer to write their own!

When it comes time to publish your work, you will of course need to acknowledge the source of *any* material that you quote or paraphrase in order to avoid plagiarism (passing off someone else's work as your own).

What are an author's moral rights?

You may have seen on the imprint page of a book a statement declaring that the author's moral rights have been asserted. Moral rights are set out under the *Copyright Act 1968*. Regardless of whether an author has assigned their copyright to another party, moral rights give authors the rights to:

- Be attributed as the creator of their work.
- Take action against another in the event of false attribution as the work of another.
- Take action if their work is distorted or dealt with in a way prejudicial to the author's reputation or honour.

Moral and ethical obligations

Regardless of genre, an author has moral and sometimes also ethical obligations in relation to their work. *Moral* obligations refer to our own principles relating to right and wrong, whereby we take into account how our actions may harm or benefit others and adjust our behaviour accordingly. With *ethical* obligations, there will be specific codes of conduct or principles set out by an external source to which one is obliged to adhere. Either may be relevant regardless of whether you are writing fiction or non-fiction.

How do morals and ethics apply to writing? Writing is a privilege, and a responsibility. Your depictions of characters and stories are necessarily subjective and, consciously or not, you make choices about *who* is visible, and what stories and themes will be privileged. It is important to be aware that you are *always* making choices when you decide to tell a particular story in a particular way from a particular point of view.

Publication is powerful. Words in print carry an air of authority and permanence that can be disconcerting or distressing. Relationships and friendships can be destroyed by writing and, more particularly, by publication. Complete strangers may also read and be adversely affected by what you write. If you are writing a memoir, you might assume that because it is *your* story, then if *you* don't mind sharing it with the world, that should be enough. However, this is not necessarily so. If you think that anyone you are writing about or depicted in your work might be unsettled, upset, offended or enraged by what you have written, then you have choices. Leaving that material out is one option; showing the person what you have written prior to publication is another. Ask:

- Should other parties represented in your story (explicitly or implicitly) be made aware that they are there?
- Is it enough that you simply let them know generally what you are doing, or is a more in-depth conversation required?
- Do they need to read ahead of publication what you have written?
- Do you need confirmation in writing of a subject's approval of content?
- Are you comfortable with being answerable to anyone after publication?
- Can you justify the position you have taken?

It is not possible to defame the dead, as they no longer have a reputation that can be damaged. Even so, people connected to loved ones can feel upset or dismayed by a depiction in a piece of writing. This can be a particular challenge in relation to crime fiction, where the events of your novel are inspired by an actual crime. If you are writing true crime, the challenges are even greater. Thus when you are writing, you may also need to think about the people connected to someone who has passed, and whether you need their consent to proceed with a particular depiction, or at least to let them know about your work. Ask:

- Who is connected to the deceased, directly or by relationship?
- Who might be hurt?
- Who might be angry and how might they express this?
- Will my story make anyone vulnerable or place them in danger?

Think carefully about possible scenarios and outcomes you want to avoid. However, in the same way it can stifle creativity to think about potential readers, such considerations may hamper your creative process or make you feel censored. So you may choose to write the first draft before considering your other obligations.

Navigating representation of others in your work

Thinking about the potential impact of your work on others does not mean you have to abandon your project, but it does allow you to consider ways in which to negotiate potential problems and lessen offence or distress. For instance, you could obscure the identity of a childhood friend or former co-worker by changing their name, or altering or leaving out a few elements of character or background that will not substantially alter the truth (or the emotional truth) of the work. You could also consider clearly prefacing in your work that your interpretation of events is entirely subjective and determined by the personal nature of memory. If your work is fiction but you think others may nonetheless choose to see themselves in it, you can insert a notice in your acknowledgements to the effect that all characters appearing in the work are fictitious and any resemblance to persons living or dead is purely coincidental.

You would do well to pay attention to checking elements of your story that may prove inflammatory to others, and also be prepared to adjust your account, even if it does mean abandoning some of the funniest or most shocking or moving passages of writing. This is particularly relevant where defamation might be present (see p. 109). When gathering information about true events from individuals, you may wish to set up your own parameters about due diligence and double-checking against other sources.

Once your work is contracted, you can talk with your editor about any red-flag areas or any aspects of representation that concern them or you. Nonetheless, while you are writing, it is a good idea to have a clear strategy about how you are going to incorporate real people and events into your work. It is easier to change course or to confront such issues earlier in the writing process than it is when a manuscript is more advanced, or submitted for publication.

Own voice considerations

Who is speaking for whom? What authority, experience or identity does a particular writer have to draw on in representing characters and points of view from cultural, gendered or marginalised positions? These are important questions a writer needs to ask when considering who is represented in their work and how they are depicted. Own voice considerations are also part of an author's moral responsibility.

In recent years, own voice considerations have become a much more visible element of the dialogue around creative work, where creators, editors, publishers and readers now think and talk more about the relationship between what is created and who created it. Cultural, gendered and other kinds of identities exist in works, authorship and audiences in multiple and complex ways. 'Own voice' writers bring authenticity to subject positions while, conversely, those who write from outside these positions may be seen to be assuming or appropriating a speaking position that is not theirs.

In the early 1990s, it was revealed that the *Australian*/Vogel's Literary Award and Miles Franklin Literary Award winner Helen Darville had faked a Ukrainian heritage when presenting her novel under the name Helen Demidenko. The revelation caused a furore, not least because it significantly altered readers' perception of *The Hand That Signed the Paper* and how it might be read, interpreted and received.

The Demidenko affair occurred a long time before #OwnVoices acquired a hashtag. And while it was an instance of deliberate obfuscation, there are many writers who write stories with the best of intentions but haven't considered why they should think carefully before adopting certain subject positions and writing from marginalised perspectives, whether in a work of fiction or non-fiction.

When we looked at an author's moral obligations, we spoke of the importance of being aware that you are always making choices when you decide to tell a particular story in a particular way from a particular point of view. Who are you speaking for? Who are you speaking over? What does your choosing a particular subject position mean, and to whom? Is there someone better placed to speak from that position?

To take a particular example in an Australian context: if you are *not* a First Nations writer, then what moral obligations do you have when depicting an Aboriginal and Torres Strait Islander person in your writing? In this country, British colonisation marked the beginning of devastating acts of systematic violence and the attempted erasure of the lives and cultures of the original inhabitants. Unsurprisingly, in that context, writing by a non-Indigenous writer that includes aspects of First Nations cultural life or practices, or that 'speaks for' Aboriginal and Torres Strait Islander peoples, can be regarded by members of these communities and others as a continuation of a long history of appropriation.

What should you do if you wish to include references to actual First Nations peoples and their country and cultures in your work? What if you wish to write about deceased or living people, or fictional characters drawn from life? There are often no hard rules for this, though particular organisations or communities may have stipulations when it comes to reproducing primary written or visual material or retelling stories, and have clear protocols in relation to naming or showing images of their deceased. The Australia Council's online publication 'Protocols for Producing Indigenous Australian Writing' sets out clear principles for ways to use or reference Aboriginal and Torres Strait Islander cultural material and to interact with their communities.

As Marda Marda author Stephen Kinnane observes:

There are a range of opinions regarding own voice writing in relation to Indigenous content. Many Indigenous writers are of a view that only Indigenous writers should deal with Indigenous perspectives or content. Then there are others, like myself, who feel that it is more important for writers to do their homework so as to arrive at an informed position from which their own creative explorations of other lives (whether they be fiction or non-fiction) must be informed by truly understanding the context of power-plays and debates regarding speaking positions. Martin Nakata speaks of a cultural interface in which peoples of different cultures arrive at understandings through intersubjective dialogue, as does Marcia Langton. Then there are authors such as Tara June Winch who have simply stated that non-Indigenous writers need to get out of the way for Indigenous writers.[1] Personally, I think there is room for all of us to explore each other's positions through imagination, but that imagination needs to be aware of the various stereotypes and tropes that it is entering into. I have written previously that Aboriginal history is layered with such traps awaiting the ill-informed. That can be the case on any aspect of diversity outside of a writer's own experience. In an interview with Bruce Pascoe he told me, 'Nothing is forbidden a writer except intellectual tact'.[2] He qualified that with 'You can't go to just one Aboriginal person and say, "Is it okay if I publish this book?" You've got to go to the community and the only way you can do that is to be a part of that community, be friends of that community. Aboriginal people have been inviting people to do that for 220 years and that invitation has generally been refused.'

1. theguardian.com/books/2019/jul/11/tara-june-winch-the-yield-andrew-bolt-unmissables.
2. *Westerly*, vol. 61.1, 2016, p. 185.

None of us would expect a writer to only write from one perspective. But we do expect writers not to simply repeat stereotypes, myths and racist or sexist or homophobic ideologies by being ill-informed. There is indeed a moral responsibility, and a creative responsibility to do the work.

Writers need to tread respectfully and sensitively. If you are *not* an Aboriginal or Torres Strait Islander person, then not using an Indigenous first-person point of view in your work is one way to avoid obvious appropriation, but own voice issues beyond this are complex and require thoughtful consideration and appropriate consultation. The best starting position is to write with respectfulness, and a good heart. And be aware that the currency and meaning of words, as well as their context, changes over time – sometimes very quickly – and from group to group.

When seeking cultural advice or expert guidance, recognise that such work will require time and effort, and be prepared to pay an appropriate reader's fee.

When seeking permission to use material, be prepared for individuals to be reluctant to assume the responsibility of granting permission for the inclusion of material that pertains to an entire group. You will also need to be aware of any individual's capacity to be a spokesperson for a group, and their position within it.

Remember that responsibility for what you write lies with you, not with the people whose permission you seek. If you feel you need to seek permission to use something, perhaps that material shouldn't be there in the first place.

Beyond the vital work of your own self-education, another step you can take is to seek the services of a sensitivity reader – someone who specialises in reading your work for the purpose of drawing your attention to racism, problematic gender representation, stereotyping, or other kinds of bias that may not have occurred to you.

If you are editing or workshopping the work of a First Nations, CALD or LGBTQIA writer, or a writer living with disability, start by assuming there is much you don't and can't know or understand about the experience of that writer. Begin with a conversation about how you may best work together. Ascertain their own intentions in relation to their work and remain alert to your own assumptions.

If you *are* an own voice writer, you can of course choose whether you wish to explicitly identify yourself and in what context.

In thinking about these issues and your obligations, you could explore some of the posts and opinions of writers in the own voice space: search the #OwnVoices hashtag or follow own voice publications like *Liminal* magazine as forums for discussions of representations of identity, including race, culture, disability, sexuality, gender or other forms of diversity. A number of links are included in Chapter 11 as places to start your reading.

Obtaining a subject's consent

If you are writing non-fiction such as biography, memoir, true crime, a travel book or a piece of investigative journalism, and interviewing people for your research, then you need to be transparent with your subjects about your intentions at the time you are gathering material for your work. It could be wise to seek formal sign-off or consent from the people you interview if you think you may include their words or their viewpoints in your work.

If your work is at the narrative non-fiction end of the spectrum, you may be gathering material in an informal way. You may chat with subjects without recording your conversation and channel their material into your work through a series of impressions rather than direct quotes or specific representation. You may also choose to change names of real people and alter their identifying features.

Once the work is written and before it is published, think about who might be affected by what you are doing and whether this requires any action on your part. You may as a matter of courtesy let certain individuals know how you have chosen to represent their stories or points of view.

When you are writing non-fiction like biography you may choose to go about the interview process in a more formal way. When speaking to a subject, one of the very first things you should do is to ask if they are willing to sign a consent or release form of interview material. There are a number of reasons for doing this early:

- Asking someone to sign a form gives them the opportunity to officially agree to or refuse your request.
- A signed consent form represents a formal agreement between parties.
- It puts both parties on notice that whatever follows is on the record.
- It gives you freedom to use material knowing you have the back-up of the consent form should disputes arise later.

- It protects you from anyone who wishes to challenge the content of your work or who wishes to dispute what was said.
- It protects you if, for instance, a series of small revelations from separate parties leads to a composite 'bombshell' revelation that individuals may not feel they signed up for when agreeing to talk to you.

A consent form template may be available from a university ethics department, a magazine or newspaper. If you create one yourself, it should contain the following elements:

- Your name and particulars of the project.
- The form of documentation of the interview (audio/visual).
- Notice that a transcript of the interview may be created.
- Notice that the records will be stored.
- Purpose for which the work is intended (e.g. publication, presentation).
- A signature of the person acknowledging the purposes of the project and giving their consent.
- Date, address and contact details of the person signing.

If you are interviewing someone, you would be wise to make a digital recording of each interview (with the interviewee's consent) and a typed and dated transcript afterwards. Then, if anything is disputed, you have these documents to hand.

If you are researching a biography or history, where objectivity and rigour will lend authority to the final work, then think carefully about who you are going to interview, and how. If you are interviewing members of a particular group – say a large family – it can be sensible to approach the person who has the greatest authority in that group and who is prepared to speak for the whole. A 'black sheep' or outlier is going to present a version of events that may be disputed by 'inliers'. Of course everyone is entitled to their own opinion, but if you have the approval of a central authority figure and spokesperson, your own job will be much easier.

If you are writing non-fiction and your work involves research and interviewing subjects, it's a good idea to read the Media, Entertainment & Arts Alliance's Journalist Code of Ethics. Even if you are not a journalist, this document sets out the kinds of things to bear in mind when gathering material for a story.

Self-care

Strange as it may seem, self-care is another form of authorial obligation in the context where you are committing representations of yourself or others to a text with the intention of publication. During the writing process you should determine and clarify for your own wellbeing what your limits are in relation to writing about your own mental health or trauma. Writing can 'get things out' and have a healing quality, but it can also stir things up and be very painful.

The act of writing can take a toll: it can make you vulnerable in ways you have not anticipated and, after publication, readers may feel as if they have a right to interrogate you because of what you have shared in your book. It is good to think these things through in advance and ascertain whether you need to take steps to be more self-protective than you were in the first flush of writing a draft. Remember, post-publication, that embarrassing anecdote or distressing incident or unverifiable assertion is something that you may find yourself having to discuss publicly or see misinterpreted in a review, or defend against legal scrutiny or an outraged subject. This is not to say you should abandon writing your desired story, but rather consider the implications of publicly being its author and thinking how the decisions you make in the writing process can best prepare and protect you.

Defamation

Defamation occurs when the depiction of an individual injures their reputation or standing without good cause. The purpose of defamation law is to protect the reputations of individuals – how they are referred to in the public domain, and how images of them are used.

As stated earlier, you cannot defame a dead person. But you may still have to deal with uncomfortable personal fallout if someone takes umbrage at your depiction of the deceased.

Generally, you cannot defame a corporation (being an entity of more than ten people) because you cannot 'hurt its feelings'. But you *can* defame corporations of under ten people, and not-for-profit organisations.

Whether material in your work is defamatory is something your future publisher will consider, and they may advise that you seek legal advice to clarify whether material is defamatory or not. Because both publisher and author, as parties to a contract, can be jointly sued, it is not in the publisher's interest to proceed to publication knowing a work may contain defamatory material. They are certainly keen to avoid a scenario in which a book must be withdrawn or suppressed for legal reasons. Publishing contracts generally include a warranty clause stating it is the author's responsibility to ensure there's no defamatory material in the work.

Nor is being sued in *your* interests! If what you say is substantially true and you have evidence to prove it, then you have a good defence, but it is still important to ask whether you would wish – or could afford – to slug a matter out in court to determine who is right.

While writing, keep issues of potential defamation in mind, or at the very least flag material for a future publisher's attention. If you are writing fiction, you should let your editor know which characters are based on real people. If those characters are rather less than model citizens and can be linked to a real-life person through context (e.g. an inept detective in a particular metropolitan police station in a particular era), then defamation may be an issue. In the late 1980s, Tasmanian ALP Senator Terry Aulich claimed he'd been defamed by a portrayal of a character known as 'The Senator' in Amanda Lohrey's political novel *The Reading Group*. In that case, the year-long negotiations resulted in a cash settlement.

Extra care should be taken when writing narrative non-fiction. You may think you have a premise for a true crime book based on a story you have heard around town. You'll need more solid evidence than pub and online gossip to avoid a defamation case. Is real evidence there? How will you go about uncovering it? Do you have the skills and resources to do so? Before you get in too deep, ask whether you should instead turn this story into crime fiction, altering recognisable details with creative touches.

Seeking a manuscript assessment before submission

Writers considering submitting their work for publication sometimes ask if they ought to pay for their manuscript to be reviewed or assessed in order to iron out any obvious glitches and give it the best possible chance to stand out among others when it lands on the publisher's desk.

A manuscript assessor is paid to review a writer's work and provide feedback. They can provide the writer with general areas for improvement or they can respond to a more specific brief – a request for expert input in a particular area, or to focus on plot or assist with structure or grammar or continuity issues. For some writers, having a manuscript assessed before submission is a part of their process. Beyond this, is it worth doing? Keep in mind that a glowing report from a manuscript assessor will have little impact on a publisher: they will make up their own mind about a manuscript rather than be persuaded by someone who has been paid to write a report.

If you *do* elect to go with a manuscript assessor, we recommend you select someone who has been recommended by word of mouth. If you engage a manuscript assessor:

- Have a sense of what you can pay and don't exceed that amount.
- Be clear about your expectations and the scope of the task.
- Do your homework before employing someone to assess your work.
- Be clear about costs upfront.
- If you plan to self-publish, ask yourself whether you may be better to spend your funds on engaging someone at the end of the process rather than at the beginning, such as a designer, proofreader or publicist.

Reasons for paying for a manuscript assessment include the following:

- Input into your work in absence of a writing group or valued critic.
- It could be a valuable partnership if you enjoy and can afford this kind of collaboration.
- You could direct an assessor to improve an area that is not your strong suit (e.g. tense, grammar, clichés) and thus tighten your manuscript overall.

Reasons against paying for a manuscript assessment include the following:

- An assessor may take your work in a direction that a publishing house subsequently asks you to undo.
- A reader's report from a manuscript assessor is often irrelevant to a publisher, who will form their own views about your work.
- If you already have constructive readers in your life, an assessor's services may be redundant.

How to know when a manuscript is ready to submit

Essentially, your work is ready to submit when you have taken it as far as you can, and you can do nothing more to improve it. Here is a checklist of questions to ask yourself to ascertain whether your manuscript is ready to submit:

- Is having readers important to me – do I actually want my work to be published?
- Does this manuscript represent the outcome of multiple drafts rather than just a first draft?
- Have I taken my manuscript as far as I can and is there nothing more I can do to improve it?
- Is my manuscript clean and error-free? (Have a trusted friend review it for any weaknesses you may have, such as shifting tenses, or grammar or spelling errors.)

If you have answered yes to these questions, then your work may be ready to submit to a publisher. And in the next chapter, we will look at how to find the right publisher to whom to submit your work.

5. Finding a publisher

- Self-publishing versus traditional publication
- The bookshop test for finding a publisher
- Submitting to a publisher
- Submission etiquette
- Cleaning the mud off a digital footprint
- Coping with rejection
- Gaining experience
- Dos and don'ts for submitting a manuscript to a publisher
- When to seek a literary agent
- Dos and don'ts for finding an agent

At some stage, after months or years of hard slog, you will finally have a manuscript that you feel is ready to be seen by a publisher. In the following chapters, we will take you through all the business of being a writer that is relevant on the road to publication. Details for the resources and organisations mentioned here are listed in Chapter 11.

Self-publishing versus traditional publication

In basic terms, 'publication' means that a work is made available to the public. Thus, you can imagine, there are many ways of being published. Publication can be in print or online, in the form of a performance or having limited distribution such as a zine or a self-published work.

It may be that you are happy to publish your work online and to receive instant feedback from a particular community – especially if you are writing fan fiction, for instance, or a blog. Or that nothing gives you more joy than to create a zine or chapbook and run off fifty copies to sell. Or to stitch up a bespoke work on handmade paper to give to appreciative friends. Or to perform your work in front of twenty people down at the local pub. If any of these fulfils your definition of finding and communing with readers, then that is an entirely satisfactory way to proceed.

It is important to ask yourself *why* you want to be published. It is possible that the answer to this question is: 'Because I have a story that I want to hand down to the next generation of my family' or 'Because I want other parents of triplets / widget manufacturers / guinea pig breeders to benefit from my knowledge'. And if that is your answer (or something like it), then you may be an ideal candidate for self-publication. In such cases, you can reach your potential audience with ease or with just a little focused perseverance (e.g. by targeting relevant clubs or associations) – or simply by turning up to the next family reunion.

Self-publishing and other non-traditional forms of publication

Self-publishing gives you absolute control and also absolute responsibility for your product. It requires you to be the creator as well as the designer, publisher, publicist, marketer, wholesaler, retailer, distributor and events coordinator – or to employ or enlist people to help you do this. A comprehensive guide to self-publishing would take a whole book in itself. What we offer here is intended to give you an overview of self-publishing and a sense of what is involved, and whether it might be a choice that is right for you.

When you are deciding whether or not to self-publish, you will need to think hard about self-publishing's perennial challenge: distribution. Are you going to distribute your book yourself? Can you find outlets to stock it for your needs? Your local bookshop may be happy to take copies of your book on consignment – that is, they may agree to stock copies for you and pay you upon sale. At least these days you can manage control of your stock and no longer have to stash a thousand books beneath your bed as you work hard to sell them. With digital printing, you can print one book or twenty-seven, or three hundred and fifty – whatever your assess your readership to be. Or you can create an ebook and have no hard copies to shift at all.

The internet is full of ads for digital printers. Make sure you identify at least one local one and go talk to them about the services they provide, take a look at their products and get a quote. When approaching interstate or online printers, go where possible with services that have been recommended by others. Who you choose depends on your own requirements. A printer may be able to deliver some handsome-looking print copies into your hands for your own distribution. Some digital print-on-demand services will distribute your book for you, meaning that a guinea pig breeder in Badger Head can order your book online, and have a single copy printed and delivered to their door without you having to do a thing. Some printers have plants or print partners on several continents, and can print your work in the UK, the US, Europe, parts of Asia and Russia, meaning your books don't need to be posted or freighted across the planet. Some companies will be able to create an ebook file for your book, or you may need to seek out a dedicated ebook professional to make the necessary changes to your print file. As part of their distribution service, a printer may make your book's data available to the crucial places needed for discoverability, including industry databases like Books In Print, Nielsen BookData and TitlePage, as well as distributors like Amazon, Booktopia, Fishpond, along with independent bookstores, online stores, chain stores, ebook retailers, libraries and universities. Some printers may also recommend people or businesses to assist you with preparing a manuscript for print, and some may offer typesetting and cover design services in-house.

There are many reputable digital printers around – again, find other people who have self-published and following their advice and recommendations, and learn from their successes and their mistakes. It is wise to be wary: there are also any number of companies looking to take advantage of self-publishers.

Probably the best advice we can offer is: start your planning by imagining the end of the process and work your way back from there. Ask:

- Do I want to make money by publishing this book, to just break even, or is cost no consideration?
- Where will I sell my book (online and elsewhere)?
- How will I make it discoverable to others online?
- What will it look like (especially compared to other like books)?
- How much will I sell it for compared to the recommended retail price (RRP) of like books?
- How many pages will it be (i.e. what is its extent)?
- What dimensions will it be (be aware that there are industry-standard sizes and most printers have their own set sizes)?
- What paper stock will look right for my book (i.e. its colour and weight)?
- How heavy will my book be?

- What size postage envelope will be needed to post my book?
- How much will it cost to mail to others?

Using these approximations and estimates, you can begin to investigate where you will print your book. Print-on-demand printers should be able to provide you with quotes, or will have printing calculators on their sites to determine how much each book (unit) is going to cost to print, based on dimensions, extent and the kind of paper stock you choose. There are some economies of scale here: the unit cost will decrease as the print run rises. They also have shipping calculators which will let you know how much it will cost for you to freight one or a specified number of books to any particular postcode.

Using this information, you should be able to build a budget and look at your profit margin based on the RRP, the percentage a bookseller or distributor will take from each sale (usually at least 40%) and the unit cost of each book – where the print run estimated is based on the number of books you believe you can sell. You will then be able to look at the 'sweet spot' of print run versus unit cost. It may cost, for example, $10 to print a single book, $5 a unit to print 100 books, $2 to print 350 books and $1 to print 1,000. Into this budget you will also need to add quotes from professionals as you decide what assistance you will need to produce a book that booksellers will be happy to stock (if this is to be one of the means of distribution) as well as appeal to readers. Other expenses will come from set-up costs with the printer and the purchase of an ISBN (International Standard Book Number) and barcode.

If you are working on a groundbreaking, multimedia, interactive sensation, now is the time to ascertain whether such a platform is even available to create your work and to ask how it is that you will distribute it or ensure that others can find it.

Where to find people to assist you on the self-publishing journey

Local writers centres often run self-publishing workshops. These can be a good place to start looking for information. Your state's peak writing body may be another.

In order to create a professional product that can compete in the marketplace, you will most probably need to pay for it. If you are working with freelancers, you may pay someone by the hour, or at an agreed-upon sum for the project in total. A freelancer should always be able to provide you with an estimate of costs for the scope of the task, and should agree to alert you as soon as it looks as if they may need to diverge from this.

When it comes to seeking professional help for editing and proof-reading, the Institute of Professional Editors or your local writers centre may be able to recommend editors. You should ask what other work an editor has done to ascertain whether their skills are suited to your project. Decide what help you need before approaching an editor (see p. 162 for the stages of editing). Chat with a prospective editor before you begin to work with them to get a feeling about whether you will be compatible.

When it comes to proofreading, be aware that friends who are good at picking up typos may appear to have the requisite skills but there are many aspects to proofreading a book-length manuscript that only a professional proofreader will be alert to. The same can be said for designers.

If you intend to sell your book, then you will need to do your homework when it comes to choosing a designer. A book that *looks* self-published will lack 'pickupability' in a bookstore where other covers have been designed by people precisely aware of what draws a customer to pick up a book. Your cover also needs to work as a thumbnail-sized image for its promotion online. You should look at a designer's portfolio to see if they are the right fit for you. Have a look at their internal designs as well as their covers: a poorly laid-out book is fatiguing to read and readers are more likely to give up halfway through. A good place to start looking for a designer is the website of the Australian Book Designers Association.

It may be that you decide you need to hire a publicist to help you get media bookings and other promotional opportunities. Look for a publicist who has experience working in the book industry.

A booking agent can find events for you to attend. Recommendations (online and from your peers) are the best way to locate a booking agent. They will interview you to decide whether they wish to take you on.

If you are self-publishing, then all the other business of being a writer we are discussing in this book still applies – preparing a manuscript for publication, revising and reviewing content with a trusted cohort of readers, pitching your work, and finding and making connections with your audience. And you need to be aware that the weight carried by a publishing house (all the expertise offered by editorial and marketing departments, and the infrastructure of warehousing and distribution) will fall to you.

When self-publishing, the following items should appear on your to-do list:

- *ISBN.* If you would like the option to sell your book, then you will need an ISBN. It is important for self-publishers to buy their own ISBNs rather than as part of a package from a third party. ISBNs are sold through the website of the NLA, and direct from THORPE–Bowker, the official ISBN agency in Australia. If your book is part of a series it will also need an ISSN (International Standard Serial Number), also available through the NLA.
- *Barcode.* These can be bought from THORPE–Bowker or generated yourself using online software and your ISBN.
- *Imprint page.* This page contains all your book's publication details. For an example, look at the very last page of this book.
- *Prepublication data.* Regardless of whether your book has an ISBN, and regardless of whether it is a print book or an ebook, you will need to visit the NLA's Prepublication Data Service to register it in the library system.
- *Legal deposit.* Lodging a copy of your published book within one month of publication, with the NLA is a legal requirement of the *Copyright Act 1968*. Visit the website of your state library to ascertain deposit requirements, which vary from state to state.
- *Legal Edeposit.* A national edeposit (NED) scheme sets out the requirements of national, state and territory libraries.
- *Metadata.* Your book's metadata (its title, RRP, ISBN, territories available, formats etc.) needs to be provided to a number of places for your book to be discoverable by booksellers, libraries and readers. The main ones are Books In Print (via THORPE–Bowker) and Nielsen BookData. The book industry has its own global standard for metadata known as ONIX (ONline Information eXchange: a standard format publishers can use to distribute electronic information about their books to wholesalers, distributors, resellers and bookstores).
- *Register with Amazon Author Books.* You can set up an account with Amazon unprompted, or you will be invited to verify your identity if your profile has been created by Amazon from metadata elsewhere so that you can manage your own author and book profile.

Traditional publishing

You may feel an important element of your writing journey is to find an audience via the reach of a traditional publisher with established methods of distribution. Much of the rest of this chapter will be devoted to this traditional form of publication.

Your best chance at success, and by far the most efficient way of going about things, is to find the publishers that are publishing the kind of work that you write. To work out the best place to submit your manuscript, we recommend the three-step bookshop test. This is a useful exercise to do as you start to think about preparing your manuscript for submission, although you can do it at any stage of your writing if you are looking for clarity about what you are writing, and for whom.

The bookshop test for finding a publisher

Step 1

Before you leave home to visit a bookshop:

- Define the genre of your manuscript – if this is difficult, it can mean that your work is not ready yet and requires some more thinking about.
- Write a list of who you think may be in your potential audience (e.g. fantasy readers, tertiary teachers, readers over fifteen, grey nomads and their grandchildren).
- Write a blurb for your manuscript – can you condense a description of your work to no more than one hundred words?
- Write down three relevant biographical details about yourself – these should be the kinds of things that someone would be keen to know about you in the context of your book.

Step 2

Identify the bookshops that you think will sell your work. Visit as many of these as you can. The content of independent or specialty or chain bookstores can vary widely. Having identified the right bookshop, go there and ask yourself where on the shelves your own work would appear. This will bring into sharp focus the fact that you have identified a genre for your work. Do *you* read the kind of books you are writing? You should! When you are in the bookshop:

- Pinpoint the spot where your book would fit best. If your book is a children's book, then you may need to fossick around a little, depending on the ordering principle of the bookstore. Most likely children's books are grouped according to reader age, rather than just alphabetically or by genre. If you need help, ask! It's one way to start a conversation with a bookseller.

- Make a list of the books that are like your work – in genre, and also with the packaging that you think is reaching for the same kind of market.
- Examine the packaging. What is the genre and how can you tell? At what kind of audience are they aimed, and how do you know? What kind of work is the back blurb doing to entice the reader? Is the blurb pitched at readers, or another audience, such as the parents of readers?
- Make notes on format (size, paperback or hardcover), the page extent, whether they are illustrated, and whether these illustrations are in colour or black and white.
- Read the author's biographical note inside: what information does it contain? What makes it feel intimate, personal or authoritative? How does its tone relate to the book itself?
- Note the publishers of books that seem to be good comparison titles to yours.
- Then (pausing only to purchase a book) head off home to do a little more research.

Step 3

Once home, return to your notes from Step 1:

- Do you need to refine potential audience and genre in light of what you learned during your bookshop research?
- Review your manuscript blurb. Check to see that it has a hook or an angle – something that is going to make someone want to open up the book and read on. Do you need to rewrite it so that it is aimed at the intended audience. Does its length match the length of the blurbs you were reading?
- Do you need to revisit relevant biographical details in light of the author's biographical notes you read?

Now you are ready to look at the websites of publishers who are publishing the kind of work you write.

Is it possible to complete the bookshop test in a library?

Not really ... While you may find all sorts of wonderful like books in the library, the organising principles of the Dewey decimal system are not necessarily useful. Answering the question 'Where will my book fit on the shelf?' in a library will send you to a different destination than if you ask it in a bookshop. Importantly too, books in a bookshop will give you a sense of current market trends in terms of themes, content and packaging, while a library has a much broader, deeper and older range of titles.

Can you complete this test without leaving home at all?

Kind of ... It is possible to visit online platforms and look for like books, especially by following the trail of 'customers who bought this title also bought ...' Theoretically, this will give you access to a great many more books than a bookshop can hold. But the internet uses algorithms to push certain titles. It won't be as effective or efficient as a bricks-and-mortar establishment whose business it is to curate genres and titles, where you can walk around and imagine which particular shelf matches your work best. Customers will reach your book online and via algorithms, but bookshops still represent the primary point of sale for your book, and it makes sense to situate your baseline research there. (An exception may be self-published books, genre titles, or highly specialised non-fiction which may be geographically difficult to reach – depending on where they, and you, are.) A bookshop allows you to browse in three dimensions, and to think about physical points of difference and similarity between your work and others'.

> ## Ask an author: What is your advice for writers looking for the right publisher for their work?
>
> **Natasha Lester says:**
> *Read!* I hope that most writers come to writing out of a love of reading. Reading will not only show you the conventions of your chosen genre, it will also inspire you to write the best possible book. But if you read widely, you'll also start to see what kinds of books different publishers are publishing and thus which publisher may

be right for you and your book. Sometimes I think that new writers feel they have no power and that they should sign with anyone who's interested, but keep in mind that, like any working relationship, you need to feel completely comfortable – and convinced that your publisher understands your book the way you do.

Consider the pros and cons of a big publisher versus a smaller publisher. Each offers different advantages and each has their drawbacks. By *tuning into the industry* – going to writers festivals, author talks and other writing-related events – you'll start to learn more about what some of those advantages and drawbacks might be, which ones you aren't prepared to compromise on and which ones don't matter to you. Subscribe to writing newsletters and journals. Follow publishers and authors on Twitter. The more you know about the industry, the more you'll begin to understand how each publisher is different, what they look for when they build their lists, how they work with authors and therefore which publishers have an approach that might best fit with you.

Daniel de Lorne says:

Read in the genre you're writing in and look up the websites of whoever's publishing those books. Most should have a page about their submissions process and whether they accept unsolicited manuscripts.

If they do, *follow their instructions to the letter*; you don't want to end up with a rejection because of something that could be easily avoided. If they only accept solicited manuscripts, either find out how you can pitch to them in other ways or look for an agent who will sign you.

You could also join writers groups and organisations, and ask them about particular publishers and how they operate. Alternatively, you may discover that going down a traditional publishing route is not for you and your work. In that case, self-publishing may be a viable option.

Do your homework on the publishing house's reputation. Is it solid? Do they pay their authors on time? Do you have to pay them anything (a big warning!)? And remember that just because they offer you a contract, it doesn't mean you have to sign it. Get it looked over by a professional (whether that's your agent or a literary lawyer or the Australian Society of Authors) and *ensure the terms are fair.*

And Ambelin Kwaymullina says:

All aspiring writers generally think it's about finding a 'big' publisher. There's no problem with that, but if you're equating a big publisher with big success, that's not necessarily the case. Yes, big publishers have more resources, but they're mostly not going to spend those resources on your book, and advances in Australia are fairly low for most writers. Since you're incredibly unlikely to get a big cheque, it's important to focus on long-term – rather than short-term – success when identifying a publisher. I'd also add, as someone who has worked with large and small publishers, that the publicity departments with small publishers are often much better. Small press publicists manage smaller lists and can give individual books far more attention, and they also tend to be incredibly invested in their list, and 'know' the books in a way that larger publicity departments don't.

I think the key question in identifying a publisher is whether they're a good fit for your book, including how your book will sit on their list. Take a look at their publications and see what kinds of books they publish. It can be a bad idea to go with a publisher who has never published anything like your book, as they may not know how to talk about it or how to promote it.

Submitting to a publisher

When you visit publisher websites, you will see that submission guidelines vary between them. Some will request electronic submission only, or the first three chapters in hard copy, or submission during a once-monthly window in the form of a pitch and sample pages, or the entire manuscript printed in full. All will specify the genres they wish to consider. Some will request a phone call ahead of submission, or will be open only to writers from a specific region, or have some other criteria. Some may say they are currently not accepting manuscripts at all. And some will tell you that they are accepting *solicited* manuscripts only. If a publisher doesn't accept *unsolicited* manuscripts, this means that they are only willing to look at manuscripts submitted by a suitable peer within the publishing industry or, more commonly, by a literary agent (see p. 135).

So, once you have identified some suitable publishers and found that they are currently accepting unsolicited manuscripts in your genre, what next?

Following submission guidelines

It is important to remember that no matter how skilfully you present and package your submission, ultimately the person who is responsible for reading submissions in a publishing house will read your manuscript and form their own conclusions about whether or not what you have written is a good fit for their list. That said, you might think of a manuscript submission as a job interview. In this case, the manuscript assessor is reviewing hundreds or thousands of manuscripts in a year. The easier you make their job for them, the better the impression you will make. And the single most important thing you can do is to follow submission guidelines.

Along with requesting your manuscript in whole or in part, as an electronic or hard copy, a publishing house may also call for:

- An author biographical note.
- A description of your work, such as a synopsis (plot summary) or blurb (something more grabby, with a hook).
- A description of intended audience.
- Comparison to like titles.

Read the publisher's website carefully. Be alert for invitations to submit that carry any whiff of a suggestion that you, the author, may have to make some financial contribution towards the publication of your work. It can be difficult to identify a vanity publisher, but the website usually contains some clue on one of its pages, perhaps citing 'package breakdown costs' or using words and phrases like 'a contribution, to be paid by the author, to cover production and printing', 'we offer packaged services', 'we offer unique packages', 'you provide the literature, we provide the service'.

A commercial publisher will *not* require the author to provide anything other than the manuscript itself and accompanying material such as biographical details and synopsis. If a traditional publisher accepts your work, they will take the full financial risk on your book, pay you royalties (and often an advance against future earnings) and seek no financial contribution from you.

What is the publisher looking for?

When it comes down to it, the publisher is looking for a manuscript that is well conceived and well delivered, and that has a distinctive voice. You know the feeling of confidence you get when you start to read a book, and you immediately feel that you are in good hands? The kind of work that says, 'I am here to tell you a marvellous story. Buckle up, let's go for a ride'? This is what the publisher is looking for too, in raw form, in a manuscript. In our experience, the manuscript that is considered seriously is the manuscript that is readable, entertaining, well written, memorable and full of promise. It may be a bit rough around the edges or require significant work, but it also contains the diamond glint of what it will become.

The publisher will also be looking for:

- A well-presented manuscript with strong accompanying material that indicates the writer understands the context of and potential audience for their work.
- Whether a work fits their list.
- The potential in the work (not a final, polished, print-ready product).
- The marketable potential of the work.
- The author's potential as someone who is marketable with career potential, and who will be a good ambassador for the publishing house.

Some of these things (particularly the first and last items in the list) are in your control, and others are not. Later in the chapter we will talk again about taking the long view and coping with rejection. These things are all part of the business of being a writer.

When a publisher contracts a work, it may be months before the publisher or editor meets an author in person. In the meantime, it is the accompanying covering material that makes the important first impression.

Gone are the days (on the whole) when a manuscript was handwritten or typed up, and stuffed into an envelope, bearing wine stains and tufts of cat hair, with the distinct look of something that has been dropped in the bath. In these days of mainly electronic submission, it should not be too challenging to present a manuscript that is pleasantly set out in a common font in a comfortable reading size (such as 12 point, with at least 1.5 spacing), a title page, and so on. As impersonal and formal as this seems, an electronic submission still conveys to the recipient whether its submitter can follow submission guidelines and is administratively competent. An author who can follow submission guidelines shows they can and are willing to follow instructions. Other indicators that give off the heartening vibe an author is in control of their life (and thus will be good to work with) include the following:

- The author biographical note contains information relevant to the work submitted – no need to tell them you are an interstate knitting champion if you are submitting a gritty speculative fiction novel set in post-apocalyptic Wagga Wagga.
- The bio note also contains a list of awards or previous publications or performances in some way relevant to its genre.
- The synopsis or blurb responds appropriately to the publisher's requirements. If the publisher wants a full-blown, five-act synopsis containing character profiles, they will ask for one. But generally, if they call for 100 words, the blurb should be brief and snappy. Remember the back blurbs you looked at during the bookshop test? They are intended to tantalise and intrigue. They will have a hook. They won't contain spoilers. They will invite the reader to open up and dive in. This is what you also want your description to do.
- A description of audience, the stated genre of your work and who it is intended for. The publisher may be able to identify a larger or a different audience to the one you have considered, but your submission indicates that you have given some thought to your manuscript's place within the market. It is a sign that you are savvy about the connection between your book and its potential audience.

What makes a good covering letter?

A manuscript submission in hard copy will generally require you to attach a covering letter. This letter may contain any of the items mentioned above (i.e. a brief description of the work, an author biographical note and a description of the market for which the book is intended). If you are required to address the recipient of your manuscript submission in a covering letter, establish the name of the publisher or acquisitions editor in your genre, and address the letter directly to them. (Phone the publisher or look on their website for help.) Whatever you do, do *not* start any letter with that nineteenth-century nicety, 'Dear Sir', when the recipient may well be a woman. 'To whom it may concern' is a much more inclusive option.

When comparing your book to like titles, it can be wise (and flattering) to make appropriate comparisons with books in the publisher's own list. This shows you have done your homework. A good covering letter:

- Is direct, succinct and professional.
- Accurately represents your work.

- Is authentic and shows something of your personality.
- Entices the reader to take a look at your manuscript.

It is a great idea to show your covering letter or proposed submission material to a competent friend to check for typos and for clarity.

Submission requirements for the manuscript

Different genres within a publishing house may require different kinds of material to be submitted. Read the submission guidelines carefully. Where a portion of a work is called for, rather than the entire manuscript, the publisher may follow through with a request to see the rest of the manuscript if they see promise in the preliminary offering.

If you are still unsure about what you should submit after reading the publisher's guidelines, try their FAQ page. Responses to your question may vary from house to house. In you are still unsure, send a quick query to the publisher by email or give their reception a call.

Submission etiquette

There are a few things to remember when it comes to the most professional way to submit your work. Both you and the publisher are seeking to make a good impression and encourage repeat custom. It is in everyone's interests to be nice, be polite and put their best foot forward.

What are a publisher's obligations?

Bear in mind that publishers have to deal with a lot of manuscripts. Ideally, they will do so efficiently, thoughtfully and with care. On their side, the publisher should stick to the response deadline stated on their website. If they have gone past it, it's fine to contact them with a gentle reminder. In a world where there are hundreds of manuscripts flowing in and out, things sometimes go awry. But before you contact the publisher, do check your email junk folder, in case a response has landed there. And double-check whether in fact this is a publisher who says: 'If you haven't heard from us within twelve weeks, assume you won't hear from us at all.'

Legend has it that in the olden days, in publishing houses, there was a bulging cupboard of manuscripts submitted by hopeful authors that was only ever prised open on a Friday afternoon after a long lunch, for fuzzy consideration on the chaise longue. These days, it's a competitive market and the fabled 'slush pile' of yore exists mostly in the minds of authors. Especially with the advent of electronic submissions, all material can be logged and dated, and it is in the interests of publishers to review every submission in a timely fashion.

What are a submitting author's obligations?

From your side, given it can take months to hear from one publisher, it is not unreasonable to make multiple submissions to publishing houses. But do let each publisher know in your covering letter that this is what you have done.

And if manuscript competition guidelines say the work must not be under consideration with another publisher, then you should adhere to this rule for the sake of the competition judges who will have a great deal of reading to do, and to avoid an awkward conversation with a publisher later.

What if I have published my short stories or poems elsewhere before submitting them to the publisher?

In our experience, it is a positive to be able to show that you have a track record as a writer whose work has appeared in journals, anthologies and online. It shows that you are dedicated to your craft, and also that other people like what you do. When short-form work is accepted for publication in a journal or anthology, copyright should remain with you, and you should be free to offer this work to another publisher.

If you do go on to publish a short story or poetry collection, then that volume should contain a list of acknowledgements showing where particular pieces first appeared. You can assist yourself administratively by keeping a list of your publications and awards – when, where and with whom.

The situation that may give a prospective publisher pause is where you have already published a whole collection of poems or stories – in a chapbook, say, or a self-published volume or as a group project. A publisher is then likely to want to know more about the extent of duplication with the current manuscript and the reach of the original market.

Can I submit a self-published book to a publishing house?

The answer is: it depends – on the publisher and on your own situation. If your self-published work has sold 3,000 copies or more, this could be a sign either that it has met its market, or that it is displaying wonderful potential. If your self-published work is in the hands of a dozen people who share your DNA, then you are probably safe to submit it to a publisher. But if their policy is not clear from their website, drop the publisher a quick line ahead of submission asking whether they are open to considering self-published works, or at the very least let them know in your covering letter that this work has been self-published and give them a sense of sales and the extent of distribution.

Cleaning the mud off a digital footprint

If a publishing house is interested in your work, they will also be interested in you, and they may go to your social media profile to find out more. As with the job market (and with life), how you present on social media reveals a lot about you. This is the time when a thoughtful or engaging website can make a great impression, or an Instagram account with a lot of ebullient party pics can have the opposite effect. You may wish to adjust your privacy settings in anticipation of a publisher's eye being cast over your online presence. Now may be a good time to create a public Instagram, Facebook or Twitter account for your writer persona, so that you can keep your private one for friends and family. You might want to create a LinkedIn account for the 'professional' you.

Keep in mind that not only your work but *you* will be an ambassador for a publishing house. The publisher will be hoping to find an appealing package when they look 'behind' your submission – namely an articulate, interesting author with an engaging social media presence to accompany their impressive submission.

That said, it is also important to be authentic. If you *are* a scruffy, wine-drinking, fight-picking bath-reader with a brash social media presence (or even no presence at all) then there can be a story in that too – some angle for the publicist to work with when it comes time to reveal your work to the world.

Coping with rejection

There are lots of bracing tales of rejection from famous writers:

- Lauded Western Australian writer Elizabeth Jolley received a great many rejections (including thirty-nine in one year) and was fifty-three when her first book was accepted for publication.
- Markus Zusak's novel *The Book Thief* was rejected several times across seven years, and a manuscript he wrote when he was eighteen was rejected by five publishers.
- Kate DiCamillo received 473 rejection letters in six years before she published her first novel, *Because of Winn-Dixie*.
- Robert Galbraith received a number of rejections for his novel *The Cuckoo's Calling* that may not have been knocked back if it had been submitted under the author's real name, J.K. Rowling. (Not to mention her first series, which was turned down by twelve publishers.)

Rejection is only entertaining in retrospect, and never that funny when it is happening to you. The best way to minimise rejection is to submit your manuscript after having done the bookshop test (see p.119), thus maximising your chances of targeting the right publisher in the first place.

The moment you receive an email rejecting your manuscript is the moment to separate your writing self from your business self. It should be the cool administrator who dispenses manuscripts and receives rejections, rather than the passionate writer.

The 'no news is bad news' approach from a publisher can be bleak and make you feel as if you have just dispatched your manuscript into a void.

The 'thanks but no thanks' pro forma letter is at least a definitive response your administrative self can cope with.

The non–pro forma rejection 'we like you / your writing / what you are attempting but just not at this time – and we are happy to see more of your work' can by contrast feel positively exhilarating.

And if a publisher asks you to come in for a chat, or to revise and resubmit your work, then that is an opportunity worth grasping. Do it, *if* their suggestions make sense to you, and if you feel you can respond to a revision with authenticity.

If you do receive a rejection, feel free not to respond at all, or reply with a chipper email along the lines of: 'Thanks for letting me know. I appreciate you taking the time to read my work.'

If you feel the beast of bitterness rising in your chest, by all means compose an email to let off some of your feelings, but please do not press send. And do not vent on social media. The world of writers and publishers and readers is smaller than you think. In twelve months time, or twenty-four, when you are ready to submit a better, stronger novel to the same publishing house, it is your email of righteous indignation or your social media post that will chime in the assessor's mind when they read your name again. Be professional at all times. It counts for a lot.

However, a no is a no, and so it can also help if you think of rejection as a numbers game. Consider this: if a publishing house receives five hundred manuscripts a year and only publishes twenty-five, and those twenty-five are across a range of genres and some of them are by repeat authors, then the work of only a handful of new writers can be taken up in any given year. Or, if a publishing house receives two thousand manuscripts a year, and only publishes fifty, including repeat authors, then the odds are stacked against you from the start.

There are other reasons for rejection too. Maybe the first reader didn't 'get' your work. Maybe what you are doing isn't a great fit for that publisher's list, or it did not distinguish itself sufficiently above other works that were being submitted.

Or maybe your work found favour with the manuscript assessor but was rejected by the publisher or at an acquisitions meeting. Maybe it went a little way up the consideration ladder, but just not far enough.

A rejection does not mean that your manuscript is worthless, or that you are a terrible writer. It may just mean that you haven't found the right publisher yet. Or it may mean that you have chosen a genre that doesn't suit your abilities, or that you have chosen the wrong story to tell, or submitted a work when it was still too raw. This happens more often than you might think: a writer turns a piece of history into a novel, for instance, when the true story itself would have worked just fine and their style seems better suited to tell it. It could mean that your first novel isn't your best novel, but that your second or third or fifth will be better. As difficult as it may be, take heart: none of this writing is wasted because you will learn something from each attempt.

Elizabeth Jolley, Markus Zusak, Kate DiCamillo and J.K. Rowling were probably rejected for a range of reasons: their work didn't connect with its reader, or distinguish itself, or fit the publisher's list, or wasn't fashionable, or was 'undercooked', or they had simply not yet gained enough writing miles to put forward a manuscript that was 'ready'. If you *are* the kind of writer who stops writing because of rejection, that is okay. Sometimes priorities change or life asserts itself in different ways. Sometimes your day job is a good plan B.

But if you are the kind of writer who is reading this book, chances are you are going to keep writing, no matter what. Remember that writing and getting published are not the same activity. You do not need to be published to write, but you do need to keep writing to get published.

Ask an author: What's your advice for dealing with rejection?

Natasha Lester says:

Firstly, expect rejection. I don't know a single author who hasn't been rejected at some point. So treat rejection as a normal part of the writing process rather than a judgement upon you and your work.

Accept that you have a vocal inner critic who will try to sabotage you and stop you from writing – this critic will definitely use a rejection as a weapon. You have to allow your inner critic to exist, as you need its wisdom when you're redrafting and polishing your work. But never let the inner critic run the show.

I firmly believe that if I hadn't written a book, I would have always regretted it – but I would never regret having tried. Remind yourself how much you love writing, and also that you don't want not writing to be yet another thing you feel guilty about.

And always have a plan. When I submitted my first manuscript for publication, I had a spreadsheet listing all the agents and publishers I would submit to. I submitted to two names on the list at a time. When I received a rejection, I just moved onto the next name on the list. It's good to have a next step to help you move on, rather than dwell on your 'failure'.

If there's one thing I've learned over nine years, it's that getting a book published is a matter of hard work, talent and luck. You can control the first two, but not the last one. So be kind to yourself, keep working hard, keep making yourself a better writer and the luck will come to you at some point.

Daniel de Lorne says:

Do not respond immediately and definitely do not send them an email calling them a moron for rejecting your manuscript! Remember that the rejection is not a rejection of you but of your manuscript – and they are different. Do not go on social media and tell the world how short-sighted and stupid the publisher is. Instead, read the rejection and walk away. Give yourself time to process. Then go back and read it again. Closely.

Every rejection is an opportunity for reflection. Are the points they've made fair? Is the manuscript just not the right fit for them? Is there any feedback in there that you can use to improve your manuscript? If you don't agree with the feedback, discuss it with someone who knows your work to see if there's a perspective you don't understand.

If it's a 'revise and resubmit', well done! You're that much closer. You then need to decide whether you want to make those revisions. Sometimes they're going to make your manuscript better; other times they might be changes that go against your values. Either way a 'revise and resubmit' is a great opportunity. It means that the publisher likes your work. If you're willing to put in the effort to make those changes, you may have a good partnership going forward. At least they'll know you can take constructive criticism.

Sometimes the rejection will be one line with no feedback. If that's the case, don't take it personally. Save it or delete it, but either way, move on.

And Deb Fitzpatrick says:

There's only one real answer to this question: be magnanimous and gracious. This is a brutally competitive industry and there are simply not enough opportunities for every writer to be published. Bear in mind that sometimes it's also very hard for a publisher to knock back a manuscript.

If you've received a knock-back from a house that only publishes ten to twenty new titles a year in your genre, you need to frame your rejection in that context.

Beyond that, there are different types of rejection letters and it helps to know which kind you're dealing with. A letter that says something along the lines of 'Thank you for submitting your manuscript *Desperate to Get Published* to Impossible Book Publishing. Unfortunately your work does not fit our list. Kind regards, Blunt Publisher' is not throwing you any kind of bone at all. They aren't happy you wasted their time and don't invite you to do so again, so don't. Just move on.

A letter that goes 'Thank you for submitting your manuscript *Desperate to Get Published* to Possibilities Book Publishing. We like your writing very much and especially enjoyed the voice of the protagonist. Unfortunately, however, we are not able to take on your work this time. Please do consider us again for any manuscripts you write in future. Kind regards, Foot-in-the-door Publisher' is an entirely different thing. It opens the door to this house in the future, and you'd be foolish to ever forget this. You need to write another book fast and get it to them, and in your cover letter, gently remind them of their kind offer. Perhaps you even have another manuscript ready to go … Dust it off, smarten it up and get it over to them.

Finally, a letter that goes 'Thank you for submitting your manuscript *Desperate to Get Published* to Now-we're-cooking-with-gas Book Publishing. We like your writing very much and wish to discuss it with you further. There are some substantial changes we'd like you to consider. If you are open to this, please be in touch via my direct line below. Kind regards, Deal's-in-the-bag Publisher' is what you've been waiting for. Hold this joyful moment in your heart. Don't call immediately. They'll know you're insanely happy. Give it a day or two. Pretend to mull on it. Then call up, make an appointment and go in there with your most open mind.

Gaining experience

Writing is a long game. If you are lucky enough to keep your marbles and all goes well, you can write until you fall down dead at the age of 103. While you are waiting for a publishing house to recognise your worth, it's a good idea to keep gaining experience in other ways.

Consider seeking feedback on your manuscript from a fresh expert reader, but only after you have tried it with a number of publishers. And if you receive an 'encouraging' rejection from a publisher, that doesn't mean that you should rewrite a novel on the strength of a couple of lines of feedback, especially if they don't strike a chord with you. For example:

- 'This novel works well, except for the plot. I think the addition of a vampire could resolve everything.'
- 'This story would be much better if it was set in Bermuda.'
- 'Retelling this story in present tense, and from the point of view of the captain's cat, may resolve the current issues.'

Sit with such suggestions before doing anything. And don't act on them (when this will involve hundreds of hours work) if they don't make sense to you. In the meantime, there are other ways to gain experience:

- Continue to practise reaching your market through live readings and social media.
- Keep honing your writing skills with input from your community.
- Build your publishing profile by submitting short works to journals and magazines.
- Enter short story and manuscript competitions.
- Keep journalling, blogging, thinking, reading and writing.

Dos and don'ts for submitting a manuscript to a publisher

- *Do* match the publisher to your work
- *Do* read online submission pages carefully.
- *Do* follow publisher guidelines.
- *Do* let the publisher know if you are making multiple submissions.
- *Do* take care with your covering letter.
- *Do* address your letter to the right person.
- *Do* review your social media privacy settings before making your submission.
- *Do* keep building your writing experience in authentic, meaningful ways.
- *Don't* disobey manuscript competition rules.
- *Don't* take rejection personally.

When to seek a literary agent

Writers considering publication sometimes wonder whether they should first find a literary agent to represent and approach publishers on their behalf. There are times when it can be useful to have an agent, but for the writer who is starting out, acquiring an agent should not be a barrier to seeking publication. Agents are in high demand and will only take on a work or a new author they are enthusiastic to champion. Finding an agent, especially at a time when your own writing is just developing, may be a time-consuming and pointless exercise when, in any event, many publishers accept unsolicited manuscripts. For the first-time author, approaching such publishers without an agent is a reasonable and sensible way to launch one's career.

As agents work on a commission basis (generally taking 15% of an author's earnings), they will work hard to get the best possible deal for their author. It can make more sense to seek an agent when an established author's career requires lots of logistical and administrative support – things that get in the way of writing and are worth paying for to avoid.

The role of a literary agent is to represent a writer's work and seek to gain the best deal for their author at contract in relation to the advance and contractual terms. Agent representation may also mean that a publisher prioritises a review of an author's submitted work over other incoming manuscripts. Agents may set up bids for a work between publishing houses. They may also offer preliminary editorial advice to the writer before presenting a draft to publishers.

Beyond the book contract itself, agents will seek to sell subsidiary rights to film or TV producers, or publishers in other territories – to sell the work into North America, for instance, or to sell the work into translation. For this reason, an agent may withhold from a publisher certain rights in a contract. This makes most sense for writers whose works are commercial and likely to generate larger print runs. From a smaller, independent publisher perspective, taking on a book without a full suite of rights can be the difference between a book being a viable financial proposition or not, and the publisher themselves may work hard on behalf of the author to seek subsidiary rights for that book alongside its publication.

As children's writer and illustrator James Foley points out, there are different kinds of agents too – and a writer or illustrator may need an agent at different points in their career:

A *literary agent* helps you to prepare your manuscripts to the best possible level, then shops them around to different publishers on your behalf. Often they also try to organise world rights. Some people have one literary agent for their Australia and New Zealand deals, and another for international deals. Agents have contacts in the industry and they want to make sure you get the best contract possible. They generally take about 15% commission on your earnings. I haven't yet had an agent, but quite a few of my colleagues have, with varying degrees of satisfaction and success. It's important that if you take on an agent, you find someone you get along with and can trust. You're entrusting them with your career, after all.

There are also *illustration agencies*. These are businesses that source work for freelance illustrators. Some of these agencies specialise in children's book illustration.

Then there are *booking agents* (sometimes called *speakers agencies*). They help you to get speaking engagements at schools, libraries and writers festivals. Booking agents are very important to me, because talks and workshops are my main source of income, not book advances or royalties. Booking agents are particularly useful when they're based in areas of the country (or the world) where you are not so well known yet; if you want to do a book tour somewhere, booking agents have the local contacts and reputation to help you. They always take a commission; some agencies take a percentage of your speaking fee, while others add a booking fee on top of yours.

The Australian Literary Agents' Association (ALAA) is a starting point for authors seeking an agent. This site provides information about the agents' code of practice, presenting work to an agent, writers organisations throughout Australia, and festivals and events. Australian agents that do not appear on the ALAA website are listed on the ASA website, along with further advice about pitching your work to an agent.

Ask an author: Does a new writer need an agent and how do they get one?

Liz Byrski says:
I published my first eleven books without an agent and with very little difficulty. I simply submitted manuscripts to publishers who published in the genre in which I was writing. When I turned to fiction, I thought it would be good to have an agent. The agent found me a publisher and I have been published by that same publisher ever since – that's fifteen years and ten novels. However, I ended my

relationship with my first agent during that time. I did this because I was not happy with the way I was represented with them. In that period, I also published two non-fiction books with a publisher with whom I had worked before. Neither book was handled by an agent.

I did not get an agent again until I was writing my tenth novel. At this time, I wanted to make a concerted attempt to attract overseas sales. My agent now is someone whom I trust; she is totally reliable and a good friend. I am relieved to be free of having to deal with contracts and other arrangements. The best thing about having a good agent is that you feel you have someone in your corner to deal with the difficult, sensitive and important things, so you can keep your distance.

It is certainly not essential to have an agent when you first start out, but it can be reassuring, easier and more efficient than managing it yourself. If you are searching for an agent, beware that many people who advertise themselves as literary agents have little or no experience. For advice, you can contact the Australian Literary Agents' Association or the Australian Society of Authors. Do your homework first. And if you know any writers, ask them for recommendations. You may not *need* an agent, but the world of publishing is complex and relies to a great extent on personal contacts, so you may well feel more comfortable being represented by someone who knows the ropes.

Amanda Curtin says:

An agent can be an important person on your team, supporting what you and your publisher do. They can be a sounding board for new ideas, or provide answers to questions. They have expertise in many of the areas that baffle writers (contracts, licensing, rights management), and act on your behalf. They also have extensive professional contacts and networks, and are abreast of issues relevant to writers and publishers.

It's possible to work without an agent. And it can be rewarding to work with one. I've done both. Before signing with an agent, be clear on what you want out of the relationship, and don't rush into an agreement with anyone who can't provide that. Most importantly, you want 100% enthusiasm: someone who believes in you and will be active on your behalf.

When seeking an agent, do your research. Find out who could be a good fit for you by reading agents' websites. Don't approach an agent if you're a poet and they only represent writers of non-fiction. Ask writer friends about their agents, and whether they would be willing to refer you, if that is appropriate. Check the client lists of prospective agents – this is a good indication of the agent's credibility. Avoid anyone purporting to be an agent but who is actually charging fees for manuscript assessment or editing; most agents work on a commission basis.

And Holden Sheppard says:

A literary agent represents an author's interests and can get your manuscript in front of a publisher, so having an agent can be tremendously beneficial. Agents have relationships with publishers, so they can get your manuscript taken seriously, and an agented submission to a publisher, in my experience, is looked at much more quickly.

My sense, based on anecdotal feedback, is that in overseas markets like the US and the UK, having an agent is more essential than just desirable. In Australia, many of the larger publishers accept submissions from unsolicited authors – however, your manuscript will land in the slush pile and could take a very long time to be considered.

An agent is always a plus, in my view, though you should never sign to an agent who charges you an upfront or reading fee. Agents should instead take a percentage of your advance and royalties if and when they land you a publishing contract, usually 15%. And because an agent understands the legal aspects of a contract, they can negotiate better conditions and rates for you, and alert you to anything that may be unfair. A typical pitch to a prospective agent usually involves:

- A one-page query letter, giving the agent a basic idea of what your manuscript is about and why it's so amazing they should sign you right away.
- A synopsis, usually three to five hundred words, which is where you literally outline the entire plot of your novel (for non-fiction authors, you may be asked to present a book proposal instead).

- Sample pages from your manuscript, commonly the first three chapters, though I've seen variations from ten to fifty pages.

You should research agents ahead of time to make sure they represent your genre, and that they are accepting new submissions. Also, remember a rejection from an agent isn't personal: if they don't love it, they'll say no, because a manuscript needs an agent who loves and will champion it.

Dos and don'ts for finding an agent

- *Do* think about whether you actually need an agent in order to get published.
- *Do* research agents to find the right match for you.
- *Do* prepare your pitch to the agent with as much care as you would a publisher.
- *Don't* sign with an agent who requests an upfront fee.
- *Don't* take rejection from an agent personally.

At the time of submitting your manuscript to a publisher, you need to have considered the prospect that your work may be accepted for publication.

The publisher will most likely have accepted your work on the basis of its potential, and it is highly likely they have further edits in mind. And so, the revision process is about to begin all over again. Thus, you need to be sure that you have the time and the stamina for future rewrites.

But this time, at least, it will be with an editor by your side – someone who loves your work as much as you do, and who shares your vision and your desire to make your work the best it can possibly be.

6. The contract

It can be an agonising wait to hear from a publisher, even if their website specifies a response time. Perhaps you have a number of submissions sitting with other publishers. This duplication will at least hasten the long, slow waiting game. If you do receive an expression of interest from a publisher, be sure to advise the other publishers that someone else is interested. This may prompt them to look at your work more swiftly. In this chapter we will look at the different stages a manuscript passes through once it is in the publishing house if it is destined for contract.

Calls for revision

A publisher may see potential in your work, but may not offer a contract immediately. It is possible that they instead contact you by email or phone or set up a meeting to see whether or not you are open to revising your manuscript with a view to resubmission. They could invite you to do a range of things, from amending the plot, to shifting the point of view, to rewriting an academic thesis for a general market, to adding another suite of poems to a poetry collection.

While it is flattering and encouraging to be approached in this way, you need to think carefully about the publisher's suggestions. If they confirm some sense of your own deficit in the work, and provide a solution, then revise away! But if the changes suggested don't make sense, or you feel as if you would be forcing them onto the manuscript, then you need to think some more. It may be that you can come up with an alternative solution that resolves the publisher's concerns, or it may be that this is not the right partnership for you, and you should try elsewhere. After all, their request will equate to many hours work for you and may not necessarily lead to a contract. Another option you could try if you reach this kind of impasse is to offer the publisher another manuscript, if you are lucky enough to have one in the bottom drawer.

In any event, if you are invited to revise your work, then you should establish whether the publisher is open to first reading a revised sample (a chapter or so) before you embark on the task of redrafting the whole thing, to check that you are on the right track.

Generally, if a publisher is bothering to give you feedback, they are letting you know that your work is worth paying attention to. And by investing some time and effort in you, the publisher is setting you a kind of test. They are interested to know whether you are capable of taking a work that is not quite there to the point where it will cross the line.

Other forms of acceptance, however, will be much more straightforward than this. You may submit your work and then, some weeks or months later, you may receive that miraculous phone call or email containing an offer to publish.

Stages of review in a publishing house

Let us step back a moment and take a look at what has happened to your manuscript since you submitted it. Not every publishing house is the same, and so this process will vary from house to house as the manuscript makes its way from the point of submission to contract. Depending on the size of the house, one person, such as the publisher, may occupy multiple roles including manuscript assessor and editor. In larger houses, there can be a clearer designation between roles and stages of manuscript review, acceptance, editing and production. But let us take a look at how different people in a publishing house may interact with your manuscript.

Publisher

In larger publishing houses, the publisher is in control of the financial running of the company, its staff and decisions. In smaller publishing houses, the publisher will perhaps also oversee the shaping of the list of books. They may also be the editor of the work they contract. There may also be several publishers within an organisation who manage different lists, such as non-fiction, fiction or children's, overseen by a CEO or director. Or these several publishers may instead have the title of managing editor.

Managing editor

The managing editor oversees a book's production, from presenting the manuscript at an acquisitions meeting, to contracting and development of the work, to management of editors, copyeditors and proofreaders, and oversight of production and printing.

Commissioning editor

A commissioning editor is proactive in building the publisher's list by seeking out potentially successful and profitable manuscripts or authors, especially in the area of non-fiction books, celebrity books, hot topics etc. A commissioning editor is across publishing trends, drawing on market knowledge to consider manuscripts. They may commission authors to write a book on a particular topic or theme or purchase the publishing rights to titles from other territories. A commissioning editor may present a work to an acquisitions meeting (where it is decided if a work will be contracted) and they may also negotiate author contracts.

Manuscript assessor

This is not to be confused with a person of the same title who provides the service of assessing a manuscript and providing their client with a detailed report. Within a publishing house, a manuscript assessor may be the first point of contact for your manuscript. They will make an initial assessment to see if it fits with the kinds of books published by the house, and whether it is promising enough to send on to the publisher, or present to a publishing committee, or perhaps give to a second reader who will then conduct a further detailed assessment of your work.

Editor

The editor has carriage of your book from the point of contract on. The editor may edit and copyedit your work, or this role could be shared between different people. The editor may also organise and oversee the proofreading process and liaise between you and the publisher or managing editor. Sometimes editors work in-house, or they may be freelancers contracted by the publisher. We will consider the different stages of editing in Chapter 7, once your work is safely contracted!

In any event, the passage of your manuscript following submission will probably look something like this:

- Initial assessment by a manuscript assessor.
- Possible review by a second reader.
- Consideration by the publisher or managing editor.
- Presentation of your manuscript at an acquisitions meeting .
- Possible input from the marketing and communications team.
- Phone or email contact with you, the author to offer you a contract!

The publishing contract

Whatever the lead-up and negotiations, the signing of the contract marks the beginning of the formal relationship between author and publisher. The contract is a legal document made between publisher and author. It sets out the terms of agreement between the parties for the editing, production, printing, promotion and sale of a work. We will look at these in more detail below.

In essence, a contract with a traditional publishing house should reflect that the financial risk in publishing the work lies with the publisher, and it should specify which subsidiary rights the publisher has the right to seek in relation to the sale and promotion of the work itself. The contract sets out the author's obligations and protections. It should assert that copyright in the creative work remains with the author and it should provide a finite term for the publisher's right and licence in the work. The terms and conditions of a contract are there to spell out the terms of a commercial arrangement, to protect an author from exploitation, and to give the publisher and, ultimately, the author, the opportunity for commercial success.

It is exciting to be offered a contract, but it is important also to follow your gut in relation to the party you are contracting with. Along with any legal advice you seek, you need to feel comfortable that there is the foundation for a good working relationship here. Before signing, there are some questions you could ask, which will not be covered in the contract:

- Are they enthusiastic about my work?
- Are they willing to answer my questions in an open and informative way?
- Who will I be working with on my book and do I feel they 'get' it?
- What, in broad terms, is the scope of editing work they have in mind?
- Am I ready and willing to undertake this work?
- Does a proposed timetable work for me?
- Has the publisher conveyed, in general terms, what my book will look like?
- Can the publisher tell me, in general terms, who they see as the market for my book?
- Can I fulfil my own obligations towards the publisher in the editing and marketing of my book?
- Does the publisher have a plan for the promotion of my work?
- Does the publisher have a clear method of distribution?
- Are other authors happy with their experiences with this publisher?

Where more than one party is involved in the contract

Sometimes a book has been co-authored, in which case each author will be party to the contract with the publisher, and the advance and royalties will be split between them.

In other cases, for instance where a picture book has an author and an illustrator, or where there are a small number of contributors to a larger book, then separate contracts with the parties may be struck.

Managing expectations about being published

If you want to be a published author because it's going to bring in the big bucks, then it's time to change careers. Publishers rely on sales to be successful as a business, and it is in their interest to work hard for you. But the marketplace is an extremely challenging one. Overseas books are readily available. Discounts provided by online bookstores undercut bricks-and-mortar book sales. And a proliferation of screen entertainment competes with books for readers' attention.

Be prepared for the amount that you earn from publishing your book to be extremely modest. A 2015 review by Macquarie University found that the average income an author may expect to make, including *all sources of income* (e.g. grants, appearance fees, workshops, copyright and subsidiary payments), is around $62,000 per annum – and the average income an author will receive from sales of their book is just under $13,000.[3] Not a great deal has changed since 2015 in a market where massive multinationals can control book prices (and thus, how much authors and publishers receive for units sold). At the top end of this earning bracket will be the authors whose books sell in the education market, followed by genre fiction authors and literary fiction authors, with poets earning the least. Divide any earnings by the hours you have spent writing the blessed thing, and then by the hours you haven't spent earning coin elsewhere – well, you can only ask: what price happiness?

The most sensible spirit in which to enter a contract is not as if this is the document that will catapult you to fame and fortune, but understanding that this contractual arrangement will protect both you and the publisher in setting out the parameters of each party's rights and obligations. It may be that the publishing house has some very strongly performing titles on their list but this doesn't guarantee yours will become one of them. If it does, then that will be a pleasant bonus but, in the meantime, it is wise to manage your expectations on this score.

Where to find contract advice

The ASA website contains much useful information about contracts and how to understand them. In addition, the society offers a contract assessment service for a fee.

If you know authors who are published with the same publisher, you could consider speaking to them about their contract and whether it contained any terms they reviewed or negotiated, and if there are any terms in particular that you should be alert to.

---

3. Macquarie University, Faculty of Business and Economics, 'The Australian book industry: Authors, publishers and readers in a time of change: 3: Authors' income'. Previously available at businessandeconomics.mq.edu.au/our_departments/Economics/econ_research/reach_network/ book_project/authors/3_Authors_Income.pdf.

The elements of a contract

In this section, we will take a look at some of the most important elements of a contract. Please note too that contracts will vary from publisher to publisher. It is possible that your publisher may not be open to altering or adjusting *any* of the terms, and if that is the case, then your acceptance of the contract is a decision for you to make. But the publisher should still be transparent about its terms. You should not be afraid to ask questions regarding the content of the contract, and ensure you are comfortable with what you are signing.

If you have an agent, they will negotiate the terms of the contract for you, but again, you still need to be comfortable with the agent's rationale for withholding or varying different clauses in the contract.

If you are a picture book author, then an illustrator will be contracted separately and most likely subsequently to you. You should ensure that the publisher is willing to discuss the choice of illustrator and will show you samples of their work, as well as willing to seek your approval of illustrator choice before contracting them.

In order to sign a contract, you will need to supply the publisher with the following:

- Name, address and contact details.
- The title of the work. This may not be the title that goes to print. Before signing, you should ask your publisher about their intentions in relation to the title and whether you will have any input or your approval is required before signing. This level of control may diminish with subsequent subsidiary rights allocations – say, if your book appears elsewhere in translation, or in another territory where another publisher may opt for a different title that they feel will better capture their market.
- Australian Business Number (ABN): if in doubt, seek advice from the publisher, an accountant or the Australian Taxation Office.

Obligations of publisher and author within the contract

The contract should set out the publisher's obligations in relation to:

- Acceptance of the manuscript or its proposed delivery date.
- A proposed publication timeframe.

- The territories the contract applies to.
- The term of the copyright and whether copyright remains with the author.
- Proposed print run.
- Proposed RRP of the book.
- Whether the book is to be both a print book and an ebook.
- The amount of an advance.
- The royalty percentage payments to be applied in relation to number of books sold and when royalty statements will be made.
- Provision for the author to inspect the publisher's accounts.
- What subsidiary rights are to be included in the agreement.
- Terms relating to editorial changes to the work.
- Terms relating to packaging of the work.
- Information regarding copyright payments.
- How many free copies of their book the author will receive.
- The price of additional copies the author may wish to purchase.
- Details regarding termination of the contract.
- Details regarding mediation and arbitration.
- (Possibly) an option clause for future works.

From their side (and depending on the terms of the contract), the author will be required to warrant that:

- The work is all the author's own.
- The work contains no defamatory material.
- The author will adhere to a delivery date (if the manuscript has not already been accepted as is).
- The author will cover the costs of any permissions for secondary materials in the work (quotes and supply of images).
- The author will make themselves available for promotion of the work.
- The author will not publish a competing work with another publisher.

Let's take a look at some of these contract elements in further detail.

Delivery date

The contract may state that the manuscript (or 'work') has already been delivered, or that an advance will be paid upon acceptance of a manuscript at a date specified in the contract. This future date may exist because the publisher has requested that you revise your submitted manuscript or because the work you submitted was not yet complete. Check that this proposed date is feasible for you!

The delivery date clause may state the work needs to be of a standard satisfactory to a publisher. This means that the publisher will only proceed with a work if they believe they can make a commercial success of the material accepted for publication. It may mean that the contract will be terminated if the author hasn't produced what the publisher was hoping for in their revision, or (rarely, and unluckily) that another work has appeared in the meantime that will cut across projected sales of the work you are writing. These are both rare occurrences, given the publisher is already investing time and energy in you and your work, but they are there to protect the publisher should a scenario arise that is beyond their control.

Publication date

The publishing date may be twelve, eighteen or even twenty-four months away from the date of contract. This will seem very far away, and may in part have been chosen because there is a relevant anniversary or festival date that the publisher wants to exploit as an element of the promotion of your work.

It is worth noting that a year is not an unreasonable length of time in the life of the production of a book, during which your work will go through the following stages:

- Editing and copyediting (three to nine months).
- Production – design, typesetting, proofreading and possibly also indexing, collour correcting and proof approval (two to three months).
- Printing, dispatch of advances and shipping (one to three months).
- Sending out of review copies and distribution of your book into stores through sales reps (around three months ahead of the publication date).

It is likely that at the time of signing a contract you will be advised of the proposed publication date. This may be specified in broad terms within the contract itself (e.g. 'your work will appear within eighteen months of the date of this contract') to give the publisher some flexibility for unforeseeable delays (yours, the publisher's, the printer's) during the process. But your publisher may be able to be much more specific with you about the proposed publication date. The publication date determines the schedule for your book. It will be the role of your editor and publisher to stick to this schedule, whose deadlines will be dovetailed with a marketing and promotions schedule. Confirm that this schedule fits in with your own commitments over the specified timeframe.

Territories

The contract should be explicit about the territories in which the publisher wishes to hold rights for your work, and these should apply to both print books and ebooks (and sometimes audiobooks, depending on the capacity of the publisher to create them). This could be world rights, or confined to particular territories, such as North America, or Europe and the UK, or the joint territory of Australia and New Zealand. An agent with overseas contacts may seek to withhold rights on your behalf in order to sell your work in other territories. If you don't have an agent (or even if you do), you should ask how active your publisher is in different territories, and to what extent they can promote the work overseas on your behalf. The publisher should have a clear answer on the question of whether they travel overseas or have agent representation at book fairs, and whether they have a network of active agents overseas to whom they send new material. Some smaller publishers may be very active in this area because, having invested time and energy in your work, it is in their interest to make the most of the resulting product. Publishers with active overseas agents will be able to pursue the licensing of your work elsewhere, in both English language and translation.

Rather than excising certain territories from the contract, it may be that you grant the publisher a *non-exclusive right* to the territories, meaning that both you and your agent and the publisher may pursue publication in other territories.

Another model could be to grant the publisher a limited timeframe to exploit overseas rights – say two to three years, after which overseas rights revert to you.

Copyright: licensing versus assigning, legal term, copyright collection

If a contract gives the publisher an *exclusive licence* to publish your work, this means that copyright in the work remains with you, while the publisher has the right to package and market your work for the duration specified in the contract. This arrangement is a common one for traditional publishers.

The *legal term* of the contract should be clearly spelled out. The contract may state that the publisher be granted an exclusive right and licence for 'the legal term of the copyright'. This means it will adhere to the definition of 'legal term' as set out in the *Copyright Act 1968*, meaning that the publisher will have the right to sell your work for your life plus seventy years after your death (see Chapter 4).

Copyright in the writing remains with you, but this particular package, with all its edits and cover presentation, is the publisher's for the duration. Understandably, if the book is to be a bestseller or a steady earner, the publisher will be keen to continue selling it. However, every contract that grants an exclusive right and licence to a publisher should also contain a termination or reversion clause, which is intended to protect the author.

If instead of licensing, the publisher asks you *assign* your work to them, this means copyright in the contents of the work is transferred to the publisher and will not revert to you once the licence lapses (i.e. once the contract terminates and/or the book is out of print). It also means that any subsidiary income opportunities will not flow to you. If a publisher asks you to assign your work to them, you should be aware of the distinction between assigning and licensing, and ensure that the terms and payment that are being offered are reasonable. Seek advice from the ASA or the Australian Copyright Council if you wish to discuss what constitutes reasonable terms for assignation.

At the point of signing the contract, register your details with the Copyright Agency through their website. Membership is free and registration is in perpetuity, and covers all your works. The Copyright Agency offers many other valuable services to creators. The core role of the Copyright Agency is to issue licences to users of copyright-protected material, and to collect and distribute licence revenue and royalties to copyright owners who have registered with them. This revenue is collected from content users including educational institutions and federal, state and territory government copying schemes.

For the duration of your contract, the publisher will also collect a percentage of royalties from such usage of your work. The contract should contain an explicit statement about the percentage of copyright (usually around 50%) to be assigned to the author in relation to copyright collection by the Copyright Agency.

Format, print run and recommended retail price

The contract should specify the proposed format of the book (i.e. what dimensions it will have, and whether it will be hardcover or paperback). It should also state the size of the initial print run and the book's RRP. Note, though, that the contract may be worded in such a way as to give the publisher the scope to change any of these elements closer to the publication date. The publisher will make their final decision about format, print run and RRP based on shifts in the market since signing, changes in marketing direction, other like books that have arrived on the market and what they are selling for. In making these decisions, the publisher will be using their expertise to reach the widest possible market for your book.

Advance and royalties

The advance is an amount paid to the author on signing or upon delivery of their work to the publisher. It constitutes an advance payment of the money that is predicted to be earned from future sales. A bigger publisher may offer a bigger advance; an advance from a small, independent publisher will likely be more modest. The kind of advance you receive may reflect your own status as a new author or (down the track) a bestselling author. Whatever the advance, you will not receive further payments from sales (i.e. royalties) until the advance has been 'earned out'. The smaller the advance, the faster you start earning royalties.

The contract should be specific about the amount of royalties to be earned, and these should be expressed as a percentage of the RRP of a print book.

The industry standard for royalties is around 10% of RRP for print books. The contract should also state (or you may negotiate) that this percentage will escalate to a higher amount (say 12.5%) once sales figures reach a specified number, such as 10,000 copies. Such a clause is sometimes known as 'rising royalties' or 'remuneration adjustment'. The rate for royalties will be less for export sales or big discount sales to some retailers like chain stores – somewhere between 5% and 8%. The royalty rate may also vary between royalties for hardcover and paperback books.

It is less usual for royalties to be calculated on the 'net receipts' – the money actually received by the publisher on the sale of a print book – and you should be aware that this percentage will need to be closer to 17% or 18% to achieve parity with 10% of the RRP.

It is common for a publisher to withhold a percentage of the first royalty payment to cover against negative income in the next royalty period due to returns, i.e. those books that come back from bookshops because they are unsold and taking up room on the shelves. The percentage withheld should be around 15% to 20%, though it could rise to as high as 50%. The net amount should be added onto the next royalty payment once all returns have been calculated.

If the book is also to be sold as an ebook, the contract should state the rate of payment on ebook sales. Because the unit price of an ebook varies from platform to platform and because this price is not always in the publisher's control, the royalty from an ebook may be paid as a percentage of net receipts rather than an RRP. It is common for an author to receive somewhere between 15% and 35% of net receipts.

The contract should be clear on when royalty statements will be made and when royalties will be paid. The publisher should comply with any payment schedule described in the contract and pay royalties promptly – if they do not, this can be grounds for termination. A contract should also contain a clause that gives the author the right to inspect the publisher's accounts.

Subsidiary rights

A great deal of work goes into the editing and production of the book, but sometimes the modest print run and your resulting royalties can be pleasantly topped up by the publisher or an agent brokering subsidiary licences for the book. If the publisher holds subsidiary rights, they too will benefit from a percentage of the agreement. Subsidiary rights granted in a contract can include rights such as:

- The reproduction of extracts or images from a book in newspapers, journals or anthologies.
- International (translation).
- Book club and book digest (i.e. where a book is abridged or condensed).
- Adaptation into other mediums such as audio, film, TV and stage.
- Digital (including adaptation into games, apps and multimedia).
- Merchandise relating to the book.

The percentage of net receipts flowing to the author from a subsidiary licence should be stated in the primary contract, and the contract should contain an explicit provision about attaining the author's consent to proceed with any subsidiary rights negotiated.

Alterations to and presentation of the work

The contract should be clear about whether the author will be consulted in relation to editorial changes made to the work (they should be!) and it may state that design choices in relation to the final packaging of the book lie with the publisher rather than the author. In practical terms, this means that the author may have minimal or no involvement in the design of a cover, including its images, fonts, the back blurb and the overall look of the published book. (The author may also not have final say in the title of the book, particularly where that book is going into translation.) Nonetheless, the publisher may include the author in the design process to some extent. There is nothing worse, from a promotional point of view, than an author who does not like the look of their book and who broadcasts their discontent during the book's promotion.

It is important for authors to understand that the publisher has much accrued experience and expertise in relation to cover design and they make their decisions in consultation with a marketing team and with the intention of reaching the widest possible audience.

Before you sign a contract, discuss with your publisher their approach to design, if only to help you manage your expectations in this regard. And check whether you will get to sign off on the final cover of your book, as well as the typeset pages, before it goes to print.

Author copies

The contract should state how many free copies you will receive of the work (this could range from two to ten), and the discount price of any additional copies you may wish to purchase for gifts – but not for resale.

Termination

Triggers for termination can include the work going out of print, or not being reprinted within a certain period. Nowadays, it is arguable that a book is never out of print if it is available as an ebook: the contract should specify a definition for 'out of print' – preferably by stating a threshold requirement for the number of books sold in a set period. For a large publishing house, this could be something like two hundred books per year across *all* editions; for a smaller house, it could be far fewer.

The contract should also specify how and when the author can terminate a contract, such as in the event of the publisher going out of business and it should specify that rights in the content of the book (i.e. the author's own writing) will revert to the author upon termination. Note that a publisher will rarely be proactive in seeking termination. It will be up to the author to request the cessation of the contract in writing.

Upon reversion, the author is free to do with their work what they choose. While ownership of the design remains with the publisher, they may charge the author a fee for the provision of a digital copy of their final edited work to enable its publication elsewhere.

Mediation and arbitration

The contract should contain terms covering the process of what avenues of redress are open to the parties in the unhappy event that a dispute arises between publisher and author. This is an area dealt with in some detail on the ASA website, and the ASA can be a source of advice and support in the event of such an outcome.

Author warranties

At the point of signing the contract, the author will be required to warrant:

- The work is all the author's own.
- The work contains no defamatory material to the best of the author's knowledge.
- They will adhere to a specified delivery date.
- They will cover the costs of any licence fees for secondary materials in the work (quotes and images).
- They will make themselves available (within reason) at a specified time for promotion of the work.
- They will not publish a competing work with another publisher.

This last requirement is contextual. If you bring out a book on pigeon-breeding in June, followed by another on pigeon-breeding with a different publisher at Christmas, neither publisher will be pleased with the way the books compete with each other. In reality, you won't be doing yourself a favour either. The same could go for genre works: it may not be wise to bring out two similar crime series or picture books with different publishers at times that are close to each other. The best thing to do is be upfront with your publisher about your plans for future works and make sure that there won't be competing commercial interests, either for you or the publisher.

Option clause

It is possible that your contract may include a clause granting your publisher first right of refusal in relation to possible forthcoming works. This means that your publisher seeks the exclusive opportunity to be able to consider your next work with a view to contracting it before you show it to anyone else. This is not the same as a multi-book deal, in which a single contract contains reference to multiple titles.

Dos and don'ts of signing a contract

- *Do* check out your publisher's track record in relation to its treatment of authors, from a marketing, editorial and administrative point of view.
- *Do* ensure you understand the terms of the contract.
- *Do* be clear on what the contract says about RRP and distribution.
- *Do* be clear about what it says about the term of copyright and termination.
- *Do* check that your contract contains provision for rising royalties in relation to copies sold.
- *Do* ask your publisher about their performance in relation to subsidiary rights.
- *Do* be certain that you can fulfil your obligations as an author.
- *Do* ask questions or seek clarification from the publisher on anything about which you are uncertain.
- *Do* have a conversation with your publisher about their process for choosing an illustrator (if relevant) and their ideas for same.
- *Don't* sign a contract until you are comfortable with its contents.

The signing of a contract is a milestone moment in an author's career, each and every time. You should pause to acknowledge all you have done to make it this far before the hard work begins all over again!

7. The publication process

- What happens after signing a contract
- Things an author can do after the contract is signed
- Working with an editor
- The stages of editing
- Additional responsibilities of an editor
- Dos and don'ts of working with an editor
- Collaboration and working with an illustrator
- Production, proofreading and printing
- The transition from a private to a public self

Until the point of contract, you will have been working on your manuscript, perhaps in splendid isolation, or in conjunction with a writing group or a mentor. But now there is a whole team dedicated to making your work the best it can possibly be and helping you reach its audience.

What happens after signing a contract

After contract, your work will make its way through a series of stages from editing to production, printing, the arrival of review (or advance) copies, marketing and finally the appearance of your book in the world on a magical publication date.

During the acquisitions meeting when the decision is made to publish your book, the marketing and communications team will be thinking about the best ways to market your book. Even before you begin editing, you may be required to supply them with material about your book, along with your contacts and relevant biographical details, your social media profiles and website, and author headshots that will be absorbed into marketing and publicity materials (see Chapter 9 for more detail on what a marketing and communications team does). All kinds of work on your future book will be taking place within the publishing house while you prepare to embark on the in-house editing process.

After your manuscript has been contracted, a number of things occur, not all of which involve your direct participation:

- A marketing and communications strategy is devised for your book.
- Marketing and publicity materials are scheduled and created.
- Editing begins.
- There is possible collaboration with another party, such as an illustrator.
- The production process follows after editing, including cover design and typesetting, proofreading, indexing, colour checks, review of proofs.
- Your book is printed.
- Advances arrive for review and promotion.
- The bulk of the print run is shipped or freighted to the publisher or the distributor from the printer.

Things an author can do after the contract is signed

After you have signed your contract, there are a number of things you can tend to, many of them to do with forging or consolidating relationships that will be of use to you after the book is published. First, check with your publisher when they are happy for you to announce that you have a publishing deal. They may want your announcement to coincide with a social media story. Second, pay your local bookshop a visit. Hopefully you have already established an active relationship with them. Now is the time to tell them you have a contract!

Claire Miller recommends a range of other steps to take while you wait for the editing to start:

- *Fill in a contributor information form.* Once your contract is signed, you should be thinking about completing a contributor information form or questionnaire for your publisher. This is a written document that gives them a sense of who you are, what you think your book is about and who you think are your key audiences. It's good to get this done early because it gives everyone from the publisher to sales, marketing and communications staff the tools to promote your book. If you're not sent a form to complete by your publisher, consider working up a document and sending it in anyway. Things you might include are:

» Date of birth, where you were born and your citizenship status – these are needed if a publisher wants to enter you into literary awards.

» Your address, where you went to school, where you grew up, any places relevant to your book – this can help the promotions team establish local links when approaching media outlets.

» Your website and social media handles so your publisher can connect with you online and promote things you post.

» Your experience in public speaking and what you'd be interested in talking to audiences about.

» A list of your other publications and awards.

» A short official author biography (the kind you don't mind being shared in publicity material).

» What you think your book is about.

» Who you think your audience is.

» What keywords and search terms you think your audience would use to search for your book – see if you can come up with at least a dozen of each of these.

» Who you know – the booksellers, media outlets, librarians, teachers, groups and organisations that you already have a connection with.

- *Arrange publicity shots.* Most publishers will want you to get professional photographs taken. These must be in colour and of sufficient quality for use in magazines. They should be high resolution: 300 dpi at A4 is a good size. Ask around for recommendations of local photographers, or check with your publisher to see if they have someone who takes author pics in the office. Talk to the photographer about what you need. Check that they are happy for the publisher to use your photos without attribution if required. Tell them what your book is about and ask for a range of shots. You don't want formal, boardroom-style images: the headshot should fit your genre and your personality. Take a look at the style of author headshots in a similar genre before you have your own photos taken. A variety of photos is good as it allows the team's publicist to send out different images to media outlets so they're not repeating themselves. Make sure some are in landscape and others in portrait.

- *Attend to social media.* If you aren't already on social media, and you plan to be, now is the time to get onto it. Investigate different platforms. Join groups on Facebook and Goodreads. Make online connections with other authors already published and with a higher profile in your genre. Hang out where your audience is. Use Instagram to follow other writers and potential readers and observe what makes for successful and engaging content. For industry connections (booksellers, librarians, publishers and media and other writers) participate in LinkedIn and Twitter. This will help you understand what their particular communities are talking about and interested in, and you can join in the conversation as a reader before joining in as a writer. If you feel the need to separate between your private and public selves, create dedicated author pages. (See Chapter 8 for this aspect of self-promotion.)

- *Brush up on public speaking.* If you're a shy, novice or weak public speaker, now's the time to get some training. Join a Toastmasters public speaking club, or practise at a friend's book club, school or library so you can get used to talking to groups.
- *Connect through bookshops, libraries and events.* Regularly give your bookseller and librarian updates about your publishing process. Encourage their participation in your journey and your book. If you intend to do events when your book is out, start looking at what kinds your local booksellers are involved in and what you might be able to offer that fits in with their programming. Be strategic and really think about who their audience is and what works. Down the track, you'll be able to work with your publisher on what events to pitch to them. That might be a simple book signing, an author talk at a bar, or a workshop or sausage sizzle on Love Your Bookshop Day. Be targeted and creative. Go to events and launches organised by your publisher. Support your peers, get to know them and learn from them.
- *Start to think about who could endorse your book.* Down the track, your publisher may be in touch (or ask you to be in touch) with other writers to request an endorsement or 'puff quote' for the cover of your book. Think about which authors you know or are connected to, and authors of like titles. Aim to make a list of a dozen feasible suggestions.

Working with an editor

There is one thing you can be certain of: the work that is signed at contract will not be identical to the book that appears in the bookshop. The publisher and appointed editor will have a sense of what scope and areas of work are required on any manuscript, and these can be minimal or, more likely, more substantial, and could take between several months or the better part of a year to complete. You should have some sense of what kinds of changes your publisher has in mind before you sign your contract.

The editor is the person who cares about your manuscript as much as you do. Their role is to help you realise your vision while they keep in mind the expectations of your future readers. Although an editor may make proactive suggestions, their role sometimes feels more akin to that of a therapist asking questions that promote growth and self-knowledge, or an intelligent reader who poses questions for you and your brain to resolve.

Through a process of discussion and collaboration, your editor will help you make your manuscript the very best it can be. You may meet them in person or on the phone before you begin your work, or this relationship may be one that mostly takes place via email, with edits to your manuscript done with Track Changes in Word or using Google Docs, or with a method that works for you both.

In general, the stages of editing will move from the macro to the micro. Large-scale issues relating to the structure and shape of the book will take place during structural editing. You will then move into issues relating to closer reading. These stages may be addressed in a series of back-and-forth conversations and revisions between author and editor, in person or digitally. This process can take three months, or six, or nine, depending on the amount of work required. We will look in more detail at the stages of editing in the next section.

Is it challenging to work with an editor, particularly if you are used to working on your own? Not as challenging as you might think. Authors are often invigorated by this process. It is amazing after years of hard slog to suddenly have a coach by your side, someone as immersed in the process as you are, who is able to discuss the intricacies of your work with you with interest and excitement. Often, though, because they are so well acquainted with your work, the editor will home in on the same issues that have been bothering you too. Their inquiries can affirm your own suspicion about weak spots and simultaneously give you the freedom to discard material you have been hanging onto. This can be exhilarating and liberating.

One challenge can be to retain clarity about your own vision. Is the editor asking something of you that doesn't feel right or readily resolvable? Do you feel that you are reluctantly forcing a change on the work with which you are not comfortable?

A simple request from an editor can involve half an hour of thinking on their part but a month of writing on yours. While the editor is good at asking questions, their proposed solution might not always chime with you. It is important that you take the time to sit with something on which you have no clarity. If you don't feel understood, ask your editor more questions or chat with them about what is bothering you.

Keep in mind that, for all their enthusiasm and deep engagement, the process for an editor is not personal or emotional in the way it might be for you. An editor won't be offended if you don't accept all their changes, though it can be wise to accept suggestions when it comes to spelling, grammar or style, unless you have a good reason for doing otherwise. (An exception may be a poetry manuscript, when you may have a solid vision for matters relating to punctuation, word choice, layout and even spelling.) From the editor's perspective, their main role is to raise potential issues with you so that you have the opportunity to consider them and respond. If you reject an editor's query on an aspect of the text, and a proofreader or copyeditor subsequently raises this identical query, you may wish to think again about your desire to keep the text as it is. If two or three readers query the same thing, then you can be sure future readers will too.

The human brain is a remarkable thing. One of the most exciting things for editors to witness is when a writer takes a suggestion on board by responding to it in a way that is utterly transformative and brings a new dimension to the work. Ultimately, you are the author of the work, and the editor is there as an expert guide to honour your vision.

The stages of editing

While your manuscript is being edited, it may go through a number of stages. With the guidance of an editor, you will respond to their comments or queries on your manuscript during some or all of the following stages:

- *Structural or developmental editing.* Includes attention to underlying concepts, structure, scenes and plot, voice, continuity and character development.
- *Line editing.* Looks at the way language works at sentence level, including tone, syntax, extraneous word choice, sentence flow, clichés and point of view.

- *Copyediting.* Involves fact-checking, applying house style, formatting, consistency, punctuation and grammar.
- *Proofreading.* Checking for typographical errors and elements of layout once the manuscript has been typeset. Your input at this stage may be required for clarification on those things that are not simply typos.

These stages may be completed by a single editor, or different editors at different stages. The proofreader and the copyeditor may be the same or separate people. Each stage may involve multiple exchanges and review of the manuscript between editor and author, sometimes accompanied by detailed reports, or with electronic mark-ups in the manuscript itself. You and your editor may also have discussions on the phone or in person as required.

In our experience, every manuscript usually has a particular issue, something that requires specific resolution. These vary from manuscript to manuscript. For example, the issues may relate to:

- Structure (e.g. an issue pertaining to the way that the story has been put together).
- Character (e.g. whether there is a better vehicle for the story; multiple characters have the same function).
- Something that is not there but ought to be (e.g. a missed opportunity or narrative thread or an aspect or motif that feels undeveloped).
- Plot (e.g. a story that is too predictable, a crime novel that is lacking a 'twist', an unresolved or ambiguous ending).
- Authenticity (e.g. elements are anachronistic or require more research or are in some way unconvincing).
- Pace (e.g. work that feels uneven, too quick, too slow, too short or too long).

Some of these elements you may have encountered during work-shopping, whether looking at someone else's work or your own. Perhaps your manuscript has already gone through multiple drafts, edits and consultations before it is submitted for publication. But an editor is an expert at long-form work, someone who comes to your work with fresh eyes, and who can draw your attention to those parts of the text where further revision will help the work become the best it can be.

Like a coach with a training schedule and a competition date in mind, an editor should be clear about deadlines and ensure you stick to them, because the book's schedule is made in the context of the publisher's list, which involves many books and an intense printing and promotions schedule. If it looks to you that you won't be able to meet a particular deadline, then you need to communicate promptly with your editor about this, so that they can communicate with the publisher and reconsider the publishing schedule.

Ask an author: After your work has been contracted, how do you make the most of working with an editor?

Alan Carter says:

Lesson one – listen and learn. I've been lucky enough to have an excellent editor who, as well as knowing how to dot my i's and cross my t's, is well and truly across the Cato series and knows the characters at least as well as (if not sometimes better) than I do. In particular, the big-picture issues of plot, logic, character arc and motivations are vital to making a book work. I tend to send my manuscript off after I've already gone through it myself a couple of times to try and iron out the obvious lumps and fill in the gaping holes – if there's stuff you already know needs your attention, you may as well take care of it yourself first. I usually take about 90% of advice on board, usually because it's good advice. Don't be afraid to fight your corner, though – just make sure you're not wrong.

Brigid Lowry says:

A good editor is a treasure house. You are lucky if you have one. Editors do not grow on trees and will cut out all your clichés without any hesitation, and then throw you under a bus if you mix metaphors. It is said that working with an editor is like being married. I have found that you don't need to love your editor or want to sleep with them, but you do need to like them. If you are not simpatico, getting your work into its best shape will not be a pleasure. It is a team effort. Mutual respect is the key. As in a marriage, sometimes it is a good idea to shut up and listen.

It can be hard to be told things by an editor. If you are fully convinced that what they are advising is not right for you, you need to say so quietly and kindly; however, I have found – over many years – to take editorial advice under strong consideration. When I was working on *Still Life with Teapot*, my very nice editor advised removing a favourite last line in an essay. I was very attached to that line. I called my friend who has also worked with my editor. In his usual measured way, my friend told me that he had found her to be almost always right. It proved thus. Once I swallowed my pride and killed my darling, the piece was stronger.

An example of a different sort happened many years ago when I had a story under consideration by a particular journal. The editor, whose name is now in the dusty forgotten past, kept suggesting changes, like changing from first person to third, and I don't recall the other ones, but there were many. At a certain point, I gave up and withdrew the story. If you don't think my baby is pretty now, you never will.

Once you have an editor, be professional. Be honest. Be prompt. Respect deadlines. Have a coffee together now and then.

Brendan Ritchie says:

I read somewhere that insecure writers ignore all feedback, but really insecure writers incorporate all feedback. Operating somewhere in the middle ground feels like a sensible approach to getting the most out of working with an editor. Each manuscript has been contracted for a reason, and it is vital that the writer protects and nurtures the 'heart' of their work, while always looking for opportunities to make it better, bolder and more ready for the reader.

It is far more productive for an editor to highlight areas of concern in a manuscript than it is for them to simply offer praise, so it is important to celebrate the positive feedback and take the negative feedback in the spirit with which it has been written. If I see an extended passage without many edits or suggestions, I take this as a victory. Not for me against the editor or anything like that, but for the manuscript in reading as it should. If I see pages littered with corrections, questions and issues, I look at it as a challenge. How can I clean these up, one by one, and send back something that is clean and true?

In this way, I approach the larger, structural editing as a kind of search for truth. No matter how bizarre the manuscript, there should be a truth that it is communicating or at least striving towards. In some moments, this truth will be present on every line. But in other areas it may need to be teased out and refocused. A constructive relationship with an editor can be invaluable in this regard.

Sasha Wasley says:

There are, of course, different types of editors: structural editors, copyeditors, line editors and proofreaders. The structural editor is the first one you work with and this is often the most challenging part of the editorial process. Your structural editor will ask hard questions about your manuscript. Should this scene happen earlier? Can you cut this subplot? Why did this character do that? Is this character necessary? You could find yourself moving big chunks of your story around, removing thousands of words worth of waffle and killing your darlings.

To get the most out of working with a good editor, I check my pride at the door. If I didn't think my work was worthy, I wouldn't have submitted it, so it's hard to hear that someone else thinks there are problems with my book. When I receive that first edit back, I experience moments of resentment, embarrassment and even hurt. So here's a tip: read the suggested changes, then close the document and leave it alone for a day or two. *Do not* reply to your editor at this point because you might say something you regret.

Then, after you've had a chance to process, go back to your file. Revise a section at a time and address each comment or suggested change. You have three options for each: make the suggested change; make a change (but not the one they suggested); or change nothing. No-one can force you to alter your book. But remember, your editor is trying to make your book better. Stay calm, decide how to address the problem raised, and if you choose to make no changes, have a good rationale for that.

Anne-Louise Willoughby says:

An editor is a writer's best friend. Listen to your friend! Being precious about your work is fatal, while being open to changes can deliver great results. Working solidly, sometimes for years, on a manuscript can leave a writer myopic and sensitive. An editor brings fresh eyes to advocate for the future readers' experiences; they are your ticket to a cleaner, better version of your text. It is important to get to know your editor – if you're in the same place it's ideal, but travel to meet them in person if you can! It helps to establish a rapport and for you to feel safe discussing suggested changes. If you feel very strongly about not changing something, back up your position with a clear rationale, without the emotion that invariably comes with being at the end of a long, at times passionate and others frustrated, process. Be prompt implementing changes to see if the suggestions sit well by delivering on or ahead of time so that there's room for discussion. Trust your editor; it's their job to make you look good.

And Caitlin Maling says:

I think the editing process is very similar to working through constructive feedback with a workshop: you need to be open to change but very clear about what you want the final product to be. Go into it open, but with you own questions about the manuscript that you want a second set of eyes on. Be ready to articulate your choices – if you can't, maybe revisit that piece.

Some poets I've met refuse to let anyone else do their editorial work, but I've enjoyed working in person with editors more than nearly every other part of the writing process. There's something energising and challenging about collaborating physically on drafts, in seeing how someone else annotates and frames your work. I really enjoy being told 'not quite, try harder' and returning over a different coffee session with a subsequent draft that meets with more approval. For this reason, I've often found working solidly on the editing process for a month or so with regular meetings to be the most effective for me – it keeps you feverishly in the process. A lot of poetry occurs in dribs and drabs around other work and/or life, so making sure at the final stage to really give it the compressed time and energy it needs is essential.

It's a very lucky thing in poetry to have an editor who has the time to give you devoted feedback – many presses don't have the resources to provide one. So if you find yourself in a situation where you have access to one, respect the wealth of knowledge they have, and that editing is a distinct art form in its own right. I always think of poetry as fundamentally a conversation, and the editing process can be the purest embodiment of this.

Additional responsibilities of an editor

Once the editor has read your manuscript, they should advise you about any possible legal issues they can foresee such as defamation and any other moral or ethical considerations, and also confirm which quoted material or images you will need to seek permissions for. If *you* have any specific concerns about any material in your work, then you should definitely raise these with your editor.

Defamation

We looked at some of a writer's responsibilities regarding defamation in Chapter 4. However, an editor will be particularly alert to potential issues in case you have not yet identified them. The publisher may choose to seek legal advice as to whether any material in the manuscript is potentially defamatory, and what adjustments you may need to make about such content.

Moral considerations

The editor will be aware that defamation is not the only kind of damage that publication can cause. As we discussed in Chapter 4, relationships can be challenged or altered by the publication of something you have written, or people (friends, family or strangers) can be injured or upset. This is something you need to give serious consideration to.

An editor may ask you whether any characters in your work of fiction relate to actual people, and whether there is anyone who may be upset by what you have written. They may also ask whose consent you have already sought for the inclusion of people represented in your work, including those who are no longer alive but who may have relatives who care. You will be able to discuss with your editor what steps you need to take at this stage in order to square any potential issues away. Your editor may discuss with you any concerns they may have about own voice representation and ensure you are aware of potential issues of appropriation. Arriving at a position with which you feel comfortable is much easier to do now, prior to publication and before the glare of publicity is upon you.

Remember, even if your editor doesn't raise them, now is the time, rather than after publication, to deal with any issues that are bothering you.

Permissions

In Chapter 4, we looked at the question of whether you need permission to quote the work of others in your own work in. Squaring away permissions and paying any associated fees are the responsibility of the author. Remember that quoting from songs can be expensive. The cost of quoting from written material can vary widely, ranging from nothing to hundreds of dollars. Seeking permissions involves finding the copyright holder of material you wish to quote, advising them of the context of your proposed reproduction and waiting for them to grant permission for usage, including on what terms. Below is a list of information you will need to include when seeking permissions. Your editor can provide you with these.

You may also need to seek permissions to reproduce visual material such as art, cartoons or photographs. Again, you will need to write to the copyright holder, and you may also need to ask whether they can supply you with a high-resolution digital file of the same. There will almost certainly be a fee attached to this process. Any gallery or library where the primary material is housed may additionally require that you supply them with permission in writing from the work's creator/copyright holder before they will release a requested image to you.

The process of permission seeking – from finding and making contact with a copyright holder to gaining permission and/or an image – can be time-consuming (most of the time is spent in waiting for a reply!), and the sooner you start on this process the better.

How do I seek permissions?

Start by googling the life dates of the author in question to check that their work is still in copyright, or seems as if it could be. You will need to then write to the copyright holder, who is usually the publisher of the work or the estate of the author. Their details are often listed on the imprint page of a book (that page at the beginning or end of a book that lists publisher and copyright details). Some detective work may be required to find the relevant contact. Try googling 'author, title, permission' for starters. You may start by sending a short email asking the contact whether they are the right person to direct your inquiry to. Once you have established who the copyright holder is, request permission to reproduce the material in question by letting them know the following:

- Your name.
- The title of your work.
- Its genre.
- When it will be published.
- The RRP of the work.
- The territories in which it will appear.
- The format in which it will appear (paperback, hardcover, ebook).
- The estimated print run.
- The number of years you seek copyright for.
- The context of the quote's usage.

The copyright holder may respond by telling you:

- You cannot use the requested quotation.
- You can use it with attribution in your book's acknowledgements.
- You may use it with attribution and for a fee.

If you cannot afford the specified fee, you must delete the quoted material. If you do not hear from the copyright holder after several attempts, or if the trail goes cold, then you will have documentation of your attempts. Speak to the publisher about including on the imprint page a notice to the effect that every reasonable effort has been made to contact copyright holders, and that any inquiries about this should be directed to the publisher.

Dos and don'ts of working with an editor

- *Do* communicate openly with your editor.
- *Don't* be afraid to ask questions.
- *Do* ask if you have any qualms in relation to the publication of content (defamatory or relationship-challenging).
- *Do* reiterate your vision if you feel it has been lost in the process.
- *Do* act on those suggestions that feel right to you and let your editor know when they don't.
- *Do* stick to deadlines and speak up if adherence looks difficult.
- *Do* enjoy this process – it may feel like a long haul, but it will be over faster than you think.

Collaboration and working with an illustrator

The process of working with an editor is one of collaboration. Another form of collaboration occurs where you are the author but not the illustrator of a picture book.

At the point of signing, the publisher will have in mind an illustrator to pair with an author. Publishers often have a database or collection of illustrators' portfolios, and a list of illustrators they have worked with before. The publisher will choose an illustrator that they believe will have a connection with the text and bring something special to it.

As discussed in Chapter 6, the author and illustrator are contracted separately, and an author should always be consulted on – and be happy with – the choice of illustrator, and be shown examples of their work in advance of signing.

Once the illustrator has been contracted, they will produce character sketches and ideas, then a storyboard sketching out the whole book, then the final illustrations. The author should see the artwork at each of these stages and have the opportunity to provide input via the editor – an author and illustrator don't necessarily meet or interact directly. The text is edited before the illustrator receives it, but there are often further changes once the artwork is complete and the book comes together as a whole.

The most successful author–illustrator collaborations demonstrate an openness to the process, and an author can be delighted by the addition of unimagined dimensions to their text which have been supplied by a visual creative. The best illustrations will certainly complement the text rather than reproduce it.

Ask an author: What makes for a good collaborative creative process?

Ambelin Kwaymullina says:

Honesty! I have engaged in a number of collaborative processes, including writing novels with my family, with a friend, and working with editors on various books. The key to any successful collaboration is for each party to be honest with each other. If you cannot speak freely and frankly to an editor or a co-author – and have them speak freely and frankly to you – the story suffers, and so does the relationship. It's hard for writers to be honest about our work and to hear honesty about our work when we feel the stories so deeply, but really, get over yourself. Professional writers value feedback and work on creating the spaces and behaviours that allow them to receive honest opinions.

James Foley says:
There are two collaborations at play in any picture book – there's the writer–illustrator partnership, then there's the working relationship with the editor.

When picture books are made in collaboration between a writer and an illustrator, people always assume that they work closely together. Most of the time, though, the opposite is true. Most of the time, they don't communicate at all; often they don't meet until the book launch, if at all. The editor works with the writer on the words, and the editor also (or book designer) works separately with the illustrator on the pictures. This process, of separating writer and illustrator, has its merits: it streamlines and simplifies the process; it stops writers getting too involved in the illustration process and vice versa; it limits the number of cooks in the kitchen at any one time.

But when I worked on my first picture book, *The Last Viking*, that's not how it worked. I met the author, Norman Jorgensen, at a Society of Children's Book Writers and Illustrators meeting. He liked my drawings and suggested we work on a book idea together. So we did. Norman is as close as you can get to being an illustrator without actually being one – he thinks in images. We're both huge fans of cinema, so we could speak in that language when discussing how the illustrations could look – close-up here, big wide shot of a battle here, pan across here etc. And while he was throwing me ideas for pictures, I was throwing him ideas for words and scenes. We shaped the story together. Sure, there were times we wanted to throttle each other, but the story became stronger as a result of our close collaboration. What made it a good collaboration was that we got along, and we each understood what we were aiming for – we were on the same page, literally.

It's similar when working with editors. You want to work with someone who understands where you're coming from, who 'gets it'. You need a similar sense of humour. You need someone who is good at giving feedback, particularly when it's not the sort of feedback you want to hear. Conversely, and I hope I'm not making too much of an assumption here, editors might say they like working with people who are good at *taking* feedback, especially when it's not the type they want to hear.

With each type of collaboration (writer–illustrator, writer–editor and illustrator–editor) the main thing to keep in mind is that the story comes first. Egos need to be put aside and everything must be done in service of the story. Your favourite character or scene may need to be cut if the story demands it. When everyone understands that – when everyone knows that the story is in charge and that they need to put their own wants aside – then you get good collaborations.

And Meg McKinlay says:

Collaboration can be a bit of a tightrope act, a precarious balance between holding on and letting go. Whoever your collaborator is, it's absolutely key that you are clear-sighted about what it is in the work that's important to you. You need to recognise and articulate this to yourself, which is not always as simple as it sounds. This in turn enables you to be clear about this to others during collaborative processes that may follow; don't assume your priorities are self-evident, or that the work is transparent to others in this way.

The flipside of this is acknowledging what matters less, and being open to the possibility of change. It is crucial that you're able to take a step back from your work, to see it as a structure, elements of narrative pulling together in the service of a particular goal. And at the same time, to trust that others – mentors, editors and so on – may be better placed than you are to do so, to respect their expertise and advice as to how to strengthen aspects of the work with that end in mind.

I've used the term 'change' but it's often bigger than that, particularly when working with illustrators. An illustrator is a true creative collaborator in the sense that they are an equal partner in the act of creation. The text may come first in a chronological sense, but that doesn't mean it comes first in any other. Once the illustrator joins the process, they bring with them a whole new language, way of seeing and skill set into which I have no insight, but must be absolutely open to. In many ways, I think this is analogous to the collaborative process in a broader sense, no matter who you're working with. What you bring to the table may be your seventy-fifth and most perfect draft, but it is still on some level raw material, and keeping that in mind is essential.

Production, proofreading and printing

Completion of your manuscript

There is a certain stage a manuscript reaches when suddenly it feels done. You can poke it anywhere (metaphorically speaking) and it won't wobble. It is structurally sound and every word is in the right place. In our experience, editors and authors often reach this point of recognition simultaneously, and hopefully on time.

Once editing has been finalised, the manuscript is typeset – set up in a design program to look like the pages of a book – and design elements are added. Typesetting can be more complex if you have written a non-fiction book with other elements like photos, illustrations, an index and captions. Your input may be called on, perhaps regarding the layout of the pages, particularly if you are the creator of some of those visual elements. It is exciting to see your manuscript suddenly look like a real book!

The typeset pages are then proofread, preferably by someone who has not seen the manuscript at all until this moment. You may also receive a proof copy at this time for your own review, or you may receive a copy after proofreading has taken place, with a list of queries that have arisen as a result of the proofread. There will invariably be changes required at this stage as the proofreader brings fresh eyes to the manuscript.

What happens at this point if you wish to make changes? Your contract may have a clause stipulating that the cost of corrections exceeding 5% of the work will be borne by the author. Making many corrections was perhaps an issue back when typesetting was manual and time-consuming. These days, author corrections are straightforward to take in, and your editor should be willing enough to do it. But even so, now is not the time to make sweeping changes like eradicating chapters or characters, or activities more suited to the structural editing phase, not least because it increases the chances of introducing errors carefully ironed out during the editing process.

The cover

During editing, your editor, publisher or designated production manager, often in consultation with people in sales and marketing, will have sent a design brief to a designer. The brief will contain information regarding the potential audience, tone and content of your book, as well as a list of comparable book covers that have elements of the look the publisher and marketing team have in mind. The cover is your book's most important marketing tool. It will be designed in consultation with marketing and sales staff and perhaps a test audience (e.g. asking a range of children for their preferences about a range of draft designs). A number of draft covers will be presented to an in-house team to discuss and refine. At some stage your input may be invited (depending on the publisher and your contract) in relation to the look of the cover and to the content of the back blurb.

Sign-off

You should have the opportunity to fully check the final version of the typeset pages prior to print, and to sign off on final versions of both cover and internals. After sign-off, the book will be dispatched for printing, usually as an electronic file. Printing may occur onshore or offshore, taking anything from two to twelve weeks for printing, shipping and delivery.

Once the book has been set up at the printer (a straightforward process these days, given digital technology) the printer will send hard (physical) or soft (digital) proofs to the publisher to check one last time, allowing any corrections to be made before the okay to print is given.

You are unlikely to be involved in this process, unless you are also the illustrator or photographer, in which case you may need to check colour reproduction. Your publisher will also upload ebook files around the same time in preparation for your book's simultaneous release as an ebook, if that is part of the contract. Suddenly, all your writing and editing work is done.

Distributors, sales reps and booksellers

Distributors focus on warehousing stock – sometimes from a range of publishers under one very large roof – and fulfilling orders to booksellers. *Sales reps* are employed by publishers and distributors to service a geographical region or specific stores to present forthcoming titles to booksellers, usually months ahead of the actual release date. Sales reps 'sell in' these books to booksellers so that the books can 'sell through' to customers. Booksellers select and curate the books according to what they believe their customers want. Meanwhile, back at the publishing house, the marketing and communications team awaits arrivals of advance copies of your book from the printer to use in promotion.

The transition from a private to a public self

For you, for now, the work is done. How odd, after all that effort, that this should be so! Some writers have observed that it can be painful to end work with their editor. At its best, the partnership will have been a close working relationship comprising shared values, encouragement, sympathy, cheerleading, coaching and therapy sessions, with a mutual sense of shared satisfaction as you approach the finish line together. An editor can have felt like a friend, but now suddenly they become a friend who moves on swiftly to a new author. You may feel rejected or a little bit lost. It is possible of course that you never experience any of these negative sensations, but if you do, be kind to yourself. Acknowledge your feelings, and try to think of this as being part of a process. It's like an excellent holiday – sad when it's over, but leaving you with memories of an intense time, and the knowledge that you can travel again.

Biographer Anne-Louise Willoughby has commented on a feeling that took her by surprise during this time, though she has since met other writers who have observed the same thing. She likens this time to the feeling you have when you are bodysurfing and bobbing about in the ocean, waiting for the wave: there is that lull when you can see the wave coming and you know you're going to catch it, but you're not sure if it is going to tumble you in the wash or carry you gracefully onto the sand. There is an inevitability about it, but there is also the sense of the unknown. After years of effort, your book is about to appear in the world. How will it be received? What will its arrival ask of you? Will you catch a glorious wave, will it roll you, or will it just fall away moments after you have caught it?

There can be a time of disorientation and disquiet between when the book goes to print and when the marketing and communications team swings into action. It is the time when you can still be an interior, introverted kind of person, someone who will soon need to be swapped out for a public-ready figure. Children's writer Deb Fitzpatrick has some suggestions for what to do with this strange in-between time:

Ideally, you will start writing your next book, being by this time completely weary of reading and thinking about the book that's about to be published! But of course, what is ideal is not always what happens … Feeling anxious about the industry's response to your book is a huge part of this time: there is a very real sense that you've completely exposed yourself, and that other people – complete strangers! – will read your pathetic meanderings and judge them harshly. This thought is scary and is best not lingered over. My experience tells me that readers are largely kind and generous and very, very appreciative of the mammoth effort a book represents.

One productive way to fill this time is to shore up your knowledge about whatever you've written, so that during interviews, podcasts or school visits you can speak in an informed way about your book. For example, I had to review all my research on the Gilbert's potoroo before *The Spectacular Spencer Gray* came out, so I was confident when talking about it in public. I also did extra research and found this very helpful.

Fiction writers will need to be aware that they'll be asked questions about their writing techniques – voice, point of view, character etc. – and this time is a great opportunity to review and consolidate what you're going to say in response to these inquiries. I found it quite embarrassing to talk about myself as a *writer* in the early days, so having a few practice sessions is worthwhile. Often your publicist can help you with this by running a pretend interview before you do the real thing, so ask for some help when your time with the publicist begins.

In short, recognise that this is probably going to be an odd time, so just sit with it and don't overthink it. If you can, pause, take a breath, enjoy it. You have worked hard! You have written a book! Once you are required to participate in the promotion of your book, any feelings of disquiet will dissipate because there will be a host of things to do, and to tend to – and this is what we will be looking at in Chapter 8.

8. Branding and self-promotion

- Defining success
- The art of self-promotion
- Tips for how to talk about your book
- When to create a website
- Tips for setting up a website
- Why and how to participate in social media
- Tips for effective social media participation
- Allocating time to being online
- Navigating social media aversion

An author who has the backing of a publishing house and a marketing and communications team to promote them should feel supported as they step out with their book into the world. But the success of your book and how you're received by an audience depends on a range of things, only a number of which are in your control. Before we look at how your publisher can assist you, we will first look at ways in which you can promote yourself successfully, and how to establish and maintain a presence online. Many of the online tips in this chapter will be also applicable to the way you promote your book in the real world.

Defining success

In Chapter 6, we looked at managing your expectations around what might happen after your book is published. An author participates in the market with circumscribed autonomy. The 'success' of any book relies on a complex alchemy that includes some or all of the following:

- Your hard work along with the publisher's and booksellers'.
- A publisher's willingness to take risks.

- Having the right cover image to appeal to the market.
- An effective distribution network.
- Word of mouth promotion by readers.
- Booksellers actively hand-selling your book.
- Trends in the market and on social media.
- The size of the market and the state of the economy.
- Consumers' willingness to purchase books.
- The availability of opportunities for review.

Blazing fame and fortune may result from the confluence of these things in the right way, but in all likelihood, they won't. Sometimes the right book comes out at the wrong time and sinks with hardly a trace, even when the publisher is doing all they can to promote it and you.

Ultimately, to manage your expectations around success, it is probably good to ask: What constitutes success for me? Is it units sold or readers reached? If a single stranger reads and responds to my book, is *that* success? Is success to be measured by the number of book reviews and awards? Is it finding an engaged audience with whom to interact?

Over time, your answer to these questions may change, but such definitions of success can provide focus to the quest of getting your book out there. Setting parameters for 'success' can let you feel you are making progress *in context* – in the beginning your success may be defined in any number of ways: by what is a good number of books sold for a debut author, or for a small publisher, or for your local bookshop, or for books in your genre.

The art of self-promotion

In the months leading up to the publication date, your marketing and communications team, responding to required lead times, will send advance information and/or copies of your book to reviewers, booksellers, festival promoters, podcasters and bloggers. It gives these people a chance to read your work ahead of the publication date and to contemplate the package that is the book and you.

In Chapter 3, we looked at what an author brand is – the choices you make about how you depict yourself to the world. As you begin to work with a publicist in the promotion of your work, you will continue to refine this sense of your 'brand'. What is important is to remain authentic – to be able to tell your story and remain connected to your work in a way that is true to you. You have a unique set of qualities that means no other writer could have written the book you have. The publicist's job is to discover and draw on your unique qualities in the context of promotion – what hook is best used in any situation to encourage the festival planner, journalist or bookseller to bite? Will the person biting be reeled in by the book? Will they respond to the author on the end of the rod? It is important to 'fish where the fish are', but whether you or the publicist can actually hook the fish is not always something either of you can control.

When it comes to being out in the world, you are your book's primary ambassador. Book buyers are often curious about the person who wrote it. Celebrities can be writers, and writers can also become celebrities, as evidenced by long crocodile queues at festival signing tables.

Adept self-promotion is something to grow into with experience and practice. A writer comes to learn how to perform, how to speak in public, and how to describe their work and the ideas behind it in engaging sound bites or mini narratives. In person-to-person exchanges, you are not selling your book so much as yourself and the *idea* of the book. Much of what we looked at in Chapter 3 about defining your brand and being authentic applies even more now that you have a book out in the world.

Finding yourself out of your comfort zone is not the same as being inauthentic. As you promote your book, you are likely to find yourself in new and daunting situations, especially if your personality lies at the introverted end of the spectrum. First times can be terrifying, whether you are in front of a radio mic, before an audience of fifteen expectant nannas in a library, or in a lecture theatre of three hundred students. Terror and performance-adrenaline are cousins – the 'exposure therapy' of multiple events can sometimes be the best way to overcome fear. But practice and preparation, especially when you are new to publicity, always makes a positive difference. And don't forget that your publicist is there to support and coach you through it.

If you want to sell your book or if you want others to read it, it is helpful if you, as its ambassador, can talk about your book with verve. Keeping it fresh (even remembering a character's name!) can be challenging, especially at your tenth or twentieth appearance, and when your brain may be already engaged in a new work.

Tips for how to talk about your book

Here are some tips from Claire Miller for talking to others about your book:

- *Remember your who, what, why, where, when.* You're a storyteller. How would you tell it if you had only a couple of hundred words to write a story with? Translate this into the spoken word.
- *Never denigrate yourself or your book.* You've written a book and been published! That's amazing.
- *Be positive.* Which part of the writing brought you joy? Share that. Did someone else say something nice about it? Have you seen your first advance copy? What did it feel like to hold it in your hands? Start by talking about something positive, something that is making you happy. If you do wish to share a negative experience or anecdote, then tell it in a way other people can relate to – and have a reason for telling that story. Don't just complain for the sake of it.
- *Listen to yourself.* If you find yourself interesting, then others are likely to find you interesting too. Don't just rattle off a prepared script.
- *Listen to others.* This is not a monologue, it's a conversation, so do talk about your work, but leave people space to participate, comment and share their own experiences in turn. Engage the person you're talking to and respond to their cues.
- *Share.* One of the things that makes us interesting to others is our willingness to be open about information and our emotions – the behind-the-scenes of us and of the writing process. Share within the parameters of your comfort zone.
- *Don't rush.* People need to be able to follow what you are saying and are more likely to listen if you are confident and measured. Don't be too serious, but don't be too flippant either.
- *Practise.* Encapsulate your book in summaries of varying length. Give each summary a beginning, a middle and an end.
- *Prepare talks for different scenarios.* If you are a children's author, you may want to prepare a workshop, a reading and an author talk for the different age levels your book is pitched at.
- *Debrief.* After every interview and event, don't just give a sigh of relief and forget about it. Ask yourself what worked and what didn't. Make notes and review them ahead of the next event.

These tips apply to face-to-face interactions, and a number of them also apply online. So, let's look at the best way that you can manage your brand through websites and social media.

When to create a website

A website can be an invaluable author tool, and is a logical place for your audience to try to connect with you and find out more about your book. The best time to set up a website is once you have a sense of your own brand and something to promote. One benefit of setting up a website while you are still writing is that it creates a forum for potential readers to become excited by your project and follow you on your journey.

If you are a prolific writer and blogger, a website can be a good platform to build early, especially if it contains a place to promote information, reviews and news about your book after it is published, and to tell stories about the process while it is being written. If you don't tend to generate much content, it may make sense to launch a website closer to the time when you have a publication date. The site can become a simple forum for your audience (readers, media, reviewers, events organisers, librarians, teachers, peers) to reach you and learn more about your work.

Bear in mind when setting up a website that many author interactions take place not here but on social media, and so your website may function as the shopfront for you where browsers can check out you and your product. Make sure your site contains links to your social media platforms.

Tips for setting up a website

Take a look at the websites of authors you admire and ask:

- What types of information do they contain (e.g. publication lists, blog posts, reviews, event schedules)?
- Are they written in the first person or the third?
- How do they visually convey their brand (e.g. graphics, images, font and colour choice)?
- How do they convey their brand through voice and tone?
- What works well and what's easy to use?
- What opportunities do these sites provide for interaction?
- With what frequency do authors post updates?

Then, thinking about your own website, ask yourself:

- What information do I have or want to convey?
- What is my brand and what written and visual elements will I use to convey it?
- How much content will I have to provide and how often can I provide it?
- Who do I want to attract to this site, and what categories do they fit into (e.g. not only readers but media, event organisers and other writers)?
- How much interaction do I wish to have with readers?
- How much do I want to share about my life beyond my writing?
- How much time am I willing to spend working on my website?

Going through this process should give you a sense of what you would like to have on your website and how you intend to use it. When setting up your website some key elements to include are:

- A contact page – think carefully if you want to be contacted directly, or via your agent or publisher.
- An author biography for events presenters and journalists to access.
- Easy-to-download high-resolution book cover images, along with author headshots, or link to where your publisher provides these.
- Capacity to be expanded.

If you are not a web designer, now is the time to invest in professional help. An unprofessional-looking website is *not* better than having no website at all. Whenever you can, use an editor and a proofreader to review any written material before you put it online. Get friends to test-drive your website to check it is intuitive, friendly and accessible. Talk to your publisher about linking your sites and about what kinds of crossover content you can provide each other.

Ask an author: What is the importance of having a website?

Natasha Lester says:
First and foremost, a website is a place where readers can find out more about you and your books. Try to give it a personality – let the

website reflect who you are. You might only have a book out every couple of years so, ideally, to develop loyal readers, you need to give them a way to connect to you as well as your books. A website means that you can have a presence all the time, in between books, whereas books might only be on a shelf for two months.

It's also a way to connect with potential sources of income. Through the contact page on my website, I regularly get emails from libraries, schools, writers centres, writers festivals and other organisations inviting me to conduct a workshop, do an author talk or present or take part in a panel. This is a great way for writers to earn extra income to supplement their writing. Without a website, I would miss so many opportunities.

Websites help with your publicity too. You can put your media bio on there as well as book cover images, blurbs, background information about the book and lots more so that interviewers and media have all the info they need in the one place. They're more likely to write a longer and lovelier article about you if you make it easy for them.

And Meg McKinlay says:

I think an informative and up-to-date website is essential. I set mine up once my debut novel was contracted, but these days many people establish a professional web presence much earlier, along with their very first steps towards writing for publication.

There can be a few reasons for this. Perhaps you want to hang out a shingle, publicly declare your intentions. Perhaps you're taking first steps into the writing community itself. Social media has a fluid, transient quality; a website is like an online home people can visit and get a more focused sense of who you are. 'People' also means industry professionals – publishers, agents, event organisers, funding bodies. When submitting work or applying for emerging writer opportunities, include your website address; if your work piques a gatekeeper's interest, giving them the chance to easily learn more about you can only be a good thing.

Once you're contracted and then published, the role of your website will change and the material there should reflect that. An effective website can function as a one-stop shop for inquiries of all kinds, saving you valuable time in the process. If people can find the resources and information they need – book details, media-ready photographs, bios, information about speaking engagements and so on – there, a lot of email back-and-forth can be avoided. For children's writers, adding additional information about individual books and their backstories serves a similar function for the many young readers writing book reviews and school assignments.

Your website needs to be professional, easy to navigate and kept up to date with new material. You don't have to set it up yourself, although these days that is not difficult to do, but you should be able to update it yourself so this is quickly and easily done. You should also write the content yourself, in your own voice; give visitors a sense of the person behind the writer, rather than just facts.

Why and how to participate in social media

To activate another metaphor: if your website is the shopfront where your product is displayed, then the rest of social media is the local pub or café – the places you go to hang out with others. And when it comes to social media, it is important to understand where your audience is so that you can interact with them. In these places, how you converse depends on the context of where you are and who you are talking to. Tim Coronel, general manager of The Small Press Network, advises, 'Be yourself. Be comfortable with the platforms that you use. There is no point jumping in and using different platforms unless you understand how their communities and how they work.'

Flexibly inhabiting and understanding the voices of different platforms comes more easily to some than to others. If any particular platform is new to you, hang out there to work out how it operates, what its function is, what its tone is, who uses it and how. Social media platforms appear and change all the time, and you will need to change and adapt with them. But the fundamental principles of communication remain the same.

Paranormal romance writer Daniel de Lorne says:

Social media is there to serve a purpose, and that is to build a relationship with your readers, but you should do, and share, only what feels right for you and your brand. If you're forcing yourself to be on social media, whatever the channel, examine why that is so and whether it's worthwhile you being there. Ideally you want to use the platform where the bulk of your readers are, so that could be Instagram, it could be in Facebook groups, but wherever it is, you need to be sure it's worth your time. If you've decided you're going to focus on only one or two platforms, figure out what you're going to post and how it supports your brand. Remember not to spam followers with 'buy my book' posts, as that will quickly turn them off. Post content that gives insight into, and an opportunity to connect with, you and your work. Be aware that social media isn't the only way to connect with your readers. Establishing your own e-newsletter is a great way of building a following that you can talk to, often with much greater success than social media. It's not perfect, but it does give you a direct method of communication. Whatever you choose, keep in mind you are building a relationship with your readers, not just treating them as a customer to whom you advertise.

It is important to remember that, while a publisher has a certain budget to promote your work within a certain timeframe, the person best equipped to reinforce, support and supplement any promotions campaign is you. Being social shouldn't be onerous or stressful. Finding a mode of delivery that feels authentic is important, as is understanding the audience who will be receiving it.

A 2018 survey found that 91% of all social media users are on Facebook.[4] Writers are storytellers and storytelling is prioritised on Facebook, so the verbally dextrous are well equipped to interact with and build an audience in a way that doesn't involve hard-selling. But each platform has its own uses. If you're a writer-illustrator and you want to engage with parents, then Instagram, with its focus on visuals and videos, might be a good place for you to try instead.

If you don't know how to use social media, get someone who does to take you on a tour. Facebook and other platforms run online tutorials. Or ask at your local library for help. Understand hashtags and how to use them. Teach yourself how to take good photos and edit them with Photoshop, Canva or one of the many photo editing apps available, how to tweet, and how to make a fifteen-second Instagram video. Many local community and arts centres now offer short courses in photography for social media.

---

4. *Yellow Social Media Report 2018*, 'Consumers. Executive Summary', p. 4. yellow.com.au/wp-content/uploads/2018/06/Yellow-Social-Media-Consumer-Stats.pdf.

Tips for effective social media participation

To make social media work for you, Claire Miller advises that you should:

- Decide whether yours is business page or a personal one and how you'll separate the two.
- Use one or two platforms well rather than many badly.
- Pick and regularly use channels where your audience is.
- Look at *when* your audience is online and be online then too.
- Join groups and be an active member of them.
- Create an author profile on Goodreads (check first to see if your publisher has set one up).
- Participate on Goodreads by reviewing other books, sharing what you are reading, joining relevant groups, linking your blog posts to your profile, posting events and reading authors' blogs for marketing ideas.
- Soft-sell – talk about topics that are in tune with your book and your audience, or tell a story about your experience of being a writer.
- If the platform has hashtags, research which are used by your audience and start to use those too.
- Link to, tag or hashtag your publisher.
- Link to other people and organisations with like audiences (those with whom your own audience is hanging out).
- Make sure that your website and social media have links to each other and to your publisher's site.

Hancock Creative founder and director Alecia Hancock runs social media training courses for charities, not-for-profits and social enterprises. These are her recommendations for effective participation in social media:

- *Plan ahead.* The most successful social media channels have a documented playbook. Rather than posting content on a day-by-day basis, it's about taking the time to really think through your strategy for your social media channels and document what that looks like. It means the content you create will be more strategic and effective, it will drive clear outcomes and you will be able to create good-quality content much faster. Without a playbook, your content is going to be influenced by your mood, the amount of free time you have on any given day and what you've been working on earlier that day – instead of being focused, structured and productive.

- *Heed market, message and medium fit.* If your social media isn't driving outcomes for you, the problem is most likely with the market, message and medium fit. Either your market (who you're talking to), message (the content you're putting out to that market) or the medium (the channel on which you are sharing content) is not aligned to your strategy. Pulling just one of these circles back into alignment can dramatically change the outcomes from your social media.
- *Be vulnerable on social media.* The biggest mistake people make is always trying to portray the perfect, shiny version of their story instead of the more real one. If people think you've got it all together, they are going to be less motivated to support you. When you share the ups and downs, it is much more real and people are more likely to be invested in your story.
- *Encourage engagement.* I remember years ago, while working with rural fiction author Fleur McDonald, one of our most effective social media posts was when she shared that she was stumped for a good name for a sheep. So many people commented with suggestions that we were able to pick the best one and that person got a short acknowledgement in the back of the book. By including your readers in the writing journey, they feel like they are part of the book and are really invested in it succeeding.

Effective social media expression and curation turns on the idea of knowing yourself and being yourself. Ask: what can you uniquely offer? Following Alecia's advice, Claire Miller suggests you aim for posts focused on one or a combination of the following:

- *Your vision and values.* This is a topic we touched on in Chapter 3. Messages about your vision, values and goals can be powerful tools for authors. Sharing posts about what you believe in and what you stand for is a good way to find like-minded people, provided this is done in a respectful and inclusive rather than a polarising way.
- *Education.* Sharing a fact or making a statement that informs your audience adds value to your posts.
- *Engagement.* Do a poll to actively ask your audience to respond to something, such as what is their favourite opening line to a novel or what signature cocktail your detective should drink.
- *Recommendation.* Share something you have enjoyed or something you think your audience will be interested in.

- *Invitation.* Do you do lots of events? Share your forthcoming gigs in the events section of your page.
- *Taking your audience behind the scenes.* Have posts about your writing-related activities, interesting facts or elements of research, or insights into the writing process. Posts that show you ferreting out weird and wonderful facts might work.
- *Introduction/cooperation.* Include posts that begin with 'Have you met …?' or 'Did you know …?' Working with writing peers and colleagues, and featuring them on your channels and vice versa, can create opportunities for education, recommendation and conversation all in one post.
- *Showing not telling.* You don't always have to tell people what you stand for – you can show them by the links that you share.
- *Peaks and troughs.* Dial yourself up and down, emphasising site curation when you are not in 'campaign mode' to give people a break from when you have a book to sell. In the direct lead-up to the publication, it is not unreasonable to post a link to enable people to buy your book, but hanging out more generally with salespeople is not much fun.
- *Variety.* Don't utilise the same material on different platforms. The same generic content will be off-putting to people. Think about who your audience is on each platform and what your content needs to contain in order to attract them. Be surprising: post the content that breaks up the feed by eliciting an emotion or jolting people into engagement.
- *Visuals.* Visuals are an efficient tool and break up the feed. Upload a picture of what you are currently researching, or your book in a bookshop, or you talking to a book club or a picture of your work-in-progress after you dropped it in the bath. Are you an author-illustrator? Maybe look at sharing process videos showing how you draw certain elements. Start building up a database of visual materials that you can share online.

Allocating time to being online

Although it can often feel like a mindless distraction, social media is a powerful tool for a writer. You can get out and meet your audience members one by one, or you can meet many all at once on social media. It is a place you can be authentic and hone your author brand, and a place where you can interact with your audience. The scope and quantity of your interaction can depend on a variety of factors including your age, the demographic of your audience and the kinds of books that you write.

Selecting the intervals at which to provide new material is up to you. It makes sense that some of your time on social media is spent replying to people who choose to directly engage with you: talk to possible future readers and people who have taken the time and trouble to read and respond to your work.

Holden Sheppard carefully structures his social media interactions, treating it as a part-time job all on its own. His social media management tips reveal strategy and structure:

- *Schedule time in your diary or calendar to spend on social media.* I usually spend an hour or two in the late afternoon or early evening updating my social media channels, and also check in in the early morning for maybe thirty minutes. In 2016, I attended a webinar where a marketing expert told us to spend thirty minutes every day on Twitter. It sounded excessive, but I wanted to succeed, so I did what he said. It worked. The more I tweeted, the more people interacted with me.

- *Post regularly.* A regular presence shows people that you're actually active as a writer and engaged with your audience. For my Facebook author page, I tend to post three times per week; on Instagram, I aim for one post each day and maybe two or three stories; and on Twitter, I tweet several times per day. My average number of tweets per day is about twenty.

- *Be authentic.* Don't be a sales bot online who only talks about their own book and where it can be purchased. Share the real moments on your journey – the ups and the downs. Don't be afraid to show your face – literally. Sharing the occasional selfie encourages people to connect with you.

- *Select the right content for the right platform.* I don't always post the same content across all three channels, as each channel lends itself to different features. I use my Facebook author page for major news announcements about my books, media and events, and updates on my writing progress. On Twitter, I try to have more fun, posting funny anecdotes, sharing other writers' tweets, and generally doing some larrikin shitposting. Instagram is where I show my more human side and focus less on promo, so this is where I share things like shirtless gym selfies or photos of me doing hobbies like playing footy, guitar, video games or weightlifting.

- *Avoid posting extensively about your political views.* The old-fashioned advice about polite topics for dinner parties applies doubly so for social media. A lot of people are ready to argue and there can be a lot of online negativity. I personally choose not to air my views on every single matter, unless it's particularly important to me and in line with who I am as a person, such as something about gay rights. The caveat with this advice would be that if you're a journalist, or your branding as an author is explicitly political – for instance, you're an activist and you've written a book about the topic you lobby for – then of course you'd be expected to engage with politics on your feed.
- *Don't worry about follower numbers.* Don't stress about only having a few hundred followers. Follower numbers, while in some ways a valuable metric of reach and social media impact, aren't everything. I've seen many writers who have paid for, say, 20,000 followers, but when you look at their feed, their tweets have no likes and no comments – no real people are actually engaging with them at all! What you want to aim for is engagement: conversations with real people who you are connecting with organically. Over time, this will grow.
- *Reciprocity is king.* You can't expect support unless you are willing to be generous and support others.

You may find it a daunting prospect to try to hold down a part-time social media job in the same way that Holden Sheppard does. But his principles can be applied in quantities that work for you. James Foley offers a couple of additional tips:

Only post on social media as much and as often as you feel comfortable doing. People talk about the algorithms and say 'you need to post three or four or ten times a day to get yourself seen!' But what human being has time to post that many times a day? Don't let it become a chore. Don't do social media with the aim of selling books, but instead with the aim to connect with fans, fellow creatives and communities. Sales will follow. I forget this more often than I care to admit.

Make sure you have photo geotagging turned off on your phone. Otherwise people could use the information in the photos on your social media to figure out where you live. Don't panic! Just do a quick Google search for your phone model and find out how to do it. Most people on social media are extremely nice and polite, but

I've had some run-ins with really quite odd and concerning people over the years – so I'd prefer to keep my private life private.

At the time your book comes out, you won't have time to organise publicity. This kind of preparation needs to be done months in advance. Start by sharing aspects of the book and its process (illustrations, pictures of things that inspired you, landscapes, items pertinent to themes) months in advance. Closer to the release date, do something more targeted that promotes and entertains at the same time. Prepare these posts in advance so you can easily share them on social media around the release date.

If you find social media addictive, or timewasting, install an app in your phone that limits your use.

Ask an author: How do you manage your profile and maintain a dialogue with your audience while remaining authentic on social media?

Deb Fitzpatrick says:
Don't make it all about you. Be tangential. Post links to articles about writing and publishing. Be excited for other people's successes – share these! Encourage others to write, and post links to opportunities for emerging writers. Be funny; post photos of yourself being silly. And then, every so often, post something really meaningful your book has been able to achieve – perhaps you've received an email from a teacher raving about how enthused her class of reluctant readers is about your book. Perhaps you scored a great review somewhere, or a class of kids sent you handwritten letters asking you all sorts of funny questions or showing you their cute drawings. (Just check with the school first that you have permission to share!) Perhaps a young person dealing with a mental illness wrote to you telling you how much your book helped her or him and you can reflect on this.

Show gratitude for all those who've helped you on the way, and who continue to help you. For example, reply to each and every one of those children who wrote to you. Acknowledge every comment on Facebook, Instagram, Twitter and other platforms you use – show your appreciation for the time these readers have taken with your work. There are thousands of other books they could have chosen, so it really is something to be grateful for. Write a blog post showcasing the amazing welcome you've received from librarians during CBCA's Book Week, and use photos. Social media devours photos! (Again, be aware that you will need permission to use photos of children online. One way of getting around this is to photograph students from behind – show them scribbling away during a writing workshop, for example.)

Finally, share some more serious stuff with readers from time to time, such as other writers' posts about the struggle to maintain momentum in the difficult economic situation we often experience. Share the odd personal story; let yourself be vulnerable.

James Foley says:

I'm still learning and experimenting with this. I don't think people want to see you always posting the good stuff – the 'look at me and this award I just won / contract I just signed' stuff. They don't want the constant sales pitch either: 'Buy my new book! Give it a five-star review on Goodreads!' People want authenticity. They want to make a connection with you, a fellow human being.

Ask yourself why you follow the people you do on social media. What do they offer you? Is it insight into their creative process? Q&As? Candid political commentary? Witty personal anecdotes? Inspirational advice? Then ask yourself, what would you feel comfortable offering on your social media? Because that's what it is, in a way ... you're offering something to others. It's called social media for a reason. It's designed so we can make social connections with others. Sure, it has its dark side – the vapid, artificial, sanitised lifestyle promoted by Instagram influencers; the Nazi trolls on Twitter – but there's a good side too, and there are millions of great people out there who want to make a connection.

Natasha Lester says:

Social media will take as much of your time and attention as you choose to give it. So only give it enough that it doesn't detract from your writing. Writing is the most important thing to do as a writer!

I use social media to keep people up to date with what I'm doing. It's easy to be authentic because I'm simply posting images and updates about what I'm working on that day. You might see a post with an image of a pile of paper because I'm about to read through my manuscript, or a picture of a beautiful dress because I'm writing a scene featuring that dress, or a collage of reader pics of my books that readers have sent to me that week, or a snap of me out at an event.

It means my social media is easy and doesn't take too much time. I'm not trying to make it into anything more than a record of my activities as a writer. And readers love to know what goes on behind the scenes.

I always respond to reader comments; if someone takes the time to engage with you, it's only polite to reply.

And I use social media to follow other authors whose books I like. Sometimes this develops into the formation of writerly friendships and it's always good when you're on the publishing rollercoaster to have a supportive network around you.

Sasha Wasley says:

I'm lucky because I happen to run the social media accounts for a not-for-profit as a part-time job, and my role included a year-long mentorship with a respected social media agency. I learned how to plan and schedule content, run promotions and understand analytics. This was all brilliant background knowledge for my own social accounts.

I quickly discovered that trying to sell books in every post would not endear me to my followers. There must be a balance between posts offering engagement, education (giving away my expertise for free), personality and products. I also learned that people are more likely to engage with my content if I interact with them. When someone comments, I make sure to respond.

I have pulled right back on my personal social media use in the past year or so because of its addictive nature. I now focus on putting up occasional quality posts across Instagram, Twitter and Facebook. I try to make them conversational, smart and fun. I concentrate less on selling and more on building interest in the things I'm passionate about because those things are generally in my books.

It can be hurtful when reviewers share their average (or bad) ratings of your book and the temptation is to argue. I cannot stress enough that arguing with a bad review is one of the worst things an author can do. If the people watching get annoyed enough, they will vindictively one-star your book on Goodreads as revenge (even if they haven't read it). If you think a review is great, share and gush away. If it's okay but not amazing, maybe just hit the 'like' button and leave it at that. If it's bad, pretend you never even saw it.

And Anne-Louise Willoughby says:
Managing a social media profile takes effort, and consistency is the key. I have established a website where visitors can see my work and, importantly, from a positioning point of view, read the press articles relating to my work, and check in on my scheduled events and appearances. Your website can be your best résumé. This is fixed and available at all times, and doesn't rely on showing up in someone's feed. The options range from contracting a website designer to do-it-yourself set-ups; I used Squarespace and created my own with help from a tech-savvy friend and a patient daughter.

I use a public Instagram account as my main social media platform and, less often, my Facebook, which is private. My Instagram is linked to a gallery on my website as a direct feed so it automatically updates. I manually select when I want my Instagram to feed into Facebook when I am promoting an event. I aim to have a 'gentle' presence on Instagram and try to post once a week with writing-related content, while at the same time occasionally adding moments in my life that share a little about myself while maintaining my privacy. I always ask permission before I include anyone else in my posts. Posting for the sake of maintaining a presence rings hollow for me and is exhausting. Set out a clear approach to what you want your social media to communicate and stick to what you know you can sustain.

Navigating social media aversion

Social media should be a tool, not a monster. It is there to be used rather than to swallow you whole. Some writers don't use it because they don't want to enter the vortex or they wish to protect their privacy. Others may be worried about attracting criticism or negativity, about what people might find out about them, about friends' and family's reactions to a book, about making an awful mistake that goes viral for the wrong reasons, or about dropping their work into a vacuum and feeling ignored. So it is not surprising that some people are wary engagers or choose not to go there at all, especially if they feel immersion may adversely affect their mental health and wellbeing.

If you do feel wary but would still like to give social media a go, sometimes acknowledging your fears and having a plan can enable you to overcome them. Below is an exercise to do just that.

If you are a reluctant beginner, perhaps just give social media a try, knowing you can disengage at any time if you find it's not for you.

An exercise to help overcome social media aversion

Here's a suggestion for what to do if you find yourself baulking at the idea of entering the social media world:

- Make a list of the things that you most fear happening. Next to each one, write down how you'll react if it does.
- Make a plan for the worst-case scenario: if A happens I will do B, C and D. If you can't think of a B, C or D, ask your publicist or your peers for their advice.
- Now write down the best-case scenario – what you want to happen and why you're doing what you're doing: this will give you some positive goals and reasons to enter the fray.
- Put this list somewhere you can find it so you know you have a plan. Your worries are much better tucked behind the ceramic goat on the mantelpiece than causing undue anxiety in your head.

In the next chapter, we will turn from thinking about self-promotion back to looking at how your publisher's marketing and communications team can help you to promote your book.

9. Your publisher and the business of promotion

- The role of the marketing and communications team
- The stages of book promotion
- Tips for working with the team promoting your book
- Working with a publicist
- Pitching for promotion
- Festivals, panels, interviews and readings
- Tips for preparing for public appearances
- Bookshop etiquette post-publication
- Tips for a positive bookshop relationship
- A final word on being an author at large

Experience has shown us that the amount of enthusiasm an author brings to the promotional aspects of being a writer has a direct bearing on how their work is received. In this chapter we will look at how to make the most of opportunities as you introduce your work to the world. But first we will look at the team invested in making a success of you and your work.

The role of the marketing and communications team

In Australia, where over 22,000 *new* print and ebook titles are published each year,[5] competition for attention is fierce, and there is little time or space to get every book substantial shelf space or coverage. A bookshop may be listening to more than five hundred pitches a month from sales

---

5. 'The Market Down Under', booksandpublishing.com.au/articles/2018/10/02/116464/the-market-down-under-2. In 2018, the total number of books sold in Australia, including trade and academic books, was 61.1 million ('Australian Market Overview', booksandpublishing.com.au/articles/2019/02/28/126097/australian-market-overview).

reps or publishers, so the marketing strategy and storytelling for a title needs to be exciting, genuine and authentic.

The positive reception of a book assists the success of the author, and vice versa. While there is no doubt that word of mouth sells books, the management of how the package of author-plus-book reaches the public will be vital to the book's success. While you must be an active participant in your own promotion, there is a team that is also responsible for your success, and for the success of the publishing house via the sale and promotion of your book. Attractive and apt design is an important component of a book's successful reception, but a great deal hangs on the efforts of the marketing and communications team in the publishing house, who are experts in the art of selling stories.

As with the bookselling ducks cruising about on the placid lake of the bookshop, in the publishing house there is a great deal of vigorous promotional paddling going on that is never seen by authors. Some publishing houses have a marketing team, a communications team and a sales team. Some have a marketing and communications team with an external sales team. Some smaller publishers may outsource all three teams or have just one person doing the lot. There are many variations from house to house depending on the state of the market, the structure of the company and the support shown by upper management. Generally, in small to mid-sized companies, the marketing manager is also the communications manager, and the marketing coordinator may also be the event coordinator or sales support officer or publicist. Specialist social media managers and digital marketers are more common than they once were, and some multinational publishing companies have an entire department devoted to author event bookings. In this chapter we will refer to this collection of promotional people as the marketing and communications team.

The *marketing and sales support* side of the team tends to be the conduit between the producers of the book (editorial and production) and the sellers of the book (sales reps and booksellers). Their tasks are very deadline driven, with much of the major marketing push timed to happen upon the book's release or timed to coincide with major sales periods such as Mother's Day or Christmas. No matter who is on your team and how it is organised – and we recommend you find out in order to build a relationship with them – the following tasks are likely to be on their to-do lists:

- Researching the market for your book, where your audience hangs out and how to reach them.
- Advising the editorial team on the book cover and blurb.
- Briefing the sales team on the book and planned marketing campaigns.
- Presenting your books to key markets, such as bookshops and buying groups, teachers, librarians.
- Creating and distributing advance information material to support sales reps in selling the book.
- Researching, creating, monitoring and updating search terms, hashtags and phrases for online distributors and search engines.
- Creating online blurbs for websites.
- Creating partnerships with organisations who might promote the book.
- Working alongside the sales team to pitch the book to bookstores for inclusion in their catalogues.
- Creating merchandise (e.g. bookmarks, worksheets, posters, book club notes, teaching notes and flyers).
- Creating marketing materials (e.g. print catalogues and advertisements).
- Creating advertising campaigns and securing advertising space online and in print media.
- Researching and implementing re-marketing opportunities for backlist titles.
- Planning, running and creating content for social media, web and electronic direct mail campaigns – this crosses over with the publicist's role.

The *communications and publicity* side of the team tends to focus on being the conduit between an author and their audience. A member of this team may have the title of publicist, or that role may be absorbed within others. This side of the marketing and communications team nurtures relationships with the people who have existing networks and who can be encouraged to champion your book. Though this role is deadline driven and focused on the big promotional push around the release of your book, the communications side is also about finding new news: fresh stories to tell that will sell your book after its initial release and which could lead to a re-marketing campaign. This side tells the stories and, much like a support act at a music festival, gets the crowd ready for the main event – in this case, the publication of the book and the introduction of the author. Some of the things the communications and publicity side may do for an author include:

- Understanding the themes of the book.
- Meeting the author to work out hooks and angles for their book.
- Getting to know the author (e.g. their strengths, skills, goals, weaknesses).
- Devising strategies for how to promote them.
- Understanding the author's comfort zones and no-go areas to assist with handling interviews and with the book's promotion.
- Capitalising on the author's existing connections and already established community of readers.
- Creating content around the book and author (e.g media releases, blog posts, interviews, videos, podcasts).
- Pitching the author's work to festivals and other events.
- Pitching story ideas to the media.
- Providing event, media and social media training as required.
- Accompanying the author to events.
- Organising a book launch (if this is something the publisher does).
- Assisting with author bookings for events.
- Sending the author reviews and mentions of their book.
- Promoting the author's book in newsletters and industry publications.
- Sourcing opportunities for placement of excerpts from the book.
- Arranging print and radio interviews for the author.
- Planning, creating and scheduling content for social media.
- Monitoring and responding to audience engagement.

Keep in mind that both sides of the team are doing all these things not just with one but multiple books at different stages of promotion. They are busy people! In building a relationship and staying in touch with them, find out from team members how they best prefer to communicate. One long email with your comments and questions? A series of short emails? A short email requesting a phone call? You can also make clear to them (through your email subject or phone call) what is and is not urgent in your list of requests and queries.

The stages of book promotion

There is a perception that much of the activity around a book's promotion occurs in the several months around the publication date. But if that was when a book's promotion and marketing actually began, it would be way too late.

From the moment a book is presented to the marketing and communications team, they start to think what hooks can be attached to your particular work: How are they going to pitch it? What stories can they tell about it and you? Who is the audience and how are they going to reach it? What does your book offer that is unique, compelling or timely that will create a buzz? How much budget and time will they need to assign the book?

The team starts by 'warming up' all the possible conduits to a book's future audience, creating a buzz around your book. They do this by telling stories and getting people engaged, then providing those people with the tools they need to sell your book or story to their networks. This might look like 'just talking' to an observer, but this seeding phase is vital in getting the right people invested in the idea of this book. The promotions team has a wealth of pre-existing connections and relationships, and a sense of who will be a good fit for any given book. Involving who the author already knows will expand this range of connections and provide access to an invested audience who can amplify the buzz around a book. This is one very good reason for filling in your contributor information form as soon as possible after your contract is signed (see p. 158).

The first thing the team will want to know from you is who you know. Via a contributor information form or a meeting with you, they will ask:

- Who do you know in the media and in your own industry?
- What kinds of networks do you already have?
- What clubs or organisations are you a member of?
- Which is your local bookshop?
- Which members of your community can you encourage to engage with your local bookshop?
- Who do you know who will be likely to buy your book?

Your biographical details and book synopsis will inform the team about who you are and what you think your book is about (though this won't always align precisely with what they think your book is about). Your list of keywords and phrases will show them how and where you think your book fits into a broader context. The more you can do to support the team by supplying connections to your own networks, the better.

The marketing and communications team will have a range of individuals and organisations that they will target in the many months prior to the book's release. These include, but are not limited to:

- National and international sales reps.
- Specialist distributors, booksellers and book clubs.
- Ebook distributors.
- Advertising reps and booking agencies.
- Possible partner organisations (e.g. book councils, author organisations, education associations and foundations).
- Festival directors and event managers.
- Key people in cultural industries.
- Librarians, teachers and community arts officers.
- Traditional media outlets.
- Freelance journalists and reviewers.
- Bloggers, podcasters and social media influencers.
- Other authors.
- Funding bodies and sponsors.

In short, they will contact anyone who will be able to assist the book and its author gain traction in the market. These people will be approached not just once, but multiple times, using appropriate angles of appeal. When different industry people each receive a particular tailored story about the book, it means that when they get together to talk books, more information is disseminated between them, which helps to generate a buzz around the book. A marketing and communications team may refine their pitches depending on the response of the recipients, because there are always more possible angles to choose when it comes to pitching an author, their book and its ideas.

All of this early promotional work runs alongside and feeds back into both the book's cover and blurb. A unique strategy is created to remind the team what the goals are for each book and what they'll do to achieve them. The strategy provides the style rules around the book's messages, describes the audiences and where to reach them, outlines the resources and budget available, provides notes on methods of attraction and includes a timeline setting out who is responsible for tasks such as booking advertising, creating merchandise, pitching to the media, distributing catalogues etc. Depending on the publishing house, you may not have a chance to have input in this process; alternatively your input may be considered essential.

You may experience the publicity of your book as being a period of around three months, because that is when publicity is coming out, and when booksellers want to work with you, and when your book appears in bookshops. What you won't necessarily see is all the tangible and intangible work that has been, and is being, done on your behalf from the point of contract. Without the much longer lead-in created by the marketing and communications team, this intensely focused publicity period that you are experiencing would be far less effective.

Tips for working with the team promoting your book

There are a number of things you as an author can do to support the marketing and communications team. Begin by thinking of your interaction with the team as a partnership. Here are some tips from Claire Miller for how to work together to promote your book:

- *Focus on the partnership.* Don't call the marketer or communications professional the 'PR girl'. By doing so, you are making an assumption about their gender and undermining their professionalism. Most marketing and communication professionals in the book trade read books. Many will be better read than you are. They have a vast range of experience in book promotion and, most likely, a couple of degrees.
- *Communicate.* If you tell the team everything you're doing, they will be in a position to let the sales team know and to amplify your efforts. Also, this prevents you from duplicating your efforts.
- *Listen.* If a member of the team takes the time to give you some advice, you don't have to accept it, but you should carefully consider it. Find out why they think the way they do and listen to what they recommend. It's worth listening to anyone sharing their expertise.
- *Keep biographical details current.* Create bio notes in several sizes – fifty, seventy-five and 150 words. Keep them up to date and keep the team informed of any changes relating to your publications, day job, speaking experience, social media channels and website address.
- *Review your contacts.* Bring along ideas for publicity or stories to meetings with team members. And be prepared with the names of your local booksellers, libraries, newspapers and any connections who may be interested in publicising your book.
- *Say yes to training.* If someone in the team offers media training, event training or social media training, do it. Learn everything you can.
- *Say yes to opportunities.* There is enormous competition for publicity. Consider all the offers presented to you and try to do as many as you

can. Then try to make the most of them. If you do well at a community radio gig, it may help your team secure opportunities to talk to radio stations with larger audiences. The more you do, the better you'll get at publicity, and the better you are at publicity, the more PR opportunities you're likely to attract.

- *Speak up.* Do raise concerns in instances where you believe undertaking a PR gig could harm your author brand. Discuss it with your publicist to see if there are creative ways to manage the risk. If you are contacted directly for a PR opportunity that you don't want to do, refer it to the team. They can extricate you without you becoming the villain, and they will most likely redirect it to another author who may be better suited to it.
- *Be professional.* If you are consistently underprepared for interviews, or unenthusiastic or resistant to promotional opportunities, or denigrate the publishing house or are churlish, the team will channel publicity opportunities elsewhere.

Working with a publicist

The publicist's role in the marketing and communications team is to be at the frontline of your book's promotion. The publicist provides access to networks and contacts you would find difficult to reach on your own. They protect you from time-wasters. They find new ways to connect with your audience. They are your cheerleader and your risk manager. As your book gets to the point of production and release, publicists will be among the first people to tell the story of you and your book to the world. If you can get them to understand who you are and what your book is about, and if you can get them enthusiastic about both, then they will be a powerful promotional partner for you.

Ask an author: How do you make the most of working with a publicist?

Sasha Wasley says:
The first thing you need to understand is that you are just one of many authors your publicist is paid to promote. If you're a debut author, they will generally work a little harder for you.

The second thing you should know is that publicists often move very quickly from role to role in the publishing industry, so you might get a different one for each book. Transitions between publicists may result in information being lost, so make sure you keep your own records of your bookings and appointments.

Be prepared to do a lot of work to promote your own book. This could mean writing blog posts, doing interviews or making public appearances. Don't schedule any major editing, writing or family events around release time!

To work well with your publicist, try to set expectations early in the relationship. Write a list of the kinds of activities you are prepared to do to help generate publicity for your book. You may have some innovative ideas the publicist will get behind. Keep communicating with your publicist regularly so you are in their mind when opportunities arise and so you don't lose track of any author commitments. Request a publicity itinerary if they don't offer one.

Lastly, be really nice to your publicist, because they are busy people with lots of authors to look after, and they may 'forget' to offer you good promotional opportunities!

Alan Carter says:

Listen and learn. The publicist has the skills and contacts to maximise your exposure, so let them get on with the job they know best. But if you have contacts and networks of your own, share them. You might know of people or organisations of influence directly concerned with the subject matter of your book. Your own career or experience of writing your book may be newsworthy. Store up your anecdotes and polish up the song and dance routine. This is no time to be a shrinking violet.

Liz Byrski says:

Make sure you talk to the publicist and discuss how they plan to promote your book. Ask as many questions as you wish and contribute anything you can. Don't hesitate to suggest possibilities for promotion, but don't expect a huge tour and crowded venues when you are just starting.

Treat them with respect and consideration. Many of them will be juggling a number of writers, some of whom may be really difficult or have huge egos.

Always turn up on time for events! Don't blame the publicist if only three people turn up when you were expecting thirty or three hundred. It happens to all of us at some time and the publicist will be just as frustrated as you.

Stay in touch with the publicist in the weeks prior to release, and also make some notes for yourself so you are prepared to stand up and speak confidently about your book.

Amanda Curtin says:

When you're asked to contribute information and ideas for marketing and selling your book, err on the side of comprehensiveness: you may be aware of niche markets and promotional possibilities that your publicist isn't. However, also have the humility to listen to and learn from what your publicist has to say, because they are experts in their field and usually have a lot of experience to draw on when considering what might and might not work.

Speak up if you feel uncomfortable about anything. Ultimately, you're the one in charge of your own identity, and you need to remain true to that. Make sure you understand everything that's required of you, and ensure that you're able to accommodate that.

Keep the publicist informed of anything you're doing or planning on your own. By communicating and working together, you'll avoid overlap and mixed messages. In any case, it's not always appropriate for authors to make a direct approach, and your publicist can advise on that.

Ask questions, be involved, but avoid making demands or complaints. Don't take out your frustration that things are not going as well as you'd hoped on someone who is on your side, often going above and beyond what's required of them.

And Holden Sheppard says:

Your publicist will be looking for every opportunity to get you exposure in the media and also book you for events. They will also be able to give you guidance about your own marketing strategy and are an excellent resource when you are unsure of something. My top tips for making the most of working with a publicist are:

- *Keep them in the loop.* Your publicist has to juggle many authors and has to keep many stakeholders happy at once. If a library, bookshop or school contacts you directly with an opportunity, it's always a good idea to CC your publicist into your response so they are aware of it. Not only does this mean they can build the opportunity into your schedule and support you with it, but it also ensures there aren't any clashes.

- *Share your ideas.* If you have out-of-the-box ideas for your book promo, let your publicist know. They might not like every suggestion you make, but you may just have some golden ideas or ideal media contacts – so definitely speak up.
- *Let them know what you're not comfortable with.* If there are any media questions or angles you aren't comfortable with, let your publicist know. For instance, if you don't want to discuss your family life or a past trauma in interviews, your publicist can manage that.
- *Ask their advice when you're stuck.* Publicists are PR experts. If you're approached by someone for media comment or an event booking and feel uncertain, or don't know the best response to give, your publicist may be able to help you craft a suitable response.
- *Be prepared to relinquish some control.* Your publicist will take the lead on preparing your media schedule and book tour, so while working with a publicist is a collaborative process, it does mean that you need to enable them to take the lead in putting these items together. A publicist's main ambition is to make your book sell as many copies as possible and have the biggest impact it can: they are on the same page as you, so it's important to trust them. Once you've established that sense of respect and trust, having a publicist is an absolute blessing – and it frees up more of your time to focus on writing.

Should I hire my own publicist?

Publicists in publishing houses work with other publicists all the time: with festival and event publicists, local government communications teams, publicists at other publishing houses and in the retail sector, film, television and theatre. Some specific reasons to hire your own publicist might be:

- If you are self-publishing and need assistance with promotion.
- If you are working with a small publisher that requires you to hire one because they have no in-house team.

- If your personal brand is already established in another area and you already have a personal PR person.
- If you have a friend in PR with good contacts offering to do a freebie.
- When you feel like you need particular mentoring in public relations and need someone to practise interview techniques or speeches with.

In the event that you hire your own publicist, discuss this with your publisher and ensure the terms of engagement and areas of responsibility of each party are clear. The publisher has invested thousands of dollars in your book and won't want to risk that investment on an unknown publicist. Put your proposed publicist in touch with your marketing and communications teams so they can negotiate how to share the workload and the vision about you and your book brand, and your goals for the book.

It is also important to be aware that it can be annoying for a journalist to be contacted multiple times by multiple publicists representing the same person.

Pitching for promotion

Both you and the communications and marketing team will need to pitch your book in order to promote it. People respond better to stories than stats, and storytelling is a great way to establish connection. We have already looked at pitching in Chapter 3, and in Chapter 8 we looked at self-promotion. Now we will look at those occasions when you will formally be called upon to pitch your book. The effectiveness of these pitches may determine whether someone chooses to buy or review your book, or invite you on to a festival panel.

The communications and marketing team will be able to work with you in thinking about the various ways to package your pitch and develop stories that link to contemporary events, themes or topics, and how to present to the different kinds of people you will be pitching to. Let's take a look at some of these categories.

The in-house team

The first people you will find yourself formally pitching to will be your in-house marketing and communications team. They need to hear your pitch for several reasons:

- So they can represent you accurately.
- So they understand who you think is the book's audience – keep in mind this won't always align with their ideas.
- To arm them with good stories so they can get their existing networks excited about you and your book.
- Because this demonstrates that you will perform well in interviews and events.
- To show them which areas you need to improve in.
- So they can share your excitement in the book you have just written.

There are a number of things you can write down or think about to prepare for this first pitch:

- Your unique selling point – there are probably other books out there that are like yours, but what makes yours unique?
- What other books inspired your writing or are similar to yours?
- Why did you write the book?
- What is unique about *your* background? What is *your* expertise?
- What are the search engine terms that may relate to your book?
- What anniversaries or media focuses make your book timely?
- Consolidate all that you've discovered by listening to your audience thus far and share it with the team.

The media

Talking to a journalist can happen as part of a formal interview or may occur at networking events or perhaps online via Twitter. Whether you've already secured an interview or are trying to, you need to tailor your responses to show the journalist that you are aware of the kinds of audiences that their media outlet is trying to reach. If you're going into a media interview, listen first to the program or read articles by the journalist. Understand who you will be talking to and what their interests are. This will help you think about what kinds of questions they may ask.

Here is how to best prepare for media interviews, scheduled or not:

- Keep an eye on the local and national media – particularly book media. Subscribe to industry news sources such as Books+Publishing and ArtsHub. Read the features and reviews in the arts section. Follow journalists writing on topics relevant to your book.

- Ask how your personal background might align with an outlet's audience – for instance, if you identify as LGBTQIA, you may be able to get a feature in publications and websites like *Star Observer* or *OUTinPerth*; if you're a First Nations person, the *National Indigenous Times*; if you're over sixty, *Have a Go News* or *The Senior*.
- Review the media outlet's advertising section on their website to understand their demographic, and your relevance to their audience.
- Keep in mind that a good story trumps all else, so aim to be proficient at giving clear, economical sound bites about you and your work.
- Ask yourself why your work is timely – do you have an event coming up, is your book related to something that's in the news, is there a 'world day' that's relevant to your subject matter and to the journalist you are talking to (e.g. International Women's Day, Zero Discrimination Day)?
- Ask yourself how your book is relevant to particular regions – did you grow up in the media outlet's distribution area, is the book set there, did you go to school there?
- Make notes and take them with you. Have a list of facts, names, dates and events so that if the journalist asks you something specific, you have these facts to hand. Prepare some anecdotes or sound bites to share with the interviewer.
- Have a sense of what key points you need to hit in any interview (e.g. your book title, a forthcoming event or anniversary). Check with your publicist if they have any additional points. Work these into your responses as naturally as possible if the journalist does not cover them.

Your audience

You may encounter your audience through the media, events, book clubs, social media etc. There are ways you can prepare to talk to this actual or theoretical cohort if you have given some thought to the following:

- Who is your audience? This is where all that listening and research becomes useful. By this stage, you should have a very clear idea about who your audience is, you will have spent some time interacting with them and you will be ready to introduce your own work.
- If you've been invited to speak somewhere, find out who the audience is going to be so you can adjust your story accordingly. Think ahead about points of commonality so you can converse in an honest way that's comfortable and true to who you are.

- If you turn up to a library and there's only one person at your talk, that one person could become your biggest ambassador for the book, so adjust your expectations and use the occasion as an opportunity to engage with and inspire that one person.
- When online, find out what engages your audience and participate in conversations with them. Think about ways to tell your story gradually, over time, in your own voice without any advertising speak.

Festivals, panels, interviews and readings

Public appearances are a way authors can directly connect with their audiences, find new readers and supplement their incomes. Your publicist may be looking to place you in as many public events as possible to build your profile and sell your book.

Every writers festival has its own themes, and is curated by a festival director with particular vision and tastes. There are many more writers than there are spots to fill in a festival, and established writers who draw an audience will of course be a priority for event organisers. Your publicist will need to cast the net wide to capture opportunities for you. Although you are just one of many unknown new writers, your book may fit with the theme at a festival, or your expertise or particular story may be perfect for a panel at a conference or symposium or a school event.

When attending events, do your homework so you understand the demographic of an audience, especially if your public appearances are taking place in the same city or town: keep it fresh, and don't duplicate material if you think there will be overlap between this and other audiences.

For children's authors, events in schools, including writing residencies, can form a significant part of their income even when these do not present direct opportunities to sell books. It is paramount that children's authors like engaging with their readers and potential readers, because they are going to spend a lot of time with them!

For poets, public readings or performances are often where a poet's audience congregates and where the majority of book sales may take place.

Writers centres regularly offer residencies, which involve an element of interaction with members, be that via readings of work in progress or workshops during the writer's stay. A writer who is willing to run a workshop on their genre or in their area of research or interest is more likely to find themselves being chosen over a 'non-interactive' author.

A note on being paid for public appearances

The ASA website has suggested rates of pay for authors and illustrators for appearances at events in public and at schools, as well as for residencies and for illustration work. It is vital that writers are rewarded for their professional expertise and do not attend events on the promise that it will give them a chance to sell their books or that it will give them exposure. Though not every event can afford to pay writers, you should not find yourself funding publicity ventures or being out of pocket for travel or accommodation to do so. Even so, you may not be awarded per diems (daily living expenses) for attending a particular event. And if the event is in the regions, you may find yourself a guest in somebody's house rather than being put up at more formal lodgings.

Be clear about the terms being offered at the time of an invitation. When contemplating the fee, it is good to ask: Does what I am being offered, in *these* circumstances, feel reasonable to me? What are the benefits of my doing this event? If you feel you are being exploited, or that you will wind up resenting what is being asked of you, it is certainly your choice to refuse an invitation, or ask your publicist to talk to event organisers to adjust or negotiate arrangements with which you are not comfortable.

One exception is that you should not expect to receive payment for an event hosted by a bookshop, such as a launch or book club event, because the bookshop is providing its staff, infrastructure, time and reader connections to promote and sell your book.

Tips for preparing for public appearances

The roles of the author and event organiser

In order to make the most of any public appearance, it is wise to read any brief carefully and ensure you understand the following:

- Who your audience is, and what their expectations may be.
- Who any other presenting participants will be.
- The mode of your contribution (e.g. discussion, presentation, reading, workshop).
- The duration of your session and how it may fit into a broader program.
- What you are definitely expected to cover.

- What is and isn't appropriate to discuss at this event.
- Whether there will be a place for merchandise and information related to your book.
- Whether books will be sold at this event, and by whom.
- Whether you will require a Working with Children Check.
- Whether you will require your own public liability insurance – this may be pertinent for events held in public spaces.

In turn, an event organiser should let you or your publicist know:

- Your rate of pay.
- Relevant details about accommodation and travel.
- What time they would like you to arrive, and what time the event itself will commence.
- Who else will be involved.
- The duration of the event and how long you will be expected to speak, plus any time allocated for discussions or Q&As.
- Whether there will be breaks and refreshments.
- What is available in terms of technology (e.g. microphone, audiovisual equipment).
- Availability of photocopying or printing for handouts if required.

Practical ways to prepare for events

Sometimes the more prepared and in control of your material you are, the more spontaneous and relaxed you appear to be, whereas if you are winging it, it shows. Preparation can turn terror or nerves into positive energy. If you have thought deeply ahead of time, this can also help you change direction on the spot if anything takes an unexpected turn. An event organiser may send you a full brief and runsheet about your event. If they haven't, or if there are gaps in the information, you should do the following:

- Contact your panel moderator or event MC if they haven't yet contacted you so that they can advise you of the parameters of the event.
- Find out whether you are expected to do an acknowledgement of country, or whether this role will fall to an MC.
- Find out who will be doing the introduction.
- Request biographical notes of your fellow participants so you can think about points of connection between you in advance.

- Read up on the place/organisation/event you are visiting so you understand the context of your participation.
- Promote the event on social media if it is a public event.
- Think about the content you are going to deliver and make notes.
- Select a number of short readings in advance so you have options.
- Practise reading your performance material aloud.
- Practise delivering your content in conditions similar to the real thing (at a podium, standing in front of people).
- Decide what props and surfaces during your presentation.
- Prepare any audio or visual material to accompany your appearance.
- Advise your event organiser of your technology requirements.
- Put PowerPoint presentations or material for printing out on a USB.
- Pack a copy of your book, business cards and relevant merchandise.
- Think about what strategies you will use if an event is not going well.
- Rehearse aloud questions that may put you outside your comfort zone.

Ask an author: How do you make the most out of public appearances?

Ambelin Kwaymullina says:
Engage with people. Sounds simple, right? But most writers find this hard because most writers are introverts. But if you're going to be a professional writer, especially if you are hoping for this to form a significant part of your income, you need to practise the social skills necessary to be at ease with other people. This includes learning how to talk about your work. You don't want to be sitting in silence on a stage, or in conversation with a bookstore owner who might promote your work, and be unable to figure out how to explain what you've written. And you need to be able to say things in a manner that is short, not long – there's no time on a stage or in the brief conversations you'll have at festivals etc. to expound on your work at length.

Amanda Curtin says:
Understand that you can't avoid public speaking, so it's worth investing in trying to get better at it – whether that means undertaking some training, or attending lots of author events and analysing what makes a good presentation, or reading how-to books. Practice is

everything. Always rehearse out loud speeches, talks and question responses (even if you've not been given questions in advance, you can usually predict what you'll be asked). If possible, try to simulate the event conditions: sitting or standing; with/without a lectern; with a hand-held/fixed/no microphone; holding notes or a book or a slide show remote control. Based on this, you might need to adjust your presentation, or ask for a microphone or a lectern or a side table. While rehearsing, remember to breathe – diaphragm breathing, not shallow upper-chest breathing.

Prepare for the event by asking questions: What type of event is it (talk, panel discussion, interview)? How long will you be speaking? Are technical facilities available? Will someone be introducing you? Will there be a Q&A? Do they want a reading?

If you'll be reading, prepare more than one passage and be flexible (the discussion might favour one over another). Stick to any time limits given. Mark up your book or print passages separately; edit out anything that won't work out loud or out of context.

Above all, consider the audience: think about why they're here. Prepare your presentation in the way you think will best engage them, meet their needs and (hopefully) exceed their expectations.

Deb Fitzpatrick says:

Be appreciative of every opportunity you're offered. Don't be arrogant, ever. Thank the organisers for having you and be genuinely interested in your audience, and the people behind the scenes who are arranging the chairs, the tea and coffee and the sound system. Offer to help set up and pack away.

Be prepared! Don't hesitate to ask the organiser for any clarification on the content of your session if need be. When you're starting out, it may be reassuring to have lots of notes with you – do whatever you need to feel organised and prepared. Heavy reliance on notes will diminish as your confidence and experience grows. Think about what you're going to say before you arrive at the venue and practise saying it out loud.

Once there, be sure to welcome people as they arrive and put people at ease by chatting until kick-off time. If the audience senses you're relaxed, they will be relaxed too, and the entire session will be smoother for it.

Be really honest. Don't try to project something you think the audience wants to see – be your genuine, daggy, funny, vulnerable self, and they will be so appreciative. The ability to strip away any pretence is important, I believe. The audience will see you as human and just one of them, which you are, and that's a winning formula.

Make sure your publishing house knows about the event and ensure your books will be available for sale if book sales are part of the event. If not, consider having a small box of books with you in your car in case someone expresses an interest in buying one.

Meg McKinlay says:

First, be clear about what your goals are for each appearance. You can't make the most of something unless you know what that represents to you. If your appearance has been organised by a publicist or another third party, it's worth asking them what their priorities are, too. There are many potential outcomes you can't control – having the goal of selling a certain number of books, for example, is a sure way to disappointment – but many others you can. Personally, my primary goal is always to connect effectively with the audience, whether that's a room full of wriggly preschoolers or a handful of adults in a book club – to deliver something satisfying for them while authentically representing myself and my work.

To this end, and to any end I suspect, preparation is key. Get as much information as you can about the audience and their expectations, the venue, how you'll be expected to interact with other participants, if any. Keep the event blurb in mind; you may or may not have had a hand in putting this together, but it's what the audience is there for. Clarify timing and equipment specifics in advance. Prepare a reading if that's called for. Have a plan B and a plan C. Be prepared to throw all alphabetised plans out the window and adapt on the spot when the promised tech is unavailable, or your roomful of preschoolers turns out to be a Year 6 writing workshop.

Speak warmly about your work, as if it was your friend, because it is, but don't turn events into a sales pitch. If people are interested in you, they're more likely to be interested in your work. If they're not, that's beyond your control, but you can at least rest assured that you delivered a successful event.

Brendan Ritchie says:

At some point I realised that people are just as interested in the journey of a book as they are in what is inside it. The same thing goes for the life of being a writer. The experience of sitting in trackpants, drinking lukewarm coffee and listening to a Taylor Swift album on repeat while rewriting the same sentence over and over isn't a story I would tell my friends – isn't really a story full stop – but to a reader or fan it becomes an oddly interesting anecdote. The majority of writers don't live particularly interesting lives, but this doesn't mean that people aren't interested in them. And they're not interested in the broad strokes. If an audience has been good enough to come along to a talk, they deserve the details. Here are some examples:

- I only use four fingers to type. A thumb if I'm really flying.
- I had gastro during the creation of the whole second and third chapters and now when I read them I wonder if the paragraphs are clipped for a reason.
- A university used one of my books in a huge advertising campaign on buses and trains, but cast a hand double in my place.
- I got so attached to the default Mac desktop image during the course of a manuscript, when I updated the OS, I felt disconnected from the work for weeks.

The mistake writers can make during public appearances is to focus too much on the contents of their books. Novels can, and should, speak for themselves. Generally an audience has already read the novel in question, or they plan to in the near future. It's a better option to offer something to complement their reading.

Rachel Robertson says:

I really enjoy festivals, talks and panels, even though I'm a shy person. Once you have done a few presentations, you can feel the audience's level of engagement and learn to develop a rapport with an audience. You also learn to answer tricky questions, which memoirists in particular get asked all the time. I always do specific preparation for each presentation or event and focus on the topic or theme provided and the type of audience expected. I also earmark in advance a number of possible passages to read aloud, practise reading them at home, and time them. In this way, if I'm unexpectedly invited to read some of my work, I know which bits I can read and how many minutes each extract will take.

Sometimes there can be pressure on writers to be humorous, especially if other authors on a panel are funny. It is okay to resist this, to talk about an issue seriously and to read a section of your work that is serious or moving rather than humorous. People often appreciate an engaged and thoughtful discussion so long as you don't take *yourself* too seriously. I find it is also good to read in advance the work of other authors with whom you are sharing a panel or presentation. Not only is this good manners, it also helps you make links between your work and theirs. It is always good to be generous and supportive towards other writers, in public and in private.

Holden Sheppard says:

An appearance on a panel is more than just showing up on the day. You will usually be booked several months in advance. Depending on the nature of the event and the stage of your career, you might need to negotiate matters such as agreeing on a fee (for instance, most published authors charge standard ASA rates), contract terms, any rights associated with your appearance, whether your appearance is an exclusive, and also sorting out forms for invoicing.

You will typically be introduced to your panel chair, or festival coordinator or library programmer, via email. This is your chance to negotiate what the appearance will entail and clarify what's expected of you, not just in terms of start and finish time, but in terms of the conversation itself. Your panel chair will often run their interview questions past you a few days before the event, so you can always ask to avoid certain topics if you're not comfortable with them, or ask to have questions added in.

In terms of making the most of these events, it can be really useful to promote the entire journey on your social media channels. For instance, you might first announce that you've been booked for the event and share a link for where your followers can buy tickets. You can later share a photo of you perhaps doing some reading in preparation for the conversation. Your promoter might ask you to do a reminder post if ticket sales are slow. You might post about how excited you are when the event is just a day or two away. At the event itself, you can have some fun by tweeting some candid photos or even capturing short videos of yourself backstage for your Instagram story.

And afterwards, you can sum up how awesome the event was in a wrap-up post on social media. Of course, you don't have to do all of these things for the one event – that might be overkill – but you should feel free to share various aspects of the experience.

On a more practical level, doing events in person is great for networking. You will have the chance to meet fellow writers and panellists, your panel chair, your promoter, other staff, readers and writers in the audience, and also industry people who may attend. Arrive early, so you have time to chat to these people ahead of time, and stay back after the event to meet those who made the time to come along and see you. The conversations after a speaking gig can be great fun, with audience members responding to what you said on stage or sharing their own stories with you. Moreover, sometimes someone will hear you speaking and will ask to book you for another event.

Anne-Louise Willoughby says:

I have prepared a series of presentations that can be tailored according to the event or institution. Appearances range from a full presentation of forty-five minutes to an hour, to a fifteen-minute overview, to a panel discussion. The first presentation I prepare is a thirty-minute comprehensive presentation that serves as a foundation document for other formats. Be entertaining, tell a story while talking and bring your work to life in the moment. You are not just delivering information, you need to captivate your audience and spur them on to read your book. Write the speech in full, time it and deliver it out loud, get a feel for what it sounds like and how you feel about what you are saying. Rehearse and be familiar with your text so you can speak to your audience rather than read to them. Does it give a fully rounded picture of your work? Does it invite questions and leave room for your audience to engage with you? Don't reveal all the 'good stuff' in your presentation or interview; offer a taster, but tell them the rest is in the book! Have selected readings ready in case you are asked for a favourite passage, or if you find there is time to fill. If you are doing a live radio interview, have key points and dates written down so you are not searching for words, and, if you need to steer a tricky host, your notes will help you redirect the conversation by introducing a point that you feel is salient. Remember, don't give shorthand responses – even though you may feel you are repeating yourself at each event your audience is likely hearing it for the first time.

And David Whish-Wilson says:

The best way to get the most out of public appearances is to find a way to enjoy them. Some people like being the centre of attention, and some don't. If you are in this latter category then you need to find a way to do your job, because make no mistake, getting out into the world and talking about your work, and the ideas behind your work, is part of the job of being a writer. Public events, however much you may dread them, bring writers and readers together in a way that can't be duplicated, and for this reason they're a vital part of the broader writing and reading cultural ecosystem. They're also a great way to meet other writers, publishers and editors. An established writer friend of mine, before my first writers festival gig, gave me a copy of a book called *Mortification: Writers' Stories of their Public Shame* (HarperCollins, 2004), which is about all of the embarrassing things that have happened to writers at public events – it's a very funny book and reassuring, too, and is a reminder that whatever might happen at a public event has already happened to someone else. While there is no substitute for being well prepared, other (chronically shy) writers I know take a beta-blocker before a public event, or exercise beforehand. Another writer I know, with a theatre background, does breathing exercises before going onstage. All writers I know have one thing in common, however, and that is acknowledging that nerves (of the manageable kind) serve to sharpen the mind and are part of the process. After a while you will learn to enjoy it – it's a privilege, after all, to be able to work quietly in solitude on a project and then to be able to share your work and your ideas and worldview with others in the most direct medium possible – that of face-to-face meetings with others who share your love of the book.

Bookshop etiquette post-publication

A bookseller can be an author's best friend. In Chapter 4 we encouraged you to form a meaningful relationship with your local bookseller. We suggested that you buy books from them (rather than some global online behemoth) and endeavour to make them part of your own writing and publishing journey (in a way that's not too pushy or weird). Bookshops love authors and can be very happy to champion them (especially local authors) and to provide an interface between an author and their audience. A bookseller who is happy to hand-sell or recommend or provide an instore written review for your book can make a big difference in sales.

If you have published your book with a publisher, then they will have the means of distribution through sales reps who will approach bookshops on the publisher's behalf to give them marketing material and endeavour to persuade the bookseller that they should stock their books. Whether the book is taken up or not depends on the bookseller's sense of whether their readers will buy that book. A sales rep's pitch may include letting a bookseller know that a particular author lives in their area. Does your bookseller already know about your book because you have mentioned it to them? You've just increased your chances of them stocking your book. And sometimes, it can be as simple a matter as to judging a book by its cover. It should look attractive enough they think readers will like it.

If you are self-published, you will need to be your own sales rep. If you have a pre-existing relationship with your bookseller and they are happy to take a look at your book, that's great. But if you are self-published, then your book still needs to *look* right – it needs to be appealing and sophisticated enough to hold its own among all the other stock in the shop. Booksellers know their business. They know what books look good and what books will draw readers to the honey pot of the new releases table. If your book doesn't look right, then a bookseller is limited in their ability to sell your work no matter how much they personally like what is inside.

Some bookshops, particularly independents, are happy to take a self-published author's work on consignment. If you are a self-published author, the best way to approach them is to drop by in person at a quiet time and ask them if they would like a complimentary copy of your book and whether they would be kind enough to take a look with a view to stocking your book. You may wish to insert an information sheet into your book with all relevant publication details, such as:

- Title and author.
- ISBN.
- RRP.
- Terms of trade (e.g. payment and discount terms; whether books are supplied on consignment or sale-or-return).

- Publisher contact details (yours).
- Relevant author biographical details.
- Picture of the book cover.
- Synopsis.
- Key selling points about the author and the book.

Remember to choose the right time of year to make your approach. Dashing in during the run-up to Christmas to entreat a harried bookseller is an approach unlikely to bear any festive fruit. Similarly, if you want to have a conversation with a bookseller, choose times of the day that are not peak periods. If the bookshop is open in the evening, this is often a more mellow time in which the bookseller may be happy to have a chat.

If you can find someone in the shop who likes your book enough that they choose to write an instore review (a 'shelf-talker') for your book, that's great, but don't give your book to the bookseller expecting that it will definitely be read, because yours is just one book in this category and is competing against all the other books being promoted by sales reps, and booksellers have a lot of books to read.

A word of warning if you are self-publishing: it is a mistake to think of your bookseller as the person who will provide all the service and distribution that a publisher or distributor does (e.g. keeping an eye on stock, ensuring your book has appropriate accompanying marketing material and is at the right price point). Booksellers won't appreciate authors who check on sales every few days and demand to know why their book isn't face out / on the counter / selling better. And you yourself will need to continue to drive readers towards the shop to buy your book via social media and participation at events.

Even authors published by more traditional means can be the source of some irritation for a bookseller. From time to time, a publisher may receive a call from a bookseller reporting on their interactions with an author (frequently a new author) who has manifested in a rather dramatic way inside the bookshop.

Tips for a positive bookshop relationship

While it can be tempting to check out how your book is going at the place where the readers are turning up to buy, there are some guidelines to follow to maintain a good working relationship with your bookshop:

- *Don't be a pesterer.* Authors who demand to know why books aren't on the bookseller's shelves don't get the support they need from booksellers. Booksellers all talk to one another about authors they don't like and pesterers get less from publishers because they can't be trusted to be good brand representatives.
- *Encourage pre-ordering.* Invite friends and relatives to pre-order from their local bookshop. Booksellers talk to each other and publishers monitor advance orders – if you can create some pre-publication buzz, that can lead to your book being more widely stocked and supported by bookshops.
- *Don't panic if you can't find your book.* If your book's not on the shelves after an extensive and thorough search at least a week and a half after the official publication date, and you're absolutely positive you know the bookseller's audience and that your book is a perfect fit for their shelves, then ask your publisher to approach the bookshop again.
- *Remember bookshops stock work that is 'fresh'.* If the last copy of your book is sold, it is possible the bookshop won't reorder another copy unless they feel that there is still some demand for the book.
- *Don't assume your book will sell.* Just because your book is on the shelf, this doesn't automatically mean it will sell. It is your own work at events and on social media, connecting with readers and building an audience, that can make the difference. This is doubly so if you are a self-published author.
- *Seek consent for book signings.* If you are going into a bookstore to sign books, you must let the publisher know first and also ask the bookshop's permission. It is not okay to turn up unannounced with your pen unless you are Jimmy Barnes. Booksellers will often be delighted to have you sign copies, but make sure you embellish the title page only with your signature. (The title page is the one that has title, author's name and publisher's logo on it.) Adding a date or the name of the bookshop along with your signature means the book cannot be returned to the publisher in event of a non-sale, and this is annoying for booksellers.
- *Be a strategic rearranger.* Is it okay to sneak into a bookshop and put your book face out? It all depends on the bookseller. Some recognise that an author will do whatever it takes to sell their book and find this subterfuge kind of charming. Others find it downright irritating.
- *Take photos in bookshops.* A bookseller will most likely be very happy for you to take a photo of you and your book, with or without the bookseller in it, especially if you tag them in your socials too. If it seems

appropriate to ask, then ask (this could be a good excuse to chat to the bookseller). Otherwise, go for it.

- *Don't expect appearance fees.* Don't expect or ask for payment to make an appearance at a bookstore.
- *Promote your local.* Encourage your friends to buy your books and the books of others at bricks-and-mortar stores. Be this kind of book buyer yourself. A bookshop can't support writers if it is not supported by readers, and everyone has a role to play in this.
- *Be informed about events.* When asked to do an event, find out as much as you can about what the bookstore expects from you on the day and ask, or offer suggestions about, what you can do for them. Make sure you nail down logistics like arrival time, parking, microphone and audiovisual materials well before the day of the event and that you have a sense of the layout of the store and where you will be speaking from, and where the audience will be.
- *Go above and beyond at events.* When asked to be at a bookstore for an event, don't leave it all to the bookseller. They are doing you a favour in providing the venue, but it is up to you to supply the crowd. Go above and beyond in your support of that event. Invite friends and family, promote it on social media in an interactive and interesting way, and do everything you can to show your support for the store.
- *Be gracious at events, especially to the staff!* Everyone is there at the event because they want to sell your book. Even if everyone is going over the top on promotion, sometimes events are fabulous and sometimes they're lacklustre. It is what it is and nobody is to blame. Charm the bookseller, charm the one stranger who turns up, do all that you can to create ambassadors for your book. If you are lucky enough to have an instore signing, be prepared to engage with customers who may otherwise be reticent about approaching the expectant author sitting beside a pile of books. Try to be friendly but not awkward (in what can be a very awkward situation).

A final word on being an author at large

The role of your promotions team is to create opportunities. They give people the chance to hear about the book or author and they create opportunities for people to read the book and talk about it. Ultimately it is up to you to make the most of those opportunities.

In the lead-up to publication, your supporters, networks and friends will also be responding to who you are and what you have established already by way of contacts. You shouldn't cut yourself off from the world at this stage of the process unless you have a spectacular reason why.

At the beginning of Chapter 8 we outlined the complex alchemy that contributes to a book's success. To give your book the best chance in a challenging environment, you will need that magical combination of people responding to you and liking your book enough to recommend it to others. You will need to stay connected to the world around you: the fact your book is sitting in a bookshop doesn't mean your work is done. Be present on social media, engage with your audience and remain accessible in the world so that your audience, if it is out there, knows where to find your book. To encourage good fortune to come to you, participate in the process in an informed, enthusiastic and authentic way.

Like the lifespan of a butterfly, the life of a book can be fleeting, especially compared to the amount of time it took you to write it. Giving it your all within this timeframe is the best way to create a little longevity or to begin to establish yourself as the kind of writer people would like to hear more from.

And so … having made your way out into the world, how on earth do you find your way back to your desk to begin the next book? Is it possible to write for a living? What do other writers wish they'd known sooner about being a writer? Let us sally boldly forth into the penultimate chapter!

10. Writing as a career

- The challenges and joys of book promotion
- Second-book syndrome
- Boundaries and work–life balance
- Writing for a living
- What they don't tell you about being a writer
- The end is just the beginning

Writing has its challenges. There are plot holes and structural disasters; there can be a whistling void in the place of sweet prose. Some days all you see are clunky lines, failed stanzas, recalcitrant protagonists, and furious exes bristling at your window. Writing is also a joy: it can be the thing that gets you out of bed, the thing you give up a social life for to embrace a life of rice and home-brand yoghurt. It is the job that doesn't require a boss or an office – though a door that shuts and a desk can be nice. The hours are flexible and there is no retirement age. You can work from bed, the beach or in a carpark while you wait to pick up the kids. You can work in your own brain through boring meetings, piles of dishes and insufferable encounters at parties. Writing can be joyful for the introvert, whereas promotion can represent a level of discomfort that is sweat-inducing and makes you groan aloud in recollection. For the extrovert, the reverse may be true. In this chapter, we are going to take the broader view and think about writing as a career.

The challenges and joys of book promotion

Remember: writing and publishing are not the same thing. Publication isn't compulsory, and nor is reaching a wide audience. You may decide that a sufficient audience comprises your immediate family, or the five members of your writing group. But if you *do* choose to seek publication, and are fortunate enough to be published, then it is worth working hard at promotion even if being published might be a dream come true, but the same can't always be said of promotion.

Here are some possible lows:

- Finding yourself next to Andy Griffiths at a signing table.
- Discovering that for you it's personal, but to others it's just another story, another product.
- Feeling judged or misunderstood.
- Feeling exposed or falling into the trap of believing what others say about you.
- Being insanely busy and still not being recompensed for the promotion of your work.
- Reaching the moment when the first rush of enthusiasm for your book is over and the phone stops ringing.
- Realising that just because you're successful in other areas of your life, doesn't mean you'll be a successful author.
- Recruiting one audience member at a time, which is relentless and ongoing.
- Coming to terms with the fact that competition is fierce and there are never going to be enough promotional opportunities.

And here are some of the joys:

- Making friends. As you go around promoting your book, you find people who think and feel as you do and they sometimes become your tribe.
- Collaborating with other authors and industry colleagues is a privilege.
- Sometimes, someone gets it. They really like what you've written. And sometimes it's only by being out there that you get the chance to discover this firsthand.
- It's satisfying to see some seemingly random or small piece of promotion lead to something much greater.

Second-book syndrome

After you have been 'on the circuit' talking about your book, how do you retreat to the desk and rediscover your quiet, contemplative self? One challenge that may present itself at this stage could be the fabled 'second-book syndrome' – how do you follow your first work with your next? If you have found your groove, your audience, and a genre that suits you, this may never be an issue, but sometimes – and despite this – it is.

Author Brendan Ritchie has some observations about getting back to the desk:

> There is often a significant period of time between contracting and publication. Given the many steps involved in taking a manuscript through to print – redrafting, structural editing, line editing, copyediting, proofing, production, marketing – this is no wonder, but I now realise how important it is to move from project to project, irrespective of the publishing process. Months spent waiting for an edit to come back or a publication date to arrive are better spent plunging into a new project and building some momentum. This also becomes very relevant once your book is published and people ask the inevitable and flattering question of what is next. In order to publish frequently (and I understand that what is considered 'frequent' for one writer might be anything but for another) writers need to remain sharp and productive and understand the realities of the publishing machine.

Every new work invariably presents its own conundrum. There may be a series of false starts as you look for the story that fires you enough to sustain a new book. And once you embark, there may be a knot or a challenge in this new work you have not encountered before. But maybe that's okay: there would be little point in writing the same book twice. If it is not interesting to you, it won't be interesting to the reader.

Thus the creative process starts again, but now you are a little more seasoned, with a better understanding of the process. It may be swifter to find your voice this time around, and you may start out with a sense of who you are writing for, because you have already met some of them.

Boundaries and work–life balance

Being a writer can be wonderfully absorbing. When you think of all the things that need to be done *apart* from writing a manuscript, it can seem like a full-time occupation, though often it is not practical for it to be so.

Life has a way of demanding the writer's attention, as do those aspects of life where money needs to be made, bills paid and food put on the table. For some, there is the matter of partner expectations, the thorny question of who will feel guilty if they neglect domestic duties, who is going to feed and exercise the livestock, or mind the children and keep the wolf from the door. Holding your space and finding time to write can sometimes feel like a ridiculous, insurmountable challenge.

Obviously, being a writer is not compulsory. But some of you will feel that it is. If only to make you feel you are not alone, we asked our authors their thoughts on balancing the writer's life with all their other obligations.

Ask an author: How do you manage your work–life balance?

Deb Fitzpatrick says:

To be honest, I've long stopped believing in the possibility of a genuine work–life balance.

Devoting myself to writing usually means removing myself from the family home for chunks of time, and while I do get a great deal done in these periods, there are also the concomitant family outcomes: younger children who – quite reasonably – act out their feelings about your absence in the days after your return, a rightly worn-out husband, and a home resembling a weapons testing site that takes at least as long as your absence to return to its former state.

If I focus on the family, creative frustration builds. Ideas will bounce around my mind, stories plead to be written down, but kids need to be collected, taken places, cheered for, cooked for and emotionally supported. I signed up for that when I chose to become a mum, so I really have to check myself when I grumble too much about not being able to 'get anything done'. There will always be other writers producing more and better works than me. Perhaps time will free itself up as my awesome young people get older.

My approach in these time-crunched days is to front up to the computer every morning and write until I have at least seven hundred words down. If I do that for five days, I'll have about 3,500 words down in a week. If I can maintain that for three months, I'll have around 40,000 words in the bag. That is a first-draft manuscript for me. It does feel doable. Most of my books have been written in this way – as Anne Lamott says, 'bird by bird'.

Finally on this point, it's worth saying that three of my six published books were written *before* I had my children – though they weren't published until after I'd had kids. So I suppose I made hay while the sun shone, in those pre-childrearing years, and even though those early rejections and near misses were hard going, persistence won out. Write when you can!

James Foley says:

I don't. I'm still learning. And when life changes (e.g. when a first child comes along), then work and life need to find a new balance. It's a constant juggling act.

One aspect to this is figuring out the work location that works best for you in your current situation. Some people find that a home studio works well, while some work elsewhere – a café, a library, in their car by the beach, or an actual studio space. I've tried all these types at different times and each has their merits.

I've been working from a spare room at home for the last few years, and that's worked well, but it does lead to me working late many nights (because I can). The advantage over the last two years has been that I can spend time with my toddler and wife at home during the day. But I'm about to go back to having a studio outside my home; I'm going to share a workspace with friends. It's partly to avoid the easy distractions at home, but I'm also hoping that by having an external studio I can leave the creative work there, then come home and wind down instead of working all hours.

Part of having a good work–life balance is being honest with yourself about how much time you need to complete a task, and making sure you communicate that with your publisher to ensure you can meet your deadlines comfortably. If my deadlines fall at super busy times of the year, or if one project takes too long and starts to knock into the next project's allotted time, then I have to start working all hours and my work–life balance goes out the window.

Then of course there's all the basic self-care stuff – exercise, sleep, healthy eating – even meditation and mindfulness. I need to ensure I make time for these, otherwise I burn out; when these pillars fall down, then everything else falls down pretty quickly too.

Another aspect to this is learning to say no to things. If you say yes to every project and opportunity that comes along, then you don't end up with enough time for anything. A creative friend said that when you say yes to one thing, you're saying no to something else. And sometimes those are things that you shouldn't say no to – sleep, exercise, health. Sometimes you miss out on great opportunities that you never knew were around the corner because you've already booked yourself up to the eyeballs with other projects you felt like you had to say yes to. So don't be afraid to say no.

Meg McKinlay says:

This is something that changes over time. Most writers starting out are juggling many other responsibilities and squeezing writing time into the cracks of those. At this point, it's natural to develop a habit of making the most of every spare moment, forsaking downtime and even sleep so you can get words on the page. For me, there was no real balance at this stage, just a mad scramble to try to keep all the balls in the air.

Over time – fourteen years and eighteen books later – I've transitioned slowly into full-time writing and am also at a point in life when I have fewer personal responsibilities. I've had to unlearn that habit of scrambling and squeezing and approach my writing in a more structured way. The creative wheels are always turning, but in terms of the actual work itself I try and keep a loose version of 'office hours', where I can symbolically leave the 'office' – being my home study – at the end of the day, setting the work down. This enables a kind of separation between work and family/home life, which I find essential.

Whatever stage you're at, I'd also say: sometimes put writing last. Sometimes life is just bigger. Kids need you. Parents need you. You need a mental health day or week or month. You don't always have to be writing. You don't have to do the whole *Butt-in-chair!, Writers WRITE!, 1,000-words-a-day-or-die!* thing espoused by many 'helpful' guides. You can keep things percolating in the background, remain active in the creative process, even if you're not actively putting words on the page or moving forward in a tangible way. You don't stop being a writer just because you're not writing. The story will wait.

Brendan Ritchie says:

The reality for most Australian writers is that they will need to supplement their writing income with other work in order to stay afloat. This means that work–life balance quickly becomes work–work–life balance, and infinitely more challenging.

Finding and protecting regular writing time is crucial. The nature and length of these blocks of time will obviously depend on work and family commitments. I generally need some time to warm up into my writing, and don't deal well with a fixed end point, so, as a parent, this really only leaves the late evenings.

I prefer to move through a draft swiftly, over the course of an intensive few months if I can, then stop writing altogether for a time while I gather my thoughts (and some kind of social life!) in preparation for the next draft or project.

The topic of 'other' work is obviously dependent on all kinds of factors such as qualifications, geography, opportunity and dependants. I have found that working in a separate field to writing can offer a better balance than taking on associated jobs such as copywriting, teaching and lecturing. It's natural to gravitate towards these types of roles, and sometimes they're all we can find, but in my experience they can also lead to an oversaturation. Writing, or talking about writing, all day, only to return home to do the same in the evening, is a difficult proposition. Haruki Murakami's combination of running a jazz bar in the evenings and writing during the day still strikes me as creative utopia.

And Rachel Robertson says:

I try to think not about 'work–life' or 'work–family' balance but rather life balance. This is because work (writing and teaching) is important and meaningful to me; it is part of my life, not an impediment to it. Nonetheless, balancing my life has been challenging. I have a son with a disability who requires significant support and I am our breadwinner. So, like many women, I am always juggling multiple demands.

How do I manage? Well, firstly, I think it is important to remember that we live and work in an inequitable system and that the need to juggle multiple demands is a result of systemic, political and personal issues. Many women do the invisible 'wife-work' for their family, friends and workplace; that is, the work not listed on our position description but which is valuable or necessary to achieve our home or workplace outcomes. This might include reading draft work by other writers, passing on opportunities to younger writers, writing letters of support for other people's grant and residency applications and so on. These are good things to do, but they take time and energy. Being a sole or main carer for a child, spouse or parent is also very time-consuming and exhausting. Writing is not lucrative and so many of us have another full- or part-time paid job.

So it is important to: set and maintain boundaries; support other writers but don't say yes to everything asked of you; be strategic in your choices; ask for help when you need it; and finally, do what *you* value (don't just aim to please others).

Nobody really knows how to achieve life balance. But surely it must help to make deep connections with people who nurture you, make you laugh and support your creative ambitions.

Writing for a living

All of this leads to a question that weighs on the minds of that small portion of the population who feels driven to write, no matter what. Let us assume that you do not have a university scholarship, a generous benefactor or have stumbled into an inheritance, but instead are wondering whether it is possible to actually write for a living. It is wonderful receiving scholarships, grants and residencies that can buy you time to write. These can form an important (if unpredictable) part of your writing income, but applying for them is time-consuming in a different way, and competition for them is fierce. Plus, eventually and inevitably, they run out.

On the upside, the Australian Lending Right schemes were created to compensate writers for loss of income when their work is used in Australian public and education lending libraries. (People are borrowing your book out rather than buying it.) The schemes are known as Public Lending Right (PLR) and Education Lending Right (ELR), and can be a nice additional source of income for writers when that unexpected drop of money from them appears in your account. You should check with your publisher that your book has been registered for these lending right schemes, or you can register yourself (see p. 247 for details).

Ask an author: Is it possible to write for a living? What other kinds of income are there for writers?

Liz Byrski says:

Yes! For most people it takes some time to establish an income from their writing, but it is certainly possible. Of course, there are exceptions, for example when a first novel bursts onto the scene with huge success. For most of us, especially if we are supporting others, it is not so easy and I think it's important for budding writers to have other strings to their bow that can bring in some income.

Some people rely on feature writing for magazines and newspapers, managing to place their work on a regular basis through part-time journalism. Perhaps you have an idea for a regular opinion column on something in which you are well informed: music perhaps, theatre, sport or restaurant reviews. Some reliable regular source of income is really worth having. Try your local newspapers, or industry and business magazines, or newsletters. Local governments often contract writers for regular work. You can register a business as a professional writer, which might include work like writing speeches, advertorials, promotional material and other similar services. You will need a range of writing skills, which you can obtain through a degree in professional writing and publishing, or a TAFE course. You may not be writing what you want to write, but you will be constantly building and refining your writing and making useful contacts.

Daniel de Lorne says:

Yes, but if you want that to happen, treat it as a business, even if you're publishing with a traditional publisher. Guard your writing time and make it a priority. Learn all you can about the market, about what works to gain readers and where the best places for you to be are. There are more opportunities than ever before for authors to take control of their writing career, but it often means becoming proficient in things other than writing such as marketing and advertising.

There are also many other ways to help supplement your writing income (and in the early days it may even bring in more money). Look at the skills you have and see what you can offer as services to other authors. Are you a graphic designer? Website builder? Editor? Social media marketer? Can you sell these services or can you teach them to others? Offering online or face-to-face workshops teaching other would-be writers about craft or supporting services can be profitable too. Appearances at writers festivals also pay, and then there are contests with prize money to enter. You might also consider ghostwriting.

And then there are your rights. Do as much with them as possible such as getting a novel turned into an audiobook or graphic novel, or having it translated into a foreign language.

James Foley says:

Yes. Well, kind of. The number of children's authors and illustrators in Australia who make enough money from royalties and advances to live on is very, very small. I'd say that most either have a day job, or a spouse who covers most of the income needs, or they earn the bulk of their income from talks and workshops at schools/libraries/festivals. Royalties from books only come once every six months and you never know exactly how much you're going to get. Talks and workshops provide much better cash flow, and they're the best hourly rate you'll ever get as a writer.

There are a few other income streams as well; if you register with the Copyright Agency, you can receive payments when people photocopy parts of your work. You can also register your books with the federally funded lending right program, which gives authors and illustrators compensation for having copies of their books in Australian libraries. You'll often hear writers talk about their ELR (Educational Lending Right – for copies of books in school, university and TAFE libraries) and PLR (Public Lending Right – for copies in public libraries). ELR and PLR payments are made once a year, but only if you've registered your new books by the annual deadline.

Writers and illustrators can also receive licensing payments for foreign editions of their books, as well as adaptations (e.g. plays, musicals, newspaper serialisation, reading aloud on online services like Story Box Library). But these are generally one-offs; they're nice little bonuses.

Some writers and illustrators also teach at TAFE or universities. Some illustrators sell their original artworks from books, or sell prints of their work. The more income streams you have, the easier it is to make your career sustainable.

Nandi Chinna says:

Writers can make money writing articles, reviews, plays, novels, blogs, screenplays and podcasts. With the diminishing pool of arts funding it seems like a lot of people try to get into academia these days, because it's one of the few avenues where a writer can earn a living and still work on their craft. It would be interesting to find out the percentage of Australian writers who do make a living at their craft. American novelist Jonathan Franzen has apparently earned ten million dollars from writing his novels. That's pretty good living!

I was recently talking to one of Australia's most successful poets. He said he had been on the dole for the last two years and was finally able to get an Australia Council grant. Another extremely successful and award-winning Australian novelist was quoted as saying that he was about to look for work in the mines when he won a lucrative writing prize.

Funding for the arts in Australia is very limited and getting scarcer and scarcer. I always follow the advice of poet Mary Oliver, who said if you can't get a job in writing, then get a part-time job doing something that doesn't take too much of your thinking, imagination and energy so you can still write and survive. I think a lot of writers will get whatever work they can and try to write whenever they can. But having a varied work life is also great material for writing. The great poet Fay Zwicky said that writers have to be out there in the world doing things and living and acting in the community. They shouldn't just sit in a room and write.

Ambelin Kwaymullina says:

Possible? Yes. Likely? No. Very few authors in Australia are sufficiently successful to rely on income drawn from writing alone, especially if they have dependants. For those of us who write for children and young adults, one of the primary sources of income comes from doing school visits. You may also like to consider joining a speakers agency, through which you can be booked for sessions.

I don't personally regard not being able to write for a living as a drawback. Stories are neither written nor read in a vacuum. My own writing thrives on interaction and experiences; my life would be far more limited in scope if I didn't have a job. It's also often the case that writers are more productive with limited time than they are with time to spare. It's easy as a writer to spend too much time inside your own head, thinking about ideas that will never be stories because no-one will ever read them; limited time forces you to get words on a page. In addition to this, writing, being a solitary endeavour, can also be a selfish one. Here's a thing that's not talked about so often: the literary world can be a highly unhealthy environment that values individuals over collectives and encourages writers to unwisely believe their own press. We're just not that special. We can write; other people can do other things; and everyone's lives (and stories) matter.

And Sasha Wasley says:

It is possible to write for a living, but most of us take a while to get there. There are exceptions – those lucky authors whose books are so astonishingly good that they win awards and become bestsellers, or those for whom the stars align and a celebrity decides to endorse their novel. But more often than not, our books simply do okay.

This can be hard to swallow. We'll often spend more than full-time hours writing and yet make barely enough to pay tax on. Or we'll only earn the advance and never see any further royalties. Writing income is notoriously low and erratic.

The money I earn from writing includes advances, royalties, appearances, translation and multi-format rights sales, and writing workshops. All of this combined cannot sustain me – yet. My solution has been to keep a part-time job that allows me to keep paying my mortgage and be an author in the other half of the working week. I plan to become a full-time author in the next few years and here's how I think I will achieve it: I will continue to produce and hopefully publish a book per year to grow my backlist. I will take all opportunities to appear in a paid capacity – at literary festivals or by running workshops. I will take my own role in marketing and promoting my books (even though I don't like it). I will support other Australian authors on their journeys because the better one of us does, the better all of us do. And I will give back by staying involved in charity work because it helps me maintain perspective – and what goes around comes around.

What they don't tell you about being a writer

So, what makes any writer continue to play the writing game? Are there some shortcuts we can share with you to make this process easier? Keeping yourself informed about the business of being a writer – and being an efficient administrator and canny self-promoter – will help you with this. And preparation and practice are essential. We hope that the information contained in this book will ease the process for you and increase your chances of success, however that may be defined.

Ask an author: What do you know now about being a writer that you wish you had known earlier?

Ambelin Kwaymullina says:

That the literary world is not a king tide that has me at its mercy; that I can make considered choices about what I want to do and what I don't, and those choices can be based on what I consider to be best for my own wellbeing and that of my work. Literature can be a terribly shiny world and it's easy to be dazzled by the lights. Focus on what's real, and what matters to you. It may not be the same thing that matters to others, and that's okay. All writers should feel empowered to define success in their own terms and for me, it's partly in my own ethical storytelling and partly in the spaces I create for other marginalised writers to speak. So much of how I define success is not in the stories I tell, but in the stories I help others to tell.

Nandi Chinna says:

I think if I had known how hard writing is, how difficult it is to make a living, and how long it takes to write something, I might have been put off by the whole thing. Writing is a taxing activity in so many ways. It can be hard on your body. Sitting still for long hours over a keyboard can really hurt your body. Writing can be hard emotionally because you're often living and working in a vortex of strong emotions and feelings, often reliving traumatic experiences over and over as you edit, or struggling for long periods over something as simple as a sentence, a paragraph, or even a single word.

Writing can be very isolating. You need to take yourself off for extended periods away from friends, family and lovers, sit with yourself in a quiet room and have a lot of self-discipline. You need to go back again and again and keep working at your computer or your paper. And you do this for little or no financial benefit most of the time.

Considering all the above, why would anybody want to be a writer? If someone had told me all of this when I was first starting out, I would have nonchalantly shrugged my shoulders and carried on. Because writing is also one of the most extraordinary things you can ever do. If you love reading and words turn you on, if words stop you in your tracks, make you weep, make you bruised, make you exultant, if they shock you and hurt you and heal you, then what better thing could you do with your life than to involve yourself in creating poems, stories, songs and books?

Amanda Curtin says:

I know – I absolutely *know* – that being a writer is about the work. That's no great revelation; I think I've always known that. But what I didn't know when I started out was that sometimes you have to fight for that: fight to remember it, fight to assert it, fight to make all the other aspects of 'being a writer' secondary to that. The work is infinitely more important than your author brand or the number of followers you have on social media, and it's more important than external validations like shortlistings or events or reviews. The work has to be the end as well as the means, the place where you derive your greatest pleasure, your greatest sense of achievement – your greatest frustration, too, because it makes more sense to be frustrated about something that's in your power to work through, learn from, than to be driven to despair by a poor review, about which you can do absolutely nothing.

None of this is to suggest that other activities associated with being a writer are not necessary, or enjoyable; or that external validations are not uplifting; or that the work is some pure and shining thing and not the bloody-minded beast it very often is (see 'greatest frustration' above). But putting things in perspective helps to keep you grounded, and even if that's sometimes difficult to achieve, it's at least worth aspiring to.

Deb Fitzpatrick says:

That receiving praise is addictive and when it ebbs rather than flows, you can feel very flat indeed. There will be initial excitement about your book around publication date and in the ensuing weeks – reviews, emails from friends, interviews and congratulations – and then things dwindle a little. You might find yourself checking your emails more frequently than is normal or, indeed, healthy. Getting through this phase is about coming to terms with the cycles of writing, and resilience will be needed!

That it can take several years for a book to 'take off'. Unless you're in the instant bestseller category, your book sales are likely to grow slowly over the first few years after an initial sale 'burst'.

That you *really will not* make a living out of selling books; however, you may earn a reasonable amount by attending or facilitating related writerly events, such as public speaking, writing workshops, writers festivals, school visits etc.

That word of mouth is a writer's best friend. If a teacher or a librarian happens to read your book and loves it, s/he will almost definitely tell another, who may well tell another, and this will branch out. Before you know it, schools might be buying class sets of your books and libraries purchasing book club sets. It might seem like a slow road, but it does work, and you simply need to chip away at it, and trust that word of mouth is well known in the publishing industry as the best publicity you can get.

James Foley says:

One thing I wish I'd known before I started is how much admin is involved! When you're a writer-illustrator you're essentially running a small business. It took a while to get my head around that. I learned how to use some accounting software, and I finally had to get serious about using time management and project management strategies. Reading some books on these topics is worth your time.

I've been lucky to be able to learn a lot of things on the go, and haven't made too many massive mistakes along the way – nothing career ending, at least. So perhaps instead I should let you know what has helped the most so far.

I joined the Society of Children's Book Writers and Illustrators (SCBWI) back in 2008. It changed my life. I met my tribe, my community; I joined at the same time as a bunch of other writer-illustrators around my age, all at the very start of our careers – now we all live close to each other and are friends for life. I met my mentors, and I met editors and publishers, and I got my first foot in the door. I owe my career to joining SCBWI.

It's not enough to just join the professional associations, though; you have to get involved and turn up to events. Volunteering for things is a great way to meet people and build connections. I was the illustrator coordinator for SCBWI's Australia West chapter for three years, then the regional advisor for two. I'm now the treasurer. Being involved means I get to meet everyone in my local chapter, and also in other chapters around Australia and the world. It's extra work but it pays off in other ways (plus, you get the warm fuzzy feeling of being a part of something bigger than yourself).

When I first started, I had the luxury of a part-time public service job to pay the bills. I liked that job, plus I could pay for rent and everything else, and it gave me time to work on my earliest books. I didn't have to worry about whether the books would sell or not because I wasn't relying on them for income. Although we have this romantic image of the full-time author ('How great that you get to follow your passion! You must be so happy!'), the reality is that it's a very odd, unpredictable, erratic and challenging job. Don't get me wrong – it's also fun, and I'm incredibly lucky to do this, and I've been doing it full-time for six years now. But it's still a job, with its own pros and cons. Right now, the upsides – being able to make stories and share them with others – far outweigh the downsides.

Brigid Lowry says:
I wish I had trusted myself and my process more in the beginning. I lacked a basic confidence in my work, yet my books did well, my career flourished and I won a prize or two. I wish I had known to just sit down and write every day with a willing heart, and not have an existential crisis about myself and my writing every five minutes.

I wish I had known that I could order things from room service, back in the day, when I was put up in a flash hotel as a guest of the Melbourne Writers Festival. I lived like a church mouse on a baguette, fruit and cheese for several days, later learning that I had free rein to order what I liked, but they didn't spread the word too widely in case writers went hard on the alcohol.

I wish I had kept sending my poetry out. As a fiction writer, busily writing YA books, I wrote poetry for my own pleasure. Now that I have time to be a poet again, I don't have a solid poetry résumé, except for the first few years of my career. To be taken seriously as a poet, I should not have stopped sending work to journals, because if I hadn't I would now look really impressive on paper.

I wish I had looked after my body better. I should have taken up yoga, tai chi, Pilates and regular massages a long time ago. Sitting at a desk all day plays havoc on the back and neck, and also the hands. It is not too late to do this, I tell myself, even though I am now elderly and have various achy bits that are probably work related.

I wish I had said no to all that social stuff I didn't really want to do. More time for writing, and for relaxing – woohoo! Again, never too late to start.

Meg McKinlay says:

That I'd never have a sense of arrival, that no matter what I published or achieved, I'd keep moving the goalposts. That the perfect sentence, or the story I really want to write, would always be just around the corner, unreachable. To be honest, I *was* told this, in a roundabout way. I just didn't listen.

That you don't learn how to write a novel. You only learn how to write the one you just finished, and the next is a puzzle all its own. But that with each completed piece, you learn something about your process, your strengths and weaknesses; you bank a few more tools to carry into the next one, and this is what it is to learn your craft.

That you must always stop and look around – ahead and behind you. Take note of how far you've come and remind yourself of what you're aiming for. Particularly once you achieve publication, once writing starts to become your job, it is so important to remember and preserve the reasons you started doing it in the first place.

That there is a physical toll. Keep moving. Stretch. And those little twinges in your wrists, arms, neck? Take them seriously, as soon as you notice them.

Rachel Robertson says:

I am not sure if it would have helped to know these things earlier, but here are a few things I now know that I would pass on to others:

- You probably won't like the cover design of your books – suck it up!
- If you make any money from your writing, you are doing well (or are just lucky).
- The world doesn't suddenly change once you have a print book published (but something in you may change nonetheless).
- Shame can be a complex and surprising emotion.
- Lots of people don't read fiction/non-fiction/poetry/memoir, so don't be offended if your close friends and family don't read your work.
- You may get lovely, heartfelt emails from readers, and this can be wonderful.
- Try to enjoy the act of writing and rewriting, the tussle with language and thought, the research and the struggle of craft (rather than enjoying only the outcome).
- Practise compassion, including self-compassion.

And David Whish-Wilson says:

What I didn't appreciate when I first started out was how much the act of writing and the career of being a writer is centred around balancing anxiety. I don't necessarily mean anxiety in the clinical sense, although that has certainly played a part in my life, but also the anxiety of not knowing what is going to be written next on the page when I sit before my laptop every morning (as a 'pantser' rather than a 'planner'). Then there is the anxiety produced as a by-product of being, necessarily, a stern self-critic, as well as the anxiety produced as a by-product of thinking, 24/7, both consciously and subconsciously, about a work in progress. Once a work is completed, there is the anxiety around submitting work for publication, soon followed by the anxiety around the reception of the published work, and finally of performing the role of the writer in public.

These are just some of the various anxieties I associate with being a writer. Others include the anxiety of balancing writing with paying the bills, and of trying to be a good partner and father while my head often wants to drift off into story world. There are many others, each specific to a writer's personal circumstances, but they each need to be dealt with. To some extent, I see a certain baseline level of anxiety as the fuel that powers writing, even as the practice of writing is anxiety-producing (as opposed to being merely imaginative, or a

> daydreamer), and that of course is useful. Excess anxiety, however, has a way of lingering and becoming damaging to the writing process, and to your life more generally, and I tend to deal with it now by way of strenuous physical activity, rather than with various intoxications, as I did when I was younger, and complete breaks from writing where possible.

The end is just the beginning

Every writing journey begins somewhere. Every writer has their own voice, and every act of creativity is a unique one. As this book nears its end, we would like to salute the storytellers and poets, the articulate humans who use metaphors, characters, plots and ideas to inform, shape, enlighten and influence readers' perceptions, and contribute to literary culture.

We hope that we have been of some assistance in bringing you solid, practical advice about how to authentically and successfully bring your words to the world.

11. Resources for writers

- Organisations mentioned in this book
- Awards and competitions
- Other resources for writers
- Our contributors recommend …

Organisations mentioned in this book

The internet is hugely useful for connecting writers with writing services and communities. The organisations mentioned throughout the book appear below, along with a list of the peak writing body and library for each state and territory.

National organisations

- **Arts Law Centre of Australia** (artslaw.com.au) – provides free or low-cost advice to Australian artists and arts organisations, and fact sheets and articles about all things legal.
- **Asialink** (asialink.unimelb.edu.au/arts) – funds residencies and exchanges throughout Asia.
- **Australian Book Designers Association** (abda.com.au) – aims to promote and connect Australian book designers with the broader publishing community.
- **Australian Copyright Council** (copyright.org.au) – information and advice about copyright and moral rights.
- **Australian Literary Agents' Association** (austlitagentsassoc.com) – agent listings as well as information about writers organisations, festivals and events.
- **Australian Society of Authors** (asauthors.org) – advocacy, support, advice and information for authors and illustrators, as well as agent listings.

- **Copyright Agency** (copyright.com.au) – information about the protection of your rights from creation to publication. Also offers mid-career grants and fellowships and distributes licence revenue and royalties to copyright owners.
- **Institute of Professional Editors** (iped-editors.org) – listings of editors, proofreaders, web designers and the like.
- **Nielsen Book Australia** (nielsenbook.com.au) – database containing title metadata to enable discovery, purchase and sales measurement of books.
- **Society of Children's Book Writers and Illustrators** (Australia East and New Zealand: australiaeastnz.scbwi.org; Australia West: australiawest.scwbi.org) – connects children's book writers and illustrators with each other and with industry professionals.
- **The Small Press Network** (smallpressnetwork.com.au) – the representative body for small and independent publishers in Australia.
- **THORPE–Bowker** (myidentifiers.com.au) – has products, services, and resources to assist self-publishing authors. See also National Library of Australia.
- **Varuna, The National Writers' House** (varuna.com.au) – offers residency programs and professional development opportunities.

State and territory organisations

Support writers, support local writing and get involved in your own writing community via your local writing centre. Especially if you are not affiliated with a tertiary institution or a seasoned writing group, it's a great place to start looking for your tribe and to find out more about competitions, readings, writing development workshops and other opportunities to interact with other writers and informed readers. To find your local writing centre or writing group, google them or go through your state's peak writing body. Your state library is also a great research and information destination:

- **ACT:** ACT Writers Centre (actwriters.org); Libraries ACT (library.act. gov.au).
- **NSW:** Writing NSW (writingnsw.org.au); State Library New South Wales (sl.nsw.gov.au).
- **NT:** NT Writers' Centre (ntwriters.com.au); Northern Territory Library (ntl.nt.gov.au).
- **Queensland:** Queensland Writers Centre (queenslandwriters.org.au); State Library of Queensland (slq.qld.gov.au).

- **SA:** Writers SA (writerssa.org.au); State Library of South Australia (slsa.sa.gov.au).
- **Tasmania:** TasWriters (taswriters.org); Libraries Tasmania (libraries. tas.gov.au).
- **Victoria:** Writers Victoria (writersvictoria.org.au); State Library Victoria (slv.vic.gov.au).
- **WA:** Writing WA (writingwa.org); State Library of Western Australia (slwa.wa.gov.au).

Awards and competitions

Your **state writing centres** (see above) are good places to connect to for current lists of awards and competitions for unpublished writing. The websites of local writing centres often have lists too.

A comprehensive summary document for awards for published works is the book awards calendar, **Australian Writing Awards to Celebrate** (alia.org.au/sites/default/files/Book%20Awards%20Calendar.pdf).

Other resources for writers

Google is your best friend when it comes to accessing material to support your writing practice. Some resources and local organisations mentioned in this book (along with a few bonus listings) include:

- **Amazon.com Author Page** (authorcentral.amazon.com) – a marketing tool to enable people to discover authors and their books and discuss them, and for authors to track sales, manage their content and link to their other sites.
- **ArtsHub** (artshub.com.au) – online journalism for people who work in the arts.
- **Australian Lending Right schemes (ELR/PLR)** (arts.gov.au/funding-and-support/lending-rights) – information about the two national rights lending schemes available for published authors.
- **Better Reading** (betterreading.com.au) – website, Facebook page, and monthly live book club create forums for participants to discuss, review and recommend books old and new.
- **Books+Publishing** (booksandpublishing.com.au) – news from the Australian and New Zealand book industry, including a wide range

of newsletters that contain author interviews, articles and reviews of forthcoming titles.

- **Centre for Stories** (centreforstories.com) – a Perth-based centre for storytelling training, services, mentoring and events.
- **Copyright information:**
  - » **Australian Government** (communications.gov.au/copyright/duration-copyright) – information about duration of copyright.
  - » **Australian Copyright Council** (copyright.org.au) – fact sheets under the heading 'Basic Information About Copyright'.
  - » **Australian Libraries Copyright Committee** (libcopyright.org.au/duration-of-copyright) – includes an excellent flowchart about duration of copyright.
- *GLAAD Media Reference Guide* (10th ed.) (glaad.org/reference) – guide for journalists and creators to how to tell fair, accurate and inclusive representation of LGBTQIA stories. Useful US publication in an area where language is always evolving.
- **Goodreads** (goodreads.com) – a social cataloguing website that allows participants to create groups of book suggestions, surveys, polls, blogs, and discussions.
- **Google Earth** (google.com/earth) and **Google Maps** (google.com/maps) – research on location without leaving your desk.
- **'Literature, Resistance, and First Nations Futures: storytelling from an Australian Indigenous women's standpoint in the twenty-first century and beyond'** by Ambelin Kwaymullina – a starting point for looking at own voice issues in relation to storytelling (westerlymag.com.au/wp-content/uploads/2019/03/Kwaymullina-Ambelin-Literature-Resistance-and-First-Nations-Futures.pdf).
- *Liminal* online magazine (liminalmag.com) – exploration, interrogation and celebration of the Asian-Australian experience.
- **MEAA Journalist Code of Ethics** (meaa.org/meaa-media/code-of-ethics) – sets out obligations for journalists and makes interesting reading for writers too.
- **'Moral rights' fact sheet** from the Australian Copyright Council (copyright.org.au/ACC_Prod/ACC/Information_Sheets/Moral_Rights) – an overview of moral rights for individual creators.
- **National edeposit website** (ned.gov.au) – national, state and territory information for legal deposit of epublications.

- **National Library of Australia services:**
  - » **Creative Arts Fellowships** (nla.gov.au/content/fellowships-scholarships-and-grants) – aimed at encouraging research work within the library's collection.
  - » **ISBN** (nla.gov.au/the-australian-isbn-agency) – information and application via NLA or THORPE–Bowker.
  - » **ISSN** (nla.gov.au/the-australian-issn-agency) – information and application via NLA.
  - » **Legal deposit and National edeposit** (nla.gov.au/legal-deposit) – lodge your published print and ebook with the NLA here.
  - » **Prepublication data** (nla.gov.au/content/prepublication-data-service) – register your work in the library system here.
- **'Privilege and literature: three myths created by misdiagnosing a lack of Indigenous voices (and other diverse voices) as a "diversity problem"'** by Ambelin Kwaymullina (alphareader.blogspot.com/2016/03/privilege-and-literature-three-myths.html) – thought-provoking article on diversity and privilege perspectives.
- **'Protocols for Producing Indigenous Australian Writing'** (australiacouncil.gov.au/workspace/uploads/files/writing-protocols-for-indigeno-5b4bfc67dd037.pdf) – guide for arts practitioners involved with Aboriginal and Torres Strait Islander people, communities, cultural material and intellectual property rights.
- **Res Artis** (resartis.org) – aggregation site listing residencies in over eighty-five different countries.
- **State Library of Queensland black&write! Writing Fellowships** (slq.qld.gov.au/get-involved/fellowships-awards-residencies/blackwrite/blackwrite-writing-fellowships) – offers two annual fellowships for unpublished manuscripts by Aboriginal and Torres Strait Islander writers.
- **Sweatshop** (sweatshop.ws) – based in Western Sydney, provides opportunities for writers from Aboriginal and Torres Strait Islander and non-English-speaking backgrounds.
- **The Wheeler Centre** (wheelercentre.com) – a central Melbourne literary hub for all things books, literature and ideas.
- **Trove** (trove.nla.gov.au) – a one-stop shop for a rich range of historical cultural texts available from various archives, libraries and museums around Australia.

- 'Twenty Ways to Talk about Creative Nonfiction', Sondra Perl and Mimi Schwartz, *Writing True: The Art and Craft of Creative Nonfiction*, Houghton Mifflin, 2006.
- 'What to Expect When You're Expecting' blog post series (annabelsmith.com) – an author's perspective into the editing and publishing process presented by Annabel Smith and many guests.
- Young Australian Writers (facebook.com/youngauswriters) – the largest Facebook community for young and emerging writers.

Our contributors recommend ...

Where do practising writers turn for advice, guidance and inspiration? We asked our contributors for their top three personal resources – book, organisation or online – and the reasons for their choices.

Liz Byrski

- *Becoming a Writer*, Dorothea Brande (Macmillan, 1996, or ebook). This is an inspirational and practical guide to creative writing, which has been in constant demand ever since it was first published in 1934. Brande deals with essential things that create a *writing magic*, from originality and the ability to see things in different ways, to writing to schedule, imitation, criticism and harnessing the unconscious.
- *How Our Lives Become Stories*, Paul John Eakin (Cornell University Press, 1999). A brilliant book on how we use our lives as subjects in writing, from autobiography to memoir and creative non-fiction, grounded in the vantage points of literature, philosophy and psychology.
- *Three Steps on the Ladder of Writing*, Hélène Cixous (Columbia University Press, 1994). This is a moving and inspirational exploration of the 'science of writing', exploring process and the importance of moving beyond the superficial.

Alan Carter

- *A Novel in a Year*, Louise Doughty (Simon & Schuster, 2007). An excellent how-to book with good advice on everything from setting up your writing space, through quarantining your writing time, to plotting and writing and dealing with blockages.

- **Australian Society of Authors website** (asauthors.org). The ASA has good advice on pay rates, publishing contracts, and resources and such, along with the websites of your state writing organisations.
- **CrimeReads website** (crimereads.com) and its partner **Literary Hub** (lithub.com) are great resources for the bigger picture and bigger ideas sides of writing and reading, with articles on specific authors, books, genres and themes. Good for broadening the mind, particularly if you've got writer's block.

Nandi Chinna

- *A Book of Luminous Things: An International Anthology of Poetry*, **Czeslaw Milosz (ed.)** (Mariner Books, 1998). This anthology is wonderful for its depth and variety. It provides a great selection of poetry from across languages and cultures.
- *Macquarie Thesaurus* (Macquarie, 2007). My most useful and treasured possession, this resource is great for finding alternative ways and words to make your writing sing.
- *Staying Alive: Real Poems for Unreal Time* and *Being Alive: The Sequel to Staying Alive*, **Neil Astley (ed.)** (Bloodaxe Books, 2002, 2004). These are two anthologies I turn to regularly for inspiration and solace. I believe that reading is the greatest learning tool for writers.

Tim Coronel

- *How to Market Books*, **Alison Baverstock and Susannah Bowen** (6th ed., Routledge, 2019). If I had to recommend one book about the book industry to aspiring authors, self-publishers, publishing students or seasoned booktrade insiders wanting a skills update, this would be it.
- Subscribe to **Books+Publishing** (booksandpublishing.com.au). I am a little biased as I worked for this ninety-nine-year-old Australian book industry news service for many years, but it really is an essential service for anyone who needs insight into the publishing world.
- If you are interested in self-publishing, or perhaps even brave enough to be considering setting up your own small publishing company, writers centres run a number of courses that run you through all the steps necessary to get started. This one from Writing NSW is a good example: **Self-publish Your Book with Joel Naoum** (writingnsw.org. au/whats-on/courses/online-self-publish-your-book-2020/).

Amanda Curtin

- **Macquarie Dictionary and Thesaurus Online** (macquariedictionary. com.au). I love the convenience of working with the *Macquarie* on-screen rather than consulting the bulky print version, and having a yearly online subscription means you are always working with the most up-to-date data on Australian language.
- *The Art of Fiction: Notes on Craft for Young Writers*, **John Gardner** (Vintage, 1991). While the prose does feel dated (e.g. it uses masculine pronouns), I still find this book more illuminating than any other on aspects of the craft of writing fiction, and on the 'why' of writing.
- *Style Manual: For Authors, Editors and Printers*, **Snooks & Co** (6th ed., John Wiley & Sons, 2002). Although in need of updating, this remains the standard Australian reference book for matters of style and consistency, and is an indispensable part of any writer's library.

Daniel de Lorne

- *Digging Deep into the EDITS System* **lecture package, Margie Lawson** (margielawson.com). This lecture series is a must for not only finding out what needs to be improved in your writing, but how to do it.
- *The 'W' Plot ... or the Other White Meat for Plotters*, **Karen Docter** (karendocter.com). This is a thorough and helpful system for plotting your novel (if you're a plotter, that is).
- *Save the Cat: The Last Book on Screenwriting You'll Ever Need*, **Blake Snyder** (Michael Wiese Productions, 2005). Although this book is targeted at screenwriters, it is valuable for other writers too, and teaches you how to write loglines, develop characters and structure your work.

Deb Fitzpatrick

- *Bird by Bird: Some Instructions on Writing and Life*, **Anne Lamott** (Anchor, 1995). Wise, gentle and honest, this is both memoir and practical writing guide. Full of gems large and small – like 'If your character suddenly pulls a half-eaten carrot out of her pocket, let her' – this is a writing guide for life.
- *Juicy Writing: Inspiration and Techniques for Young Writers*, **Brigid Lowry** (Allen & Unwin, 2008). A fabulous and funky how-to guide for young and old; this book is always with me when I run creative writing workshops. Brigid's hippie-poet voice winds through every page. Students, teachers and I love this book!

- *On Writing: A Memoir of the Craft,* **Stephen King** (Scribner, 2000). Like many people who rate this masterful writing memoir, I am not a reader of horror or crime fiction or King's other works. This is compelling and honest. Prepare to be seriously impressed.

James Foley

- *The Artist's Way: A Spiritual Path to Higher Creativity,* **Julia Cameron** (TarcherPerigee, 1992). This is a bestselling book and a self-help guide for recovering creatives. It changed my life.
- *Art and Fear: Observations on the Perils (and Rewards) of Artmaking,* **David Bayles and Ted Orland** (Image Continuum Press, 1993).
  A thought-provoking book about why we make art, and how to overcome the fear that stops us.
- *Show me a Story!: Why Picture Books Matter: Conversations with 21 of the World's Most Celebrated Illustrators,* **Leonard S. Marcus** (Candlewick Press, 2012). An excellent collection of interviews with the most successful children's illustrators from around the world. Insightful and inspiring.

Deborah Hunn

- *The Writer's Reader: A Guide to Writing Fiction and Poetry,* **Brenda Walker (ed.)** (Halstead Press, 2006). A very useful collection of essays by Australian writers and academics on key creative issues and problems across a range of genres.
- *How Fiction Works,* **James Wood** (Picador, 2018). The ability to read widely and engage critically with narrative technique is crucial for writers. This insightful and skilfully written book will enhance your reading skills and your pleasure in reading.
- *The Collected Essays of Virginia Woolf,* **Virginia Woolf** (Benediction Classics, 2011). Woolf's insights on her own writing and that of myriad others remains an education and an inspiration.

Ambelin Kwaymullina

- **Reading While White** (readingwhilewhite.blogspot.com). This is a US website that critically examines racial bias in literature and offers useful analysis for anyone interested in cultural and racial inclusivity in literature.

- **Publisher websites**. Identify publishers you might like to be published by and start checking in on their websites to get an idea of what they publish and how they talk about the books.
- **Author websites**. Identify your favourite authors, follow their websites, blogs and/or Twitter accounts to get an idea of what writing is like from the people who are doing it.

Natasha Lester

- *Still Writing: The Perils and Pleasures of a Creative Life*, Dani Shapiro (Grove Press, 2014). This is not a how-to book exactly, but it has some of the best advice I've ever read about the 'endurability' needed to become a writer.
- Australian Writers' Centre podcast **So You Want to Be a Writer** (writerscentre.com.au/category/podcasts/so-you-want-to-be-a-writer-podcast). This podcast is an excellent resource of author interviews, links to writing articles, and lots more.
- **Australian Society of Authors** (asauthors.org). You can join the ASA as an affiliate member if you're unpublished and that gives you access to industry wisdom, advocacy, a terrific newsletter and lots more.

Brigid Lowry

- *Poemcrazy: Freeing Your Life with Words*, Susan Goldsmith Wooldridge (Three Rivers Press, 1997). An enthusiastic guide to the world of words, full of workshop ideas and joyous ways to get the writing zing happening.
- *Bird by Bird: Some Instructions on Writing and Life*, Anne Lamott (Anchor, 1995). An oldie but a very goodie. Heaps of terrific writing information, and damn funny too.
- *Handling the Truth: On the Writing of Memoir*, Beth Kephart (Avery, 2013). The best book I have read on the genre. Passionate, punchy and inspiring.

Meg McKinlay

- *Art and Fear: Observations on the Perils (and Rewards) of Artmaking*, David Bayles and Ted Orland (Image Continuum Press, 1993). Part philosophical and part practical, this is both a reassuring and challenging examination of what it means to make art, to find your own voice, and to continue along a creative path in spite of its inherent challenges.

- **Society of Children's Book Writers and Illustrators** (scbwi.org). For aspiring children's writers, SCBWI will provide you with a wealth of resources, connect you with a supportive local or online community and offer invaluable professional development opportunities.
- **Writing WA** (writingWA.org). For writers in general, and West Australian writers in particular, this website is a repository of invaluable information, opportunities, and potential points of connection.

Caitlin Maling

- *Princeton Encyclopedia of Poetry and Poetics*, **Alex Preminger** (Princeton University Press, 1974). There are approximately one billion words for the different schools, techniques and types of poems and this book defines them all.
- *The Making of a Poem: A Norton Anthology of Poetic Forms*, **Eavan Boland and Mark Strand** (W.W. Norton & Company, 2018). Eavan Boland and Mark Strand have assembled an intriguing sample of the key forms in English-language poetry. Arranged chronologically, it shows how forms mutate and continue to have relevance.
- *Poetry Magazine* (poetryfoundation.org/poetrymagazine). Still the gold standard in journal publications for poetry, the website also offers a rich repository of poetry published over past centuries, often with audio recordings and individual poem guides.

Georgia Richter

- **The Fremantle Press Podcast** (fremantlepress.com.au/the-podcast) contains all kinds of conversations between writers, editors and industry people. If you enjoyed reading different author perspectives in this book, then this podcast will appeal to you.
- **Google Books Ngram Viewer** (books.google.com/ngrams). Choose your field (English, English Literature Literature, Chinese, Russian, Spanish, American), and plug in any word for an instant graph of its popularity in any year in the last two centuries. A fun tool for writers and editors to assist with historically accurate language use.
- *Yacker: Australian Writers Talk about their Work*, **Candida Baker** (Pan Macmillan, 1986). A book I referred to many times as a keen young writer. This three-part series is full of conversations with writers and was part of my inspiration for including writers' voices here. I loved reading about other practitioners and their take on their craft.

Brendan Ritchie

- *What I Talk About When I Talk About Running,* **Haruki Murakami** (Knopf, 2008). An unconventional and revealing memoir on writing (and running!) by one of the most enigmatic novelists around.
- *On Writing: A Memoir of the Craft,* **Stephen King** (Scribner, 2000). This book offers tangible insights on topics such as writing process, inspiration, characterisation, syntax and redrafting – all written in King's captivating voice.
- *TEXT Journal of Writing and Writing Courses* (textjournal.com.au). This A-ranked academic journal offers twice-yearly articles, reviews, poetry and prose from some of Australia's most notable creative and literary theorists.

Rachel Robertson

- *The Situation and the Story: The Art of Personal Narrative,* **Vivian Gornick** (Farrar, Straus and Giroux, 2001). A slim and sophisticated look at personal essay and memoir; the introduction itself is worth the price of the book.
- *Writing True: The Art and Craft of Creative Nonfiction,* **Sondra Perl and Mimi Schwartz** (Houghton Mifflin, 2006). A useful and comprehensive introduction to writing creative non-fiction including writing prompts and exemplar readings.
- *Stasiland,* **Anna Funder** (Penguin, 2018). A brilliant work of creative non-fiction by an Australian writer that demonstrates the power and range of well-written narrative non-fiction based on comprehensive research.

Holden Sheppard

- *On Writing: A Memoir of the Craft,* **Stephen King** (Scribner, 2000). Part memoir, part guide to the writing craft, this book is a resource beloved by many, including me. King's advice is clear-sighted and no-nonsense: it is highly motivational and I found it life-changing.
- Janet Reid's blog, **Janet Reid, Literary Agent** (jetreidliterary. blogspot.com). This New York City literary agent is a legend in the blogosphere, and reading her blog about being an agent and what she looks for in new projects taught me almost everything I know about agents and publishing. She also runs the incredible **Query Shark** blog (queryshark.blogspot.com), where writers send in their query letters and she dissects them for the benefit of all her readers.

- **Writer's Digest** (writersdigest.com). While I learned most of what I know about writing craft at university through a creative writing degree, or via mentors and editors, I learned a lot of what I know about publishing from the Writer's Digest website. They have an incredible range of resources for writers, including some helpful interviews with writers, editors, agents and publishers – an absolute goldmine for writers at any level.

Sasha Wasley

- **Australian Society of Authors** (asauthors.org). Even if you don't join, I love the ASA website because it includes recommended rates of pay for authors invited to speak or give a workshop. I would not have known what to charge without this website.
- **Romance Writers of Australia** (romanceaustralia.com). When you join, you will be added to a group of peers, receive newsletters and opportunities to contribute to anthologies and have the chance to attend their annual conventions.
- **Literary Hub** (lithub.com). A curated website full of stories, podcasts, reviews and articles about writing, reading and books.

David Whish-Wilson

- *Writing Fiction: A Guide to Narrative Craft,* **Janet Burroway and Elizabeth Stuckey-French** (7th ed., Longman, 2006). This is the best prose fiction handbook I've come across.
- *How Fiction Works,* **James Wood** (Picador, 2018). This is a good primer in how to read critically, both in your own work and the writing of others.
- *Westerly* (westerlymag.com.au). This is my local Western Australian literary journal, which has been running for more than sixty years. My advice is to find your own local journal and read back through the years.

Anne-Louise Willoughby

- *The Heart Garden: Sunday Reed and Heide,* **Janine Burke** (Vintage Australia, 2005). For me, *The Heart Garden* represents the perfect balance in biographical writing, vividly creating the world of Sunday and John Reed and the complex relationships with the artists that were central to that world, while historically contextualising the whole.

- *Dear Writer,* **Carmel Bird** (Penguin, 1988). *Dear Writer* is an engaging crash course on writing that was first published over thirty years ago, with a revised edition released in 2013. I recommend it to fiction writers to hear Bird's personal and literary voice giving sound advice through her charming device of letters addressed to her 'Dear Reader'.
- '**Design and Truth in Biography**', **Arnold Rampersad** (South Central Review, vol.9, no.2, 1992, pp. 1–18). Pulitzer Prize–nominated biographer Arnold Rampersad is an emeritus professor at Stanford University. This journal article provides enormous reassurance and guidance with regard to my obligations as a biographer.

Contributor biographies

Liz Byrski is a novelist, non-fiction writer, former journalist and ABC broadcaster, with more than fifty years experience in the British and Australian media. She is an adjunct associate professor at Curtin University and has taught writing in the University's School of Media, Creative Arts and Social Inquiry. She is the author of ten bestselling novels, including *A Month of Sundays* and *The Woman Next Door*; and author of twelve non-fiction titles including *In Love and War: Nursing Heroes*, *Getting On: Some Thoughts on Women and Ageing*, and *Remember Me.*

Website: lizbyrski.com

Alan Carter is an award-winning crime author and sometimes television documentary director who divides his time between Fremantle and Tasmania. His Cato Kwong series – *Prime Cut*, *Getting Warmer*, *Bad Seed* and *Heaven Sent* – has been published in the UK, France, Germany and Spain. *Prime Cut* won the Ned Kelly Award for Best First Fiction in 2011. The fifth in the Cato Kwong series, *Crocodile Tears*, will be released by Fremantle Press in 2021. His first novel set in New Zealand, *Marlborough Man*, won the 2018 Ngaio Marsh Award for Best Crime Novel, was shortlisted for the Ned Kelly Award for Best Fiction 2018 and is also published in Germany. The sequel, *Doom Creek* was published by Fremantle Press in 2020.

Facebook: @AlanCarterAuthor | Twitter: @carter_alan28

Nandi Chinna works as a research consultant and community arts facilitator. With a background in yoga and meditation, Nandi uses mindfulness and meditation, slow walking and immersion in nature to facilitate creativity. Nandi's poetry publications include *Our Only Guide is Our Homesickness* (Five Islands Press, 2007), *How to Measure Land* (Picaro Press, Byron Bay Writers Festival Poetry Prize winner, 2010), *Alluvium* (with illustrator Andrea Smith, Lethologica Press, 2012), *Swamp: Walking* *the Wetlands of the Swan Coastal Plain* and *The Future Keepers* (Fremantle Press, 2014 and 2019).

Website: nandichinna.com
Instagram: @nandichinnapoetry | Twitter: @ChinnaNandi

Tim Coronel is the general manager of The Small Press Network and an industry adjunct lecturer in publishing and communications at the University of Melbourne. He has worked in the book trade in many capacities for thirty years, including as a bookseller, reviewer, journalist, editor, publisher, publicist and publishing consultant.

Website: timcoronel.com.au | Facebook: @timcoronel
Twitter: @Tim_Coronel

Amanda Curtin is the author of novels *Elemental* and *The Sinkings*, short story collection *Inherited*, and a work of narrative non-fiction, *Kathleen O'Connor of Paris*. She has won numerous awards for short fiction, been shortlisted for the Western Australian Premier's Book Awards and the Western Australian Writer's Fellowship, and been nominated for the Alice Award (a national biennial award honouring Australian women who have made a long-term contribution to literature). Amanda has been granted residencies/fellowships at Art Omi, United States; Tyrone Guthrie Centre, Ireland (through the Australia Council); Hawthornden Castle, Scotland; Sun Yat-sen University, China; and the Tasmanian Writers' Centre. She has a PhD in Writing and has worked as a book editor for many years (accredited through IPEd). She lives in Perth with her husband and an opinionated Siamese cat, and works in a backyard studio among magpies, doves and old trees.

Website: amandacurtin.com | Facebook: @AmandaCurtinAuthor
Instagram: @amandalookingupdown | Twitter: @lookingupdown

Daniel de Lorne writes about men, monsters and magic (often with a bit of mayhem thrown in too). In love with writing since he wrote a story about a talking tree at age six, his first novel, the romantic horror *Beckoning Blood*, was published in 2014. In his other life, Daniel is a professional writer and researcher in Perth, Australia, with a love of history and nature. All of which makes for great story fodder. And when he's not working, he and his husband explore as much of this amazing world as they can, from the ruins of Welsh abbeys to trekking famous routes and swimming with whales.

Facebook: @danieldelorne |
Instagram: @ danieldelorne | Twitter: @ danieldelorne
Goodreads: goodreads.com/danieldelorne

Deb Fitzpatrick is the author of six novels for adults, young adults and children. Her two YA novels (*90 Packets of Instant Noodles* and *Have you Seen Ally Queen?*) were named Notable Books by the Children's Book Council of Australia; two of her books have been shortlisted in the West Australian Young Readers Book Awards (WAYRBAs); and her first middle grade book *The Amazing Spencer Gray* was published in the US in 2017. Deb loves using stories from real life in her novels and tries to include her kids' names in her books wherever possible. Deb has a Master of Arts (Creative Writing) and regularly teaches creative writing to children, young adults and adults; she loves motivating writers. Deb is the recipient of a 2020 May Gibbs Children's Literature Trust Creative Time Residential Fellowship to write her next novel. Her latest book is *The Spectacular Spencer Gray*.

Website: debfitzpatrick.com.au | Facebook: @debfitzpatrickwriter
Instagram: @debfitzpatrick9 | Twitter: @DebFitzpatrick2

James Foley makes picture books, middle-grade novels and comics for kids. He's the author-illustrator of the S.Tinker Inc. graphic novel series for middle readers. *Brobot* (2016), *Dungzilla* (2017), *Gastronauts* (2018) and *Chickensaurus* (2020) star Sally Tinker, the world's foremost inventor under the age of twelve, and Joe Tinker, her stinky baby brother. James illustrated the Toffle Towers series written by Tim Harris, and *Total Quack Up!* (2018), an anthology of funny short stories with proceeds going to charity. James's books *My Dead Bunny* (2015), *In The Lion* (2012), *The Last Viking* (2011) and *The Last Viking Returns* (2014) have all scored several honours, including children's choice awards, shortlistings in the CBCA Book of the Year Awards, and selection to the International Youth Library's White Ravens list. James is an ambassador for Books In Homes and Room To Read Australia. He is a massive Marvel movie nerd and comes from a long line of queuing enthusiasts.

Website: jamesfoley.com.au | Facebook: @jamesfoleybooks
Instagram: @jamesfoleybooks | Twitter: @Jamesfoleybooks
YouTube: @jamesfoleybooks

Deborah Hunn is a lecturer in creative writing in the School of Media, Creative Arts and Social Inquiry at Curtin University in Western Australia. Deborah completed a PhD at UWA in 2000 and has taught over the last three decades at universities in Western Australia and South Australia. Her creative and academic work has been published in a range of anthologies, edited collections and journals, and includes short stories, creative non-fiction, academic essays on literature, film and television, and reviews. Her short story 'Endless Winter' won the 2013 Patricia Hackett Prize.

Facebook: @How to be an Author in Australia
Twitter: @deb_hunn | LinkedIn: deb-hunn-52051816

Ambelin Kwaymullina is an Aboriginal writer and illustrator from the Palyku people of the Pilbara region of Western Australia. She is the author-illustrator of multiple picture books and a young adult dystopian series, The Tribe. Her latest novel, *Catching Teller Crow* (co-written with her brother Ezekiel), won the Victorian Premier's Literary Award for Writing for Young Adults and the Aurealis Award for Best Young Adult Novel. Ambelin's books have been published in China, South Korea, the United Kingdom and the United States.

Natasha Lester managed the Maybelline brand for L'Oréal Australia before becoming a writer. She then returned to university to study creative writing, completing a Master of Creative Arts at Curtin University as well as her first novel, *What is Left Over, After*, which won the T.A.G. Hungerford Award. She has now published five historical novels including the *New York Times* and *USA Today* bestseller *The French Photographer*, and her books have been translated into many languages and are sold all around the world. *The Paris Secret* is her latest book. When she's not writing books, she loves to collect vintage fashion, read, travel, dream about Paris, and have fun with her three children. Natasha lives in Perth, Western Australia.

Website: natashalester.com.au | Facebook: @NatashaLesterAuthor
Instagram: @natashalesterauthor | Twitter: @natasha_lester

Brigid Lowry has an MA in Creative Writing, and has published poetry and short fiction for adults, as well as eight books for teenagers. *Guitar Highway Rose* and *Juicy Writing: Inspiration and Techniques for Young Writers* are two of her prize-winning YA titles. Her latest book is *Still Life with Teapot: On Zen, Writing and Creativity*, Fremantle Press, 2016. Her forthcoming book, *A Year of Loving Kindness to Oneself, and Other Essays*, will be published by Fremantle Press in 2021. Brigid believes in op shops, coloured pencils, vegetables, oceans, floral frocks and postcards, and fostering creativity in herself and others.

Caitlin Maling is a Western Australian poet with three poetry collections out through Fremantle Press, including the latest, *Fish Song* (2019). She was the holder of the Marten Bequest in Poetry and the Department of Culture and the Arts (WA) international scholarship for her MFA studies at the University of Houston. She received her doctorate in English in 2019 from the University of Sydney.

Website: caitlinmaling.com | Instagram: @caitlinmaling

Meg McKinlay is the author of eighteen books ranging from picture books and young adult fiction through to poetry for adults. Her work has won a number of awards, including the Prime Minister's Literary Award for Young Adult Fiction, the Queensland Literary Award for Children's Writing, the Aurealis Award for Best Children's Fiction, and the Davitt Award for Best Young Adult Novel. Her most recent titles are middle-grade novel *Catch A Falling Star* and picture book *How to Make a Bird*. Raised in central Victoria, in a TV- and car-free household, Meg was a bookish kid, in love with words and excited by dictionaries. A former academic at the University of Western Australia, where she taught Japanese, English literature and creative writing, Meg lives near the ocean in Fremantle, where she is always trying to carve out more creative time.

Website: megmckinlay.com | Facebook: @megmkinlayauthor
Instagram: @megmckinlay |Twitter: @ MegMcKinlay
Carrier pigeon: the blue birdbath by the flowering gum

Claire Miller worked for Lothian Press before relocating to the Netherlands to market the country's first satellite communications company during the ISP boom. Upon her return, Claire worked as an events manager and marketer for Tourism WA and the University of Western Australia. She joined Fremantle Press in 2008 and is the marketing and communications manager. As well as running individual book campaigns, Claire produces the Fremantle Press podcast, creates and runs workshops for the Four Centres Emerging Writers Program and oversees the City of Fremantle Hungerford Award and the Fogarty Literary Award. She has been a Small Press Network committee member since 2018.

LinkedIn: claire-miller-691aa939

Georgia Richter has an MA (Creative Writing) from the University of Western Australia and is an IPEd Accredited Editor. She has taught creative writing, professional writing and editing at the universities of Melbourne, Western Australia and Curtin. After working as a freelance editor, Georgia joined Fremantle Press in 2008 as fiction, narrative non-fiction and poetry publisher. She has a passion for sharing advice and ideas with new writers and encouraging them to support each other through community building. With Claire Miller she has conducted workshops for the Four Centres Emerging Writers Program, along with many workshops and presentations in universities and the community. She is proud to judge the City of Fremantle Hungerford Award and the Fogarty Literary Award.

Facebook: @How to be an Author in Australia
LinkedIn: georgia-richter-7588465b

Brendan Ritchie is a novelist and academic with postgraduate qualifications in the fields of creative writing and screenwriting. In 2016, Brendan was awarded a Doctor of Philosophy in Creative Writing within an Excellence Scholarship at Edith Cowan University. Fremantle Press published his debut young adult novel, *Carousel*, in 2015. *Carousel* has been critically acclaimed and was longlisted for the 2016 Gold Inky Award. Brendan has subsequently published a sequel, *Beyond Carousel*, alongside poetry and academic articles in various notable publications. He lives in the south-west of WA with his wife and daughter, and works as an academic at Edith Cowan University. He has several novel-length projects in development.

Website: brendanritchie.com | Twitter: @BrendanRitchie

Rachel Robertson is a Western Australian writer and senior lecturer in the School of Media, Creative Arts and Social Inquiry at Curtin University. She is the author of *Reaching One Thousand* (Black Inc., 2012, 2018), which was shortlisted for the National Biography Award 2013, and was the winner of *Australian Book Review*'s Calibre Prize for an Outstanding Essay in 2008. She is co-editor of *Purple Prose* (Fremantle Press, 2015) and *Dangerous Ideas about Mothers* (UWA Publishing, 2018). Rachel's creative work has been published in journals and anthologies such as *Westerly*, *Island*, *Meanjin*, *Griffith Review* and *Best Australian Essays*. Her academic interests include Australian literature, life writing, the essay form, creative non-fiction, creative writing pedagogy and disability studies.

Website: rachelrobertson.net.au

Holden Sheppard is an award-winning author born and bred in Geraldton, Western Australia. His debut novel, *Invisible Boys* (Fremantle Press, 2019), won the 2018 City of Fremantle Hungerford Award, was shortlisted for the Victorian Premier's Literary Awards and named as a Notable Book by the Children's Book Council of Australia. Holden's writing has been published in *Griffith Review*, *Westerly*, *page seventeen*, *Indigo Journal* and the *Bright Lights, No City* anthology. He has written articles for *10 Daily, Huffington Post*, the ABC, *DNA Magazine* and *FasterLouder*. He graduated with honours from Edith Cowan University's writing program and won a prestigious Australia Council ArtStart grant in 2015. Holden has always been a misfit: a gym junkie who has played Pokémon competitively, a sensitive geek who loves aggressive punk rock, and a bogan who learned to speak French. He lives in Perth's northern suburbs with his husband.

Website: holdensheppard.com |Facebook: @HoldenSheppardAuthor
Instagram: @holdensheppard | Twitter: @V8Sheppard

Sasha Wasley was born and raised in Perth, Western Australia. She composed her first literary work before she could write – a poem, orated improv-style in the kitchen at five years old. A known literature nerd in high school, Sasha went on to spend several hundred years at university and completed a PhD in feminist literature in 2006. As the career opportunities for experts in feminist literature were somewhat scarce, Sasha worked as a copywriter for a number of years. Her debut novel was published in 2015, after which she gave up her copywriting business to pursue a fiction-writing career. Today, she lives and writes in the Perth Hills region with her partner and daughters. A lover of nature and animals, Sasha spends her free time pottering in the garden with her flock of backyard chickens.

Website: sashawasley.com | Facebook: @sashawasleyauthor
Instagram: @sashawasley_author | Twitter: @SDWasleyAuthor

David Whish-Wilson is the author of novels *The Summons*, *The Coves* and four crime novels in the Frank Swann series: *Line of Sight*, *Zero at the Bone*, *Old Scores* and *Shore Leave*, along with *True West*. A historical fiction, *The Sawdust House*, is forthcoming with Fremantle Press. His non-fiction book, *Perth*, part of the NewSouth Books city series, was shortlisted for a WA Premier's Book Award. He writes essays, short fiction, reviews, and the text for public artworks. David lives in Fremantle and coordinates the creative writing program at Curtin University.

**Website: davidwhish-wilson.com | Facebook: @davewhishwilson
Instagram: @davidwhishwilson | Twitter: @david whish-wilson**

Anne-Louise Willoughby's career in journalism spanned thirty years in Western Australia, first training as a newspaper cadet in the 1970s before moving to magazine publishing with Swan Publishing and Australian Consolidated Press. During her career as a freelance journalist, Anne-Louise was a feature writer for Australian newspapers and magazines, contributing WA editor to *Belle Magazine*, and produced a weekly column for a subsidiary of Newscorp. Her magazine work has been syndicated internationally. During her PhD candidacy at UWA, Anne-Louise worked as a lecturer and tutor in creative writing with a particular interest in memoir and biography, and continues to teach in the theory and practice of creative writing. Anne-Louise's biography of Australian painter Nora Heysen, *Nora Heysen: A Portrait*, was published by Fremantle Press in 2019. She lives in Fremantle, Western Australia.

**Website: annelouisewilloughby.com
Instagram: @annelouisewilloughby**

Acknowledgements

This book had its beginnings in the workshop series run by Fremantle Press for the Four Centres Emerging Writers Program facilitated by marketing and communications manager Claire Miller and publisher Georgia Richter. It was also sparked by a conversation between Georgia Richter and lecturer Deborah Hunn about the wealth of experience that published authors have to offer other writers. It has grown out of many further conversations between them, and Georgia and Deborah have also gratefully received input from the team at Fremantle Press: CEO Jane Fraser, children's publisher Cate Sutherland, marketing and communications coordinator Chloe Walton, and events marketing assistant Tiffany Ko. Special thanks for the focussed and helpful input from Fremantle Press editor Armelle Davies, and the very many contributions from Claire Miller, who encourages and promotes her authors with passion and dedication. Thanks to Naama Grey-Smith for her additional research, intelligent proofreading and insightful comments, Carolyn Brown for her lovely, cheery design and Alisa Dodge for her elegant index.

Special thanks to Tim Coronel, general manager of The Small Press Network and industry adjunct lecturer in publishing at the University of Melbourne, for his reading, sage commentary and suggestions. Thanks to Stephen Kinnane for his review of, and contribution to, the own voice material in Chapter 4. We thank Alecia Hancock and Anna Hill of Hancock Creative, whose guidance and experience over time helped inform the material about online promotion and social media. Thanks to Alan Sheardown and staff at New Edition Bookshop, Jane Seaton of Beaufort Street Books, and Nadia Giacci of Planet Books for their booksellers' perspectives.

Thanks too to Michael Earp (The Little Bookroom), and Allyce Cameron and Aisling Lawless (Dymocks Morley and Joondalup) for their observations about booksellers during the 2020 Business of Being a Writer program at the Perth Festival Literature and Ideas Weekend, and to all the additional authors who have been generous with their advice on The Fremantle Press Podcast.

From the 2019 Business of Being a Writer program at the Perth Festival Writers Week, we are grateful for self-publishing tips from authors Annabel Smith and Wendy Binks, and printer Debbie Lee (Ingram Spark); grants, residencies and awards advice from Gail Jones, Alice Nelson and Wenona Byrne (Australia Council Director of Literature); and Tim Coronel (The Small Press Network), Lisa Shearon (formerly of Hancock Creative) and author-illustrator James Foley for their insights into what writers need to know about marketing and PR.

Finally, we thank the writers who directly contributed to this book with careful thought and unbridled enthusiasm, and from whom we continue to learn so much about the business of being a writer. It is a privilege to work with you.

Index

First published 2021 by
FREMANTLE PRESS

Fremantle Press Inc. trading as Fremantle Press
25 Quarry Street, Fremantle WA 6160
(PO Box 158, North Fremantle WA 6159)
www.fremantlepress.com.au

Copyright © Fremantle Press, 2021.
The moral rights of the authors have been asserted.

This book is copyright. Apart from any fair dealing for the purpose of private study,
research, criticism or review, as permitted under the *Copyright Act*, no part may be
reproduced by any process without written permission.
Enquiries should be made to the publisher.

Cover photograph by Bibadash, shutterstock.com.
Design by Carolyn Brown, tendeersigh.com.au.
Printed by McPherson's Printing, Victoria, Australia.

 A catalogue record for this
book is available from the
National Library of Australia

ISBN 9781760990046 (paperback)
ISBN 9781760990053 (ebook)

Fremantle Press is supported by the State Government through the
Department of Local Government, Sport and Cultural Industries.

Publication of this title was assisted by the Commonwealth Government
through the Australia Council, its arts funding and advisory body.